Professional Practice

n Counselling and Psychotherapy

Sara Miller McCune founded SAGE Publishing in 1965 to support the dissemination of usable knowledge and educate a global community. SAGE publishes more than 1000 journals and over 800 new books each year, spanning a wide range of subject areas. Our growing selection of library products includes archives, data, case studies and video. SAGE remains majority owned by our founder and after her lifetime will become owned by a charitable trust that secures the company's continued independence.

Los Angeles | London | New Delhi | Singapore | Washington DC | Melbourne

Professional Practice
in Counselling and Psychotherapy

Ethics and the Law   Peter Jenkins

Los Angeles | London | New Delhi
Singapore | Washington DC | Melbourne

Los Angeles | London | New Delhi
Singapore | Washington DC | Melbourne

SAGE Publications Ltd
1 Oliver's Yard
55 City Road
London EC1Y 1SP

SAGE Publications Inc.
2455 Teller Road
Thousand Oaks, California 91320

SAGE Publications India Pvt Ltd
B 1/I 1 Mohan Cooperative Industrial Area
Mathura Road
New Delhi 110 044

SAGE Publications Asia-Pacific Pte Ltd
3 Church Street
#10-04 Samsung Hub
Singapore 049483

Editor: Susannah Trefgarne
Editorial assistant: Charlotte Meredith
Production editor: Rachel Burrows
Marketing manager: Camille Richmond
Cover design: Lisa Harper-Wells
Typeset by: C&M Digitals (P) Ltd, Chennai, India
Printed by CPI Group (UK) Ltd, Croydon, CR0 4YY

Library of Congress Control Number: 2016961358

British Library Cataloguing in Publication data

A catalogue record for this book is available from
the British Library

ISBN 978-1-4462-9663-9
ISBN 978-1-4462-9664-6 (pbk)

At SAGE we take sustainability seriously. Most of our products are printed in the UK using FSC papers and boards.
When we print overseas we ensure sustainable papers are used as measured by the PREPS grading system.
We undertake an annual audit to monitor our sustainability.

Contents

Lists of figures, tables, boxes and exercises

List of figures

List of tables

List of boxes

List of exercises

About the author

Peter Jenkins is a counsellor, trainer, supervisor and researcher. He has worked as a student and staff counsellor in college and university settings for the past 30 years. During this time, he has developed a particular interest in exploring ethical, professional and legal issues in counselling practice. He has run over two hundred workshops on these topics, aimed at addressing the current concerns of practitioners. He has been a member of both the BACP Professional Conduct Committee and the UKCP Ethics Committee, and has published around one hundred articles on law and ethics in the professional counselling press. His publications include *Therapy with Children*, as co-author with Dr Debbie Daniels (second edition, Sage, 2010); *Counselling, Psychotherapy and the Law* (second edition, Sage, 2007); and online modules for Counselling MindEd and other training material, such as *Counselling Confidentiality and the Law* (2013, Counselling DVDs).

Acknowledgements

First, thanks are due to the BACP, for kind permission to quote extensively from the *Core Curriculum for Accredited Courses* (2009) and the *Ethical Framework for the Counselling Professions* (2016) for educational purposes; John Mellor-Clarke, Managing Director of CORE IMS; Professor Michael Barkham, Professor Chris Evans and Dr Frank Margison, of the CORE System Trust; Professor Keith Hawton, Centre for Suicide Research, University of Oxford; and Cheryl Lund and Nina Markham-Brew from Tameside, Oldham and Glossop Mind, for permission to reproduce material for this book.

Many people have helped me directly or indirectly in shaping my ideas and counselling practice and thus contributing towards this book, including my friends and colleagues Hazel Batchelor, Jill Collins, Dr Debbie Daniels and Andrew Webb; my former students Tom Brooks, Elisabeth Brownlee, Jo Moore, Alex Williams and Helen Wilkinson; Sarah Littlejohn, Maxine Whybrow and my colleagues from Manchester University Student and Staff Counselling Service; my colleagues from Manchester University, in particular George Brooks and Kevin Fletcher, and also Violet Baker, Liz Ballinger, Maureen Charlton, Terry Hanley, Barbara Impey, Allan Kidd, Mike Poulter, Adrian Rhodes, William West and Pam Winter; and my colleagues from Salford University, Elaine Beaumont, Gosia Bowling, Dr Liz Coldridge and Vee Howard-Jones.

Staff at SAGE have been consistently supportive in facilitating this book, with thanks owing to Edward Coats, Susannah Trefgarne, Molly Farrell, Camille Richmond and Rachel Burrows.

Finally, my thanks are due to my family, near and far, but especially Jane, Lisa, Rachel, Xav and Leo.

Introduction

This book is written primarily for students on qualifying courses in counselling and psychotherapy, as a guide to developing professional practice. Hopefully, it will also be of interest to a wider audience, such as qualified counsellors and psychotherapists, supervisors, service managers and counsellor trainers, in a wide variety of settings. It aims to fill a gap in the market by providing the kind of practical information about the 'nuts and bolts' requirements of actually beginning work as a counsellor. This is the book I wish I could have had when I undertook my own professional training.

There are numerous valuable and well-respected books on counselling and psychotherapy, many of which engage with one or other aspect of professional practice, but none of which looks directly at this as a topic in its own right. What does 'professional practice' mean here? By 'professional practice', I refer to the wide range of activities, from risk assessment to recording client notes, from working with client diversity to safeguarding, which are a key part of current therapeutic work. These professional tasks are largely independent of the therapeutic style, or orientation, of the therapist concerned. Increasingly, all counsellors are expected to assess and manage high levels of client risk, for example, regardless of their modality. Forms of professional practice will be influenced, to some degree, by the *context* of the work. There will be a different emphasis on certain aspects of professional practice, perhaps, in statutory settings, compared to voluntary or third sector settings. Nevertheless, the central core of expectations regarding professional practice, which are set out here, will remain fairly constant.

Professional practice is influenced by a number of factors, in addition to context, such as the role of ethics and the law. This book acknowledges the key role of ethics in shaping professional practice in counselling and psychotherapy, exemplified by the BACP *Ethical Framework for the Counselling Professions* (2016). Legal factors also play a major role in providing the context for professional practice, not least in terms of deciding whether, or to what extent, counselling is subject to statutory regulation. In educational terms, this book makes frequent reference to key training documents, such as the BACP *Core Curriculum for Accredited Courses* (2009). A third level of expectation is set out in terms of *competences*. These refer to the level of skill and knowledge required of counsellors working in specific roles, e.g. as a supervisor, or in the provision of specific therapeutic modalities, e.g. humanistic therapies or CBT, or in working with specific client groups, such as children and young people. Competence frameworks are *task*-based in that they 'describe what a therapist might do'. Competence frameworks break new ground, by focusing on tasks and in cutting through previously long-held *role*-based distinctions between counsellors and psychotherapists. This approach stresses that 'both counsellors and psychotherapists could offer the competences embodied in this framework, so long as they have had the appropriate training' (Roth et al., 2009: 3).

Note for students, trainers and other readers

The style of the book is that of a textbook, rather than being more discursive or theory-based. It makes frequent reference to classic texts, such as by Casement, or Schön, as a way of introducing new students to the wealth of literature on therapy which is available. This is in the hope that this will spark an interest to go on to read the originals, when time permits. The book is buttressed by regular selections from the *Ethical Framework for the Counselling Professions* and the *Core Curriculum*, in a way which is probably unusual within counsellor training. However, this style is standard practice in other forms of professional training, such as social work and nursing. No doubt, as curricula and other reference points shift and change over time, then the book's content will need to reflect this by future regular updating.

The book also makes use of case examples, often drawn from the counselling literature, and exercises to complete, either working alone or in a structured training activity. Chapters are set out with the main themes to be addressed, and with a concluding Resources section, including web-based material where appropriate. Research summaries, often of quite small-scale qualitative surveys, are included. These illustrate the role of research in providing evidence for some of the developing changes within counselling practice. Major background changes to professional practice include the widespread use of outcome measures and the establishment of the Improving Access to Psychological Therapies programme (IAPT). Each chapter has a Reference section for supervisors, which links chapter content to specific supervisory issues and interests and to relevant research summaries.

Value-based and evidence-based training

In terms of training context, there is a current vogue for an 'evidence-based' approach to curriculum design, which is largely to be welcomed. This book tries to reference relevant research findings wherever possible, in order to underpin the validity of particular developments, such as informed assessment for suicide risk, as just one example. However, there are definite limits to the value of an evidence-based approach to training and professional practice. Researching an evidence base for a particular practice can help to set a standard, for example in communicating with young people. But actually implementing an evidence-based curriculum, or competence model, then requires consistency in carrying out the assessment process, in appraising the evidence of competence and in evaluating the quality of the assessors. These are proving to be complex issues to address in practice.

There is also something of a tension between an *evidence*-based approach to training and a *value*-based approach. Much of the *Ethical Framework for the Counselling Professions* represents an expression of professional *values*, rather than claiming to be firmly based on research evidence as such. In fact, many of the most cherished elements of professional practice and training still lack convincing evidence, whether this refers to the need for students to undergo personal therapy, or the number of hours of practice required for individual accreditation, or even for training as a counsellor. These aspects of professional training and practice are much more solidly rooted in a professional peer community *value base* rather than in a solidly established and incontrovertible evidence base. Supervision is perhaps in the process of slowly moving from representing such a value-based requirement to becoming more of an evidence-based one. Research is now beginning to demonstrate the proven value of supervision, in terms of its contribution to achieving improved outcomes for therapists and their clients. However, this relatively recent development comes long after its general acceptance within the profession, as an essential component of good practice. Perhaps the evidence base for other core elements, of what is generally accepted as constituting good professional practice, will also follow suit in the near future.

Structure and content of this book

In terms of the structure and content of this book, the following diagram sets out the main flow of the material covered.

The book begins, in Chapter 1, in looking at the process of becoming a member of counselling and psychotherapy, as a new and emerging profession. It addresses the thorny issue of the statutory regulation of counselling and psychotherapy, and offers some critical perspectives on the role of counselling within the wider society. It covers the relationship of counselling and psychotherapy to other professions, such as law, medicine and psychology, and looks at the unfolding process of becoming a professional counsellor and psychotherapist.

Chapter 2 opens up the somewhat neglected topic of the organisational context of counselling practice and introduces a model for understanding counselling organisations. It discusses the impact of organisational context on counselling practice, different types of organisational culture and the challenges of working as a counsellor in what can be described as hybrid, or 'mixed', organisational cultures.

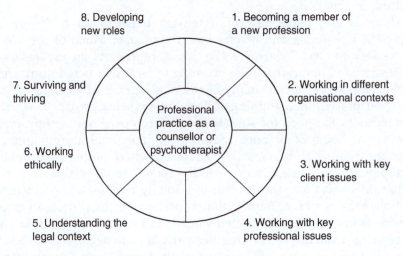

Figure 0.1   Structure of the book and chapter sequence

There is a perhaps slightly artificial distinction in Chapters 3 and 4, between client issues and professional issues, when – clearly – these areas overlap to some extent. Chapter 3, 'Working with key client issues', covers a number of central, client-related issues that are at the heart of professional counselling practice. These relate to working with difference, avoiding discrimination in counselling, working with risk and safeguarding adult clients.

The focus in Chapter 4, 'Working with key professional issues', is on issues that are more directly connected to the counsellor's professional *role* than to those issues impacting more immediately on therapeutic contact with the client. Hence Chapter 4 looks at working as a member of a multi-disciplinary team, the shift towards evidence-based practice, the 'stepped care' model of service delivery and using outcome measures to evaluate counselling practice.

Chapter 5 looks at the law and relevant legal frameworks for practice, with a particular focus on understanding the professional, legal and ethical aspects of confidentiality, data protection and the use of contracts with clients. This is followed by Chapter 6, 'Working ethically', which considers the shift from codes of ethics to more flexible ethical frameworks. It closely follows the process of applying ethics to therapeutic practice, exploring ethical principles and different approaches to ethics, and identifying and responding to ethical issues.

In Chapter 7, 'Surviving and thriving', the book looks at the process of working as a counselling student, from placement, to qualification and to the point of registration with BACP. This covers developing self-awareness and self-care, making use of supervision, preparing for placement and then qualifying and registering as a counsellor.

Finally, Chapter 8, 'Developing new roles', looks at the potential next steps for counsellors, having achieved qualification and registration as a counsellor. These steps include working as a counsellor, whether in employment, private practice or via portfolio work. Other potential post-qualifying options include developing a new specialism, undertaking further training or individual accreditation as a counsellor, or developing new roles as a group facilitator, counsellor trainer, supervisor, researcher or as a coach.

1

Becoming a member of
a new profession

Introduction

This chapter looks at what it means to join counselling and psychotherapy as a profession and what is involved in the process of becoming a 'professional' counsellor. It covers the following topics:

- understanding counselling and psychotherapy as a new profession;
- exploring the statutory regulation of counselling and psychotherapy;
- developing critical perspectives on the role of counselling in society;
- exploring the relationship of counselling and psychotherapy to other professions;
- becoming a professional counsellor and psychotherapist.

Learning context

The BACP *Core Curriculum* (2009) briefly sets out the requirement for students to develop knowledge and understanding of the history and culture of counselling in order to join and fully become a part of the wider community of therapists. The BACP *Ethical Framework for the Counselling Professions* (2016) provides a core part of what is required from students and practitioners in becoming a professional, by working to meet the appropriate standards of practice and behaviour. Extracts from both documents are included below for reference.

BACP *Core Curriculum* (2009)

9.1.A The professional role and responsibility of the therapist.

7. Understanding the values underpinning the profession, as exemplified in the Ethical Framework. (2009: 17)

9.1.D. The social, professional and organisational context for therapy:

The practitioner will have relevant knowledge to inform his or her ability to:

1. Take an active role as a member of a professional community.

2. Show a critical awareness of the history of ideas, the cultural context and social and political theories that inform and influence the practice of counselling and psychotherapy. (2009: 18)

BACP *Ethical Framework for the Counselling Professions* (2016)

Working to professional standards:

13. We must be competent to deliver the services being offered to at least fundamental professional standards or better.

14. We will keep skills and knowledge up to date by:

a. reading professional journals, books and/or reliable electronic resources

b. keeping ourselves informed of any relevant research and evidence-based guidance

c. discussions with colleagues working on similar issues

d. reviewing our knowledge and skills in supervision or discussion with experienced practitioners

e. regular continuing professional development to update knowledge and skills

f. keeping up to date with the law, regulations and any other requirements, including guidance from this Association, relevant to our work

15. We will keep accurate records that are appropriate to the service being provided.

16. We will collaborate with colleagues over our work with specific clients where this is consistent with client consent and will enhance services to the client.

17. We will work collaboratively with colleagues to improve services and offer mutual support.

18. We will maintain our own physical and psychological health at a level that enables us to work effectively with clients.

19. We will be covered by adequate insurance when providing services directly or indirectly to the public.

20. We will fulfil the ethical principles and values set out in this Ethical Framework regardless or whether working online, face to face or using any other methods of communication. The technical and practical knowledge may vary according to how services are delivered but all our services will be delivered to at least fundamental professional standards or better. (2016: 6)

Understanding counselling and psychotherapy as a new profession

So, what exactly is this new profession that you have decided to join, or which you are in the process of joining? Counselling and psychotherapy are hugely worthwhile occupations, with great job satisfaction and a strongly developing evidence base for their effectiveness in relieving human distress. However, whether they can confidently be called 'professions' in the more widely accepted sense of the word is still subject to dispute, at least in some circles. This chapter will look at some of the main features of what it is to be a member of a profession, or to act in a professional manner, which may not hold quite the same meaning.

Definition of a profession

The notion of a checklist, or list of key characteristics required of recognised professions, is a well-established format for guiding discussion on this topic. This is known as the *trait* model of professionalisation, which has been hugely influential in framing discussions on this topic. However, it has also been subject to increasing criticism for neglecting significant issues, such as power and gender. The checklist approach is, in part, a *developmental* model, holding out the possibility that different occupational groups, such as teachers and social workers, can work towards achieving full status as a profession by gradually achieving each of the required criteria. Becoming a profession involves a degree of legal recognition, when either the *title* (e.g. as a psychotherapist) or the *activity* of a particular group (e.g. counselling) becomes protected by law. This has important implications. A legally protected title (e.g. as a chartered psychologist) means that anyone claiming this status *without* being properly registered with a professional body (e.g. the British Psychological Society) or with a regulating body, such as the Health and Care Professions Council (HCPC), can be prevented from doing so. In addition, if a practitioner is subject to a successful complaint or a disciplinary procedure against them by their professional association (such as the British Psychological Society), or by their regulatory body (such as the Health and Care Professions Council), they can be removed from the register. They are thus legally prevented from practising in that role.

The trait model has been a standard feature of sociological discussions of the process of professionalisation over the last century. It still retains influence as a working approach to deciding whether occupational groups, such as art therapists, dance therapists and social workers, fully qualify as professions. The Health and Care Professions Council used this approach in deciding applications from new and emerging professions up to 2011. It has had, therefore, real application in the recent past in deciding on the value of competing claims to professional status, even if it is no longer used for this purpose. The list of criteria follows a classic trait or a 'checklist' model, despite the growing academic criticism of this approach. Aspiring professions needed to demonstrate the criteria set out in Box 1.1.

Box 1.1   HCPC criteria for considering applications by new professions for regulation

- Cover a discrete area of activity displaying some homogeneity
- Apply a defined body of knowledge
- Practice based on evidence of efficacy
- Have at least one established professional body which accounts for a significant proportion of that occupational group
- Operate a voluntary register
- Have defined routes of entry to the profession
- Have independently assessed entry qualifications
- Have standards in relation to conduct, performance and ethics
- Have Fitness to Practise procedures to enforce those standards
- Be committed to continuous professional development (CPD)

Health and Care Professions Council (HCPC) (2001) New professions process, www. hpc-uk.org/aboutregistration/aspirantgroups/newprofessionsprocess/

Exercise   Exploring HCPC criteria for a new profession

Consider the HCPC list of criteria in Box 1.1 and tick those you feel are met for counselling. Discuss and compare your answers with those of someone else, and then compare with the answers below in Table 1.1 (examples

(Continued)

(Continued)

relate primarily to the BACP as the leading body for counselling in the field, but similar responses could be supplied for the British Psychological Society (BPS,) United Kingdom Council for Psychotherapy (UKCP), British Association for Behavioural and Cognitive Psychotherapy (BABCP), etc.).

Table 1.1 Evidence of BACP meeting HCPC criteria for regulation of new professions

HCPC criteria	Commentary on evidence of BACP meeting HCPC criteria
Discrete area of activity	Continuing discussion over similarities and differences between counselling and psychotherapy. BAC added 'and Psychotherapy' to its title, becoming BACP in 2002.
Applied body of knowledge	BACP Research Panel set up in 1986; BACP peer-reviewed research journal (*Counselling and Psychotherapy Research*) published from 2001.
Evidence of efficacy	Increasing evidence of efficacy (see Cooper, 2008); however, relatively limited use of randomised controlled trials (RCTs) in this respect.
At least one established professional body	BACP is established in 1977 with current membership of around 44,000.
Voluntary register	Voluntary UK Register of Counsellors set up in 1997; introduction of Accreditation of Voluntary Registers scheme, operated by Professional Standards Authority for Health and Social Care, under Health and Social Care Act 2012.
Defined routes of entry to profession	From 2016, counsellor registration via either relevant training plus online assessment process or completion of BACP-accredited training course (the latter first set up in 1987).
Independently assessed entry qualifications	Blind online assessment process (90% pass rate) or completion of accredited training course.
Standards for conduct, ethics and performance	BACP *Code of Ethics* established 1982; BACP *Ethical Framework for Good Practice in Counselling and Psychotherapy* in 2002; *Ethical Framework for the Counselling Professions* in 2016.
Fitness to Practise procedures	BACP Complaints Procedure set up in 1983.
Commitment to CPD	CPD requirement for accreditation of individual counsellors first set up in 1983 and for all registrants from 2016.

The evidence outlined in Table 1.1 seems to suggest that BACP has already met, or is in the process of meeting, all of the criteria required by the HCPC for professional status and regulation. So, why is it still not subject to statutory regulation? This is a crucial question which will be discussed below.

Exploring the statutory regulation of counselling and psychotherapy

Counselling began to emerge as a distinct occupational group during the 1960s and 1970s, with the British Association for Counselling being established in 1977. This took a 'broad church' approach to member-ship, including as members those who used counselling *skills* as part of another profession, such as teachers. The issue of statutory regulation was first raised in 1971, with the publication of the Foster Report into the Church of Scientology (Foster, 1971), which was highly critical of the quasi-psychological methods used by Scientology to recruit, retain and control its members. It also raised the wider issue of regulating counselling and psychotherapy. However, it is telling that the Report struggled, then as now, to distinguish between the various different types of psychological practice. Hence '"psychiatry" was seen as deal-ing with emotional or mental problems, "psychology" mainly with problems of the intellect. "Counselling" was widely practised, as was "psychotherapy without a fee"' (Foster, 1971: 176). The Report con-cluded that 'It is high time that the practice of psychotherapy for reward should be restricted to members of a profession properly qual-ified in its techniques and trained...' (1971: 179).

The mantle was then taken up in the form of the Seighart Report (Seighart, 1978). This similarly struggled with resolving problems of definition:

> we have serious doubts about whether psychotherapy as a function could be defined precisely enough by statutory language to prevent evasion, without at the same time casting the net so wide as to catch many people who are outside the mischief which the statute is designed to meet. We have in mind here professions as diverse as general medical practitioners, applied psy-chologists, clergymen, counsellors and educators who do not present themselves as specialised psychotherapists, but many of whom use interper-sonal techniques in the course of their ordinary work... (Seighart, 1978: 6)

The strategy proposed was to regulate the use of the title of 'psycho-therapist', given that it was not feasible to regulate a broad social grouping, with such loosely defined boundaries to its practice and membership. Yet this first major attempt to introduce statutory regulation ultimately failed because of the continuing high levels of disagreement within the wider profession. In particular, concerns were raised by the behavioural psychotherapists. This group insisted on evidence of *therapeutic effectiveness* – and not simply of completion of *a period of training* – as a crucial precondition for the regulation of the profession (Jenkins, 2007a: 189).

Barriers to achieving statutory regulation

Disunity between the various therapists' organisations effectively ended this first attempt at achieving statutory regulation. The second major attempt developed after the failure of a Private Member's Bill in Parliament to regulate psychotherapy (but explicitly *not* counselling) in 1981. This led to a sustained round of lobbying by all the main therapists' organisations, the BACP, UKCP and others, during the 1980s, 1990s and beyond the turn of the century. Once again, this ran into substantial difficulties in trying to distinguish between counselling and psychotherapy for regulatory and legislative purposes. Another major cause of dissent among therapists was that the proposed regulatory body was to be the Health Professions Council (now the Health and Care Professions Council). This seemed to offer statutory regulation, but on a very medicalised model. Critics argued that this model was not suitable for the psychological or 'talking' therapies. Movement towards even this relatively unsatisfactory form of regulation ended with the change of government in 2010. The new Coalition government announced that the way forward would now be via the implementation of *voluntary* registers of therapists, rather than through statutory regulation. This decision ended the second attempt to achieve statutory regulation for counselling and psychotherapy. Almost 40 years of slow progress towards achieving the goal of statutory regulation was thus halted overnight.

This account suggests that the reasons why counselling and psychotherapy still do not have statutory regulation are quite complex. Progress towards regulation has been hampered by major disagreements between the different therapist bodies, over professional status and over their proven level of effectiveness in working with clients. Attempts to regulate have foundered, time and time again, on the difficulties involved in defining 'counselling' and 'counsellor' in a precise and binding manner. The situation now is that there is *partial* statutory regulation, in that psychologists are regulated in terms of title, via the HCPC. Art therapists, play therapists and child psychotherapists are also regulated by HCPC registers. Adoption counselling (although somewhat ill-defined) is regulated via the Adoption and Children Act 2002. Infertility counselling is regulated via the Human Fertilisation and Embryology Act 1990. The overall result is something of a patchwork quilt, with different outposts of title, or practice, which are regulated. There are large parts of counselling and psychotherapy which are still not regulated, and are now unlikely to achieve regulation in the foreseeable future:

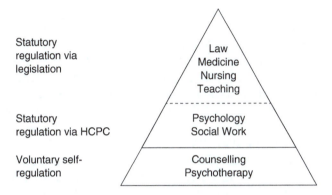

Figure 1.1   Schematic representation of different formats for statutory regulation and voluntary self-regulation for different professions and occupational groups

Exploring counselling, social work and nursing as semi-professions

There are a number of further potential answers to this crucial question of why counselling and psychotherapy are not fully recognised as professions. The following factors are important here:

- the problem of defining counselling and psychotherapy in an *exclusive manner*, i.e. which would *not* include other occupational groups that may use counselling as part of their role;
- the view that counselling and psychotherapy can only ever achieve *partial* recognition, given their limited and fixed status as a semi-profession;
- the argument that counselling adopted an *overly collaborative approach* to the process of seeking statutory regulation, which diluted its arguments and effectiveness in achieving regulation;
- the view that counselling and psychotherapy, rather than being a profession, really constitute a quite different kind of animal – namely 'a *community of practice*'.

Problems with defining counselling

One view is that counselling and psychotherapy provide therapeutic interventions to individuals, couples and groups. However, the knowledge and skill base for these interventions and responses are not unique to those defining themselves as counsellors and psychotherapists. There is a real problem in defining counselling and psychotherapy in such a way that will effectively rule out competing claims for such expertise by other occupational or professional groups, such as psychologists. This difficulty is illustrated above in the account given of the history of progress towards statutory regulation. One possible answer is that counselling is an activity that can be carried out only by trained counsellors. This runs the risk of becoming rather a circular and unconvincing argument for those outside the profession. Sally Aldridge, a key player in the process of seeking statutory regulation, recounts the example of 'a senior civil servant in the IAPT programme asking me, as the BACP representative, to answer the question "What is *counselling*?"' (2010: 368, emphasis added). Perhaps, for us as counsellors, the answer to the question 'What is counselling?' may seem fairly self-evident, or a question that can be easily answered by referring to the current BACP definition. However, the lack of clarity about counselling's definition by a powerful government representative suggests a relative lack of understanding in the wider society, about what counselling consists of and how it can be distinguished from other, similar forms of psychological support (see Box 1.2).

Box 1.2   BACP definition of counselling and psychotherapy (2012a)

Counselling and psychotherapy are 'umbrella terms for a range of talking therapies. They are delivered by trained practitioners who work with people over a short or long term to help them bring about effective change or enhance their wellbeing.'

British Association for Counselling and Psychotherapy (2012a) *What are Counselling and Psychotherapy?* Lutterworth: BACP, www.bacp.co.uk/crs/Training/whatiscounselling.php

---

Exercise   Defining counselling and psychotherapy

Devise your own working definition of either counselling or psychotherapy. Check it over. What is missing and needs to be added?

The problems inherent in trying to define counselling and psychotherapy are presented and discussed very thoroughly by Reeves (2013: 7–13) and Aldridge (2014: 2–6).

Professions, from one perspective, are essentially about the exercise of *power*. For example, the legal profession has legitimate power with regard to providing legal advice and representation. The medical profession exercises legitimate power over who can carry out specific medical activities, such as the diagnosis and treatment of illness and disease. The view advanced by Etzioni (1969) is that certain occupational groups, such as teaching, nursing and social work, are fixed and unable to progress beyond their current status as *semi-professions*. This is partly due to the fact that their core activities are hard to define in a way that would exclude other occupational groups. There is also the additional factor of *gender*, in that these are occupational groups largely consisting of women, who may find it harder to exercise power effectively within a male-dominated society (see Box 1.3). Counselling and psychotherapy share many of the features of teaching, nursing and social work, as semi-professions. However, each of these occupational groups (teaching, nursing and social work) has achieved statutory regulation, unlike counselling and psychotherapy.

Box 1.3 Characteristics of a semi-profession (Etzioni, 1969)

Their training is shorter, their status is less legitimated, their right to privileged communication less established, there is less of a specialised body of knowledge, and they have less autonomy from supervision or societal control than the 'professions'. (1969: v)

...while the semi-professionals are more supervised than the professionals, supervision is more often conducted by their own kind. (1969: xv)

Etzioni is referring here to *line management* supervision, rather than to the type of *therapeutic or consultative* supervision, which is integrally associated with counselling and psychotherapy practice (for further discussion, see Chapter 7). Nonetheless, there is a well-recognised tension for many therapists in the prospect of being line-managed by people who are non-therapists and who do not necessarily subscribe to therapeutic values, e.g. relating to client confidentiality and information-sharing. 'Privileged communication' refers here to legal powers, which protect client or patient confidentiality from access by the courts.

Sally Aldridge was a representative of BACP during the most recent attempt to secure statutory regulation for counselling and psychotherapy.

She presents an interesting argument that these are 'insecure professions' with weak occupational boundaries. At critical moments, BACP has decisively opted for an *inclusive* approach to membership (hence the earlier title referring to the 'British Association *for* Counselling and Psychotherapy', rather than *'of* Counsellors and Psychotherapists'). Until comparatively recently, BACP has been reluctant to define membership criteria in a strict and exclusive manner. It could, for example, have opted to restrict entry *only* to applicants completing BACP-accredited courses, or *only* to those achieving individual accreditation. The process of negotiating statutory regulation with sceptical government figures was perhaps hampered by BACP's adoption of a relatively self-effacing (rather than a more assertive) lobbying approach. BACP failed, therefore, to push through its own agenda with sufficient forcefulness. This collaborative approach may have been perceived as reflecting weakness, on the part of the largely female-dominated occupational group of counsellors and psychotherapists, by the largely male gatekeepers, who held the power to award or withhold institutional recognition. This is a persuasive insider view. Nevertheless, it perhaps understates the more objective barriers to statutory regulation for new professions in the post-Thatcher era. In neo-liberal market economies, the emphasis is now firmly on de-professionalisation, rather than the creation of yet more new emerging professions (Aldridge, 2010).

Counselling as 'a community of practice'

An alternative view to the concept of counselling and psychotherapy as a semi-profession, or even as an *insecure* profession, is to reframe the discussion, away from the fruitless pursuit of professional status. Wenger (1998) suggests that it may be useful to look at groups of professionals, working together in a shared culture, with common values and understandings, as constituting 'a community of practice'. This is a difficult concept to define with any degree of precision, but it embraces groups of people coming together to work on and resolve particular problems or projects. Wenger uses the term to describe something that is broader than just a team, or a department within an organisation. It may be stretching his concept somewhat, but exploring counselling and psychotherapy as just such a 'community of practice' has the merit of shifting discussion away from a relentless focus on the quest for professional recognition, in the form of statutory regulation. So what is a community of practice? Essentially, this consists of 'a community of mutual engagement, a negotiated enterprise, and a repertoire of negotiable resources accumulated over time' (Wenger, 1998: 126).

Translating from this somewhat abstract, academic language, such a community requires a shared approach towards group membership and roles, a shared understanding of task and process, and a shared experience and a means of communicating with others of like mind. This awareness of belonging to a community makes a lot of sense at an *experiential and relational* level, in that counsellors will often quickly establish good working relationships with each other. They will routinely share their knowledge and skills with other practitioners, in the service of working with the client, rather than immediately retreating behind specialisms of therapeutic modality. Of course, there will always be some exceptions to this rather optimistic scenario, but differences of modality and professional label may often be submerged by a common interest in providing effective therapy for a given client or set of clients. This approach stresses the role of *shared values*, rather than focusing on *power* as such (see Box 1.4).

Box 1.4 The key characteristics of a community of practice

Such a concept of practice includes both the explicit and the tacit. ... It includes the language, tools, documents, images, symbols, well-defined roles, specified criteria, codified procedures, regulations and contract that various practices make explicit for a variety of purposes. But it also includes all the implicit relations, tacit conventions, subtle cues, untold rules of thumb, recognizable intuitions, specific perceptions, well-tuned sensitivities, embodied understandings, underlying assumptions, and shared world views. Many of these may never be articulated, yet they are unmistakable signs of membership in communities of practice and are crucial to the success of their enterprises. (Wenger, 1998: 47)

A community of practice is a unique combination of three fundamental elements: a *domain* of knowledge, which defines a set of issues; a *community* of people who care about this domain; and the shared *practice* that they are developing to be effective in their domain. (Wenger et al., 2002: 27)

This approach to exploring counselling as a community of practice places an emphasis on the shared, but largely informal, *culture* of counselling and psychotherapy. It focuses on shared meanings and expectations, rather than on formal roles, rules and qualifications. You may find that the idea of a community of practice quickly becomes real at an experiential level, when joining a discussion, a group, workshop, or conference which is composed of counsellors, rather than activities which include a broad mix of professionals from very different working backgrounds.

Developing critical perspectives of counselling as a new profession

Clearly, the drive for recognition as a fully qualified new profession is not a straightforward or easy process. Other powerful groups and interests in society may challenge, or even ridicule, the arguments put forward by newly emerging occupational groups. Classically, other more powerful groups have criticised counselling on the grounds that counselling is 'just talking' or that 'anyone can do it'. Other established professions, such as medicine and law, may actively oppose newer groups achieving a degree of professional control, given that a profession can be defined as 'a monopoly in the public interest' (Gross, 1967: 47). Established professions, which have already achieved a degree of this type of monopoly power over specialised services, may be reluctant to admit newer occupational groups to full professional status, particularly if this step involves a reduction in their own power. The issue of how counselling and psychotherapy relate to medicine and the law therefore becomes another factor to consider in exploring the process of achieving professional status, which will be briefly touched on later.

Exercise   Exploring approaches to professionalisation

Consider one of these four approaches to the professionalisation of counselling and psychotherapy, as outlined above. Make brief notes of the positive and negative aspects of one of these for future reference.

Developing critical perspectives on the role of counselling in society

Other perspectives may be critical, either of counselling's claim to hold specific expertise, or of the ways in which this expertise may be put to use in society. Some of the main critiques and arguments about the role of counselling in this regard include the following:

- counselling and psychotherapy is a *social project*, promoting unhealthy levels of emotional vulnerability in society, based on its own vested interest in offering 'solutions' to largely invented problems of low self-esteem and trauma;

- counselling is a valuable form of *social engineering*, geared to reducing the distress of mental illness, via state-funded provision on a medical model;
- counselling is a by-product of affluence, *narrowly focused on individual change* and ignoring wider social issues of poverty and austerity.

These critiques and perspectives are briefly outlined and explored below.

Counselling as promoting social and individual vulnerability

One recent critique is by Furedi (2004), who argues that counselling seeks to exaggerate normal problems of transition and manageable anxiety in order to create a role for itself in apparently providing 'solutions' to these problems. His critique covers a wide range of applications of counselling, or 'therapy culture', to encompass trauma counselling, workplace counselling and counselling in schools and universities (see Box 1.5).

Box 1.5   Counselling and self-reliance: A project promoting a moral panic about vulnerability

I was meeting a friend in the lobby of the University of London Union. While killing time, my attention was drawn to a large poster displayed prominently on the wall. The poster was advertising one of the innumerable helplines that cater for university students. In bold black letters it proclaimed: 'The stiff upper lip went out in the 1940s'. Almost immediately, I understood that this in-your-face celebration of counselling contained an important statement about our times. The stiff upper lip was out and a new culture of helplines, support groups, counselling services, mentors, facilitators and emotional conformism was in. (Furedi, 2003: 22)

Therapeutic culture has helped construct a diminished sense of self that characteristically suffers from an emotional deficit and possesses a permanent sense of vulnerability. (Furedi, 2004: 21)

Furedi argues that therapy culture perceives people's emotions as 'objects to be managed', rather than experiences to be endured and learned from (2004: 34). In terms of his philosophical stance, Furedi is writing from a classically liberal position, in resisting pressures from the wider society, or from the state itself, which encroach on the individual's autonomy and liberty. This has much in common with a Stoic position within classical Greek philosophy, namely of developing cheerful acceptance of life's adversities (see Howard, 2000: 62–79; Vesey and Foulkes, 1999: 275–276).

In a curious way, Furedi, a critical sociologist, is echoing the views of Victorian advocates of *self-reliance and self-help*. However, his views are increasingly out of step with changing perceptions of counselling and its role in contemporary society. Market research, commissioned by BACP, has indicated a sea-change in the wider public's perceptions of counselling. By 2004, 83% of British adults have had, or would consider having, counselling or psychotherapy (Future Foundation Projects, 2004: 17). Only 18% would 'never consider having counselling or psychotherapy'. Of course, on its own this does not demonstrate that Furedi's arguments are without some justification. Simply, he is arguing a minority case, given that the public acceptance of counselling has significantly increased over time.

Furedi's approach also tallies with that held by Epictetus, another Greek philosopher, who is credited with the saying: 'Men are troubled not so much by circumstances, as by their reactions to circumstances' (Howard, 2000: 68). This view correlates closely with the crucial role of *cognition*, or *thinking*, within cognitive behaviour therapy. The link with cognitive behaviour therapy is taken up in a different way by the next writer, who claims that CBT and counselling can play a major role in addressing society's current pressing mental health problems.

Counselling as producing a happier society

Lord Layard (2006) has taken a very positive view of the role of CBT and, to a lesser extent of counselling and other therapies, as a means of addressing and reducing the current high levels of depression and anxiety within society. This approach has provided the rationale for the influential Improving Access to Psychological Therapy (IAPT) programme. This has radically transformed the entire landscape of counselling and psychotherapy in England (see Box 1.6).

Box 1.6   Counselling and social engineering: Aiming to produce a happier society

We should look for the state in which people are happiest; the guide for public policy being how we can enable people to lead the happiest possible lives. (Layard, 2006: 6)

If you focus on the least happy people and ask how they differ from other people, you will find that the single most important factor is their record of mental illness. We know that while one in six people at any one time would be diagnosed as having mental health problems, only a quarter of these people are in treatment. Therefore, it must be a major objective of our society to get treatment available and used by the great majority of those people. It means a total change in the treatment we offer people, not only for those with psychotic disorders but also for those who have clinical depression or chronic anxiety conditions. They should be offered what NICE guidelines say they should be offered: not only medication but also psychological therapies, especially CBT [cognitive behaviour therapy], but also other therapies where relevant. (Layard, 2006: 7)

From a philosophical perspective, Layard is proposing a classical *utilitarian* rationale for the IAPT policy. This is consistent with the position adopted by Bentham, who favoured social legislation geared to achieving 'the greatest happiness of the greatest number' (Bentham, in Howard, 2000: 210).

Layard's goal is, effectively, one of *social engineering*, in order to reduce levels of distress in the population. His method is to use only psychological therapies of proven value. This requires therapies to have been rigorously evaluated, usually in the form of randomised controlled trials, according to 'best evidence' standards, as applied by the medical profession in devising the NICE guidelines. In terms of counselling and professional status, this needs the former to apply standards of evidence which are derived from medicine, using a quantitative methodology, firmly set within a positivist standpoint. Counselling and psychotherapy research is thus put under the wing of medical science, rather than being able to rely on its own independently developed research criteria. It has also placed counselling and psychotherapy at a significant disadvantage to other occupational groupings, such as clinical and counselling psychology. The latter have contributed to a much more extensive evidence base, which is now available for CBT. The evidence for CBT today is substantial, as compared with an often ill-defined 'counselling', as an alternative therapeutic intervention in scientific trials for depression and anxiety.

Counselling as an alternative to social reform

Layard takes the high levels of mental illness and distress as his starting point in arguing a case for making CBT and other therapies available on a much wider scale. Nevertheless, Wilkinson and Pickett (2010) are concerned to pose the question *why* these levels are so high in the first place, given the rise of post-war affluence in many Western societies. They identify that, as societies have experienced a rising standard of living, for much of the post-war period, a real paradox has emerged. Levels of self-esteem have risen in society, but so have levels of anxiety and depression. This is a curious finding for counsellors, as our received wisdom might suggest instead that high self-esteem is an *antidote* to anxiety and depression. However, Wilkinson and Pickett claim that this self-esteem is insecure in its foundations, resting on high levels of what individuals perceive as a 'social evaluative threat'. This, in turn, produces growing levels of stress, measurable via increased levels of the hormone cortisol. From a counselling perspective, this highly insecure but increased self-esteem might be framed in terms of an *external locus of evaluation*, using a person-centred language. Self-esteem is thus high *only* if one can be sure that others constantly approve of one's behaviour, achievements and possessions. Some supporting evidence for this view is suggested by one study in Denmark, which found that taking a break from using Facebook was associated with feeling happier, for both children and adults (Happiness Research Institute, 2015).

For Wilkinson and Pickett (2010), the ultimate cause of these high levels of social anxiety and depression in many Western societies is the high level of social inequality, which increases a sense of social evaluative threat. More equal societies report lower levels of mental health problems, according to the authors (see Box 1.7).

Box 1.7 Counselling and social reform: The problems of anxiety and depression linked to 'social evaluative threat'

Politics was once seen as a way of improving people's social and emotional wellbeing by changing their economic circumstances. But over the last few decades the bigger picture has been lost. People are now much more likely to see psychosocial wellbeing as dependent on what can be done at the individual level, using cognitive behavioural therapy – one person at a time – or on providing support in early childhood, or on the reassertion of religious or 'family' values. (Wilkinson and Pickett, 2010: 238)

The solution to the problems caused by social inequality is not mass psychotherapy aimed at making everyone less vulnerable. (Wilkinson and Pickett, 2010: 32–33)

It follows from this view that social policies, such as IAPT, do not address the real underlying causes of mental distress and will therefore not be successful in resolving them. However, many counsellors will already be aware of the impact of inequality within society on mental health. They may also be aware that they can see the positive effects of their own therapeutic work in individual clients over time. They will be aware too of the growing evidence base for the effectiveness of counselling and psychotherapy in helping clients to overcome these concerns.

Exercise   Evaluating critiques of counselling

Decide which of these three social critiques and perspectives in relation to counselling is closest to your own personal views. Now, take the critique or perspective you disagree with most. What arguments can you make *against* the case you agree with *most*?

Exploring the relationship of counselling and psychotherapy to other professions

One of the ways of exploring the relationship of counselling and psychotherapy as a profession, or semi-profession, or even as a 'community of practice', is to compare them with other professional groups. Counsellors will inevitably come into contact through their work with other more established professional groups, such as doctors, psychologists and lawyers. It is important to develop a good working understanding of the roles and contributions of these other professional groups in order to build better working relationships with them.

- **Medicine**: Counsellors will often work alongside members of the medical profession in multi-disciplinary teams, for example in occupational health, or in primary care within the NHS. Counsellors may also come into professional contact with psychiatrists, when working in more specialised medical settings, such as mental health services, either in the community or in hospital settings. The medical profession is much more hierarchical and structured than counselling, with a longer period of training. Issues of diagnosis and treatment are considered to be central to medical practice. Until recently, doctors had a monopoly of prescribing drugs and medication, but it has now become possible for advanced nurse practitioners to carry out this activity, after taking the relevant training. Within psychiatry, doctors will usually refer to diagnostic manuals, such as ICD-10 (World Health Organization, 2010) or DSM-5 (American Psychiatric Association, 2013), which identify specific symptoms associated with particular mental health conditions; e.g. auditory hallucinations may be indicative of schizophrenia. Appropriately qualified doctors have the legal authority to admit patients suffering from a mental disorder to hospital for treatment, under the Mental Health Act 1983. Some psychiatrists will have completed at least some level of psychotherapy as part of their specialist training. Doctors are represented by the British Medical Association and are regulated by the General Medical Council.

- **Psychology**: Within the field of psychology, there is huge variation in terms of levels of qualification, expertise and employment. In IAPT, many counsellors may work alongside, or be employed as PWPs (Psychological Wellbeing Practitioners), providing initial support to patients or clients, regarding low-level anxiety or depression, on a stepped care model (see Chapter 4 for more detailed discussion of this model of care). PWPs will have an initial training in CBT, and provide guidance by phone or in person to clients, perhaps by guiding them towards computerised self-help programmes, through referral for exercise, or for purposeful reading of self-help guides. Other psychologists with postgraduate training may work as clinical psychologists, or as counselling psychologists, offering a range of therapeutic interventions to clients. They may provide 'high intensity' therapeutic work with clients who show more complex presentations, such as obsessive compulsive disorder or chronic depression. Psychologists, as a profession, are represented by the British Psychological Society (BPS) and are regulated by the Health and Care Professions Council. Some forms of psychological intervention are restricted to appropriately trained members of the BPS, such as the use of formalised assessments for dyslexia or autism. Increasingly, psychologists act as supervisors of counsellors, or of teams of counsellors, within the NHS and are often seen to have a stronger research base than counsellors, as active 'practitioner researchers'.

- **Law**: Counsellors may be somewhat less likely to come into professional contact with members of the legal profession, at least on a regular basis. When they do, it is often in the context of a requirement to respond to a legal request, or order, which can become quite challenging as an experience. Lawyers, like doctors, belong to a hierarchical and quite structured profession. Until recently, lawyers tended to be divided between solicitors, who provided legal advice, and barristers, who represented clients in court. This division has been eroded, as solicitors have gained the right to act as advocates in court. Barristers are represented by the Bar Council and are regulated by the Bar Standards Board. Solicitors are represented by the Law Society and regulated by the Solicitors Regulatory Authority.

Counsellors may be contacted by lawyers for access to their client records, for use as evidence in either civil or criminal proceedings. One difficulty is that counselling training rarely provides much coverage of the legal system relating to counselling, other than at a very basic level, e.g. regarding confidentiality. Counselling training, therefore, does not properly equip counsellors to write court reports on their clients, nor to appear as professional witnesses, in contrast with other professional groups, such as social workers. However, much of counselling practice is set firmly within a legal context, such as the crucial role of contracts in private practice or supervision. It is important, therefore, for counsellors to build up their knowledge and confidence in dealing with legal matters and with the legal profession as a whole (see Chapter 5).

Becoming a professional counsellor and psychotherapist

It can be helpful, in undergoing the process of counsellor training, to have a model of professional development in mind. Often these are 'stages' models of development, involving progression from lower levels of skill, to more advanced and more independent forms of practice. One such model is proposed by Dreyfus and Dreyfus (1986), who distinguish between the following levels of practitioner development:

- **Novice**: This involves a process of learning which relies heavily on the *rules* of the activity in question. A common example in early counselling skills training is the internalised injunction about 'not asking the client questions'. This is thought to take the counsellor *away* from the client's *own* frame of reference. Rules can take on the quality of being absolute and, at this stage, rather like the client, are not 'open to question'. This approach is rather rigid, but perhaps understandable, in that assessment of competence at this early stage may well be based on observable compliance with basic 'rules' of how best to communicate empathically with clients.
- **Advanced beginner**: This is where the developing practitioner can begin to discern aspects of the client's behaviour, which then

inform the counsellor's decision-making, both inside and outside the session. An example of this might be recognising that a client hearing voices may signal the onset of psychotic symptoms, which should be taken back to supervision. The counsellor, although still a beginner, can recognise limits to their own competence and seek advice and support from more experienced colleagues.

- **Competent**: Here, the therapist can apply learned 'rules' from their earlier and ongoing training, but in a more relaxed and creative manner. Hence, the practitioner can begin to *anticipate* events, *before* they unfold, without this necessarily driving the therapeutic process. An example might be where the therapist has a sense that the client is on the cusp of experiencing anger, in the context of a recent major bereavement, or that a client may be likely to experience (even an agreed) ending of therapy as abandonment by the counsellor, based on the client's description of experiences in undergoing painful losses in the past.

- **Proficient**: Here, the practitioner has an awareness of nuances, such as perhaps subtle shifts in voice tone, eye contact and appearance, which are part of an underlying, but still easily missed, pattern of meaning for the client. These nuances probably would be missed by a novice, lacking both the proficient practitioner's experience and the latter's growing ability to recognise subtle patterns of client expression and meaning, such as shame or disappointment.

- **Expert**: At this level, the therapist works in a largely intuitive (but highly effective) manner, based on their experience and their own learning. The therapist has a strong and usually accurate sense of how to work best with the client, but may find it hard 'in the moment' to identify exactly *why* a certain emotional response was given. Therapist responses at this level may be governed more by immediate context and the sensed relationship with the client, rather than by reference to rules learned back in the early stages of training. An example might be where an experienced practitioner decides to vary the agreed length of sessions to two hours, after quick consultation with the client concerned, or to offer a video session in place of the usual face-to-face meeting.

The following example gives a flavour of how this process of learning can become internalised:

> I learned all the rules and so I came to a point – after a lot of effort – where I knew the rules very well. Gradually, I modified the rules. Then I began to use the rules to let me go where I wanted to go. Lately I haven't been talking so much in terms of rules. (Dreyfus and Dreyfus, 1986: 66–67)

Exercise   Evaluating your own professional development

What stage are you currently at in terms of your own professional development? What do you need to achieve in order to be confident about moving on from, or at least remaining at, your current stage as a practitioner? Select one aspect of the criteria from the BACP *Ethical Framework for the Counselling Professions* (2016) to work on, and set a specific goal to achieve over the next month.

Becoming a professional

The chapter so far has suggested that counselling and psychotherapy may not have reached full recognition in terms of their achieving full status as a profession. There is, however, an important distinction between being a member of a profession and being a *professional*. This is not simply in terms of being paid – counsellors are required to act and behave in a professional manner, even when giving their services for free, perhaps as a student or as a volunteer working towards accreditation. So what does being (or becoming) a professional counsellor involve?

Some standards of professionalism can be set out fairly easily. Counsellors need to be competent to provide therapy. This is easily said, but working to develop skills may often involve practising at the very edge of your own level of confidence and skill. Every counsellor will have worked with a potentially suicidal client for the first time at some point in their career. A crucial point here is the need to appreciate the need for ongoing support and consultation with other more experienced colleagues and to recognise your own limitations. One paradox is that counselling (apart from with couples and in groups) may largely be delivered on a one-to-one basis, but is, in many ways, a very *collegiate and collaborative* process, based on *sharing knowledge*, whether through continuous professional development (CPD) or through taking part in group supervision, hence the emphasis in the *Ethical Framework for the Counselling Professions* (BACP, 2016) on collaborative work with colleagues. Accurate record-keeping may be another aspect of this, because colleagues and service managers may need access to client records to maintain continuity of care to a given client. The counselling relationship is primarily a relationship between the client and the counsellor. However, it is also, at least in part, a relationship between the client and the *agency* that the counsellor represents and is a volunteer for, or is employed by. Records are one aspect of collaborative practice in that another counsellor may need access to records to provide counselling in your absence or once you have left the agency.

Counsellors are increasingly expected to keep up to date with the fast-developing evidence base for their work. This can be done by reading professional journals from BACP, and from the more specialist divisions, such as for workplace counselling, or counselling children and young people. Many counsellors are resistant to research, perhaps seeing it as an academic exercise and unrelated to their ongoing practice. It is worth making a habit of reading at least one research article from journals such as *Counselling and Psychotherapy Research* to keep up to date with practice with your own client group, or to begin to develop new specialist interests.

The concept of becoming a professional has been open to some criticism in the past, in almost implying a rigid separation between the person and the professional role, as a kind of 'mask' that professionals sometimes wear. Counselling training makes it very clear that therapy is about *being* as well as *doing*. Being role-bound, as a therapist, is likely to come at the cost of being congruent, empathic and authentic in client work, and more generally in all our personal relationships. The BACP *Ethical Framework for the Counselling Professions* (2016) stresses the importance of self-care, both physical and psychological, in managing the stresses as well as the pleasures of therapeutic work.

In the main, these are probably quite conventional and well-established standards of being a professional. Others may be more subtle, being based on interpersonal communication with clients and colleagues. Time-keeping is critical for counsellors, through being in place and 'prepped' by reading notes from a previous session, with the counselling room already set out in its usual way, before client work begins. Emails need to be responded to quickly and courteously. How we dress as counsellors is also significant, in terms of the messages we may give off to potential clients, colleagues, or members of other professions. What is seen as appropriate dress, or appearance, may vary according to context and audience, with probably a higher incidence of suits being worn among workplace counsellors, perhaps, than among counsellors working with young people. As counsellors, we may not be a formally recognised profession, but we still need to impress clients, colleagues and members of other occupational groups and professions, as being fully and recognisably *professional* in what we do.

Summary

This chapter set out the key features of what it is to be a profession and discussed some of the problems experienced by counselling and psychotherapy in their bid to achieve statutory regulation. Different models of professionalisation were considered, such as counselling as a semi-profession, and as a community of practice. Social critiques and perspectives of counselling were outlined, in terms of counselling undermining self-reliance, ignoring social inequality, or making a major contribution to reducing mental health problems in society. The relationship of counselling to other professions, such as medicine, psychology and the law, was briefly noted. Finally, a model of the stages of professional development was suggested, together with some of the main features of what it means to be a 'professional', as an aid to understanding the differing demands and opportunities available at different points of our overall development as therapists.

Resources

Research

Aldridge, S. (2010) 'Counselling – an insecure profession? A sociological and historical analysis'. Thesis submitted for the degree of Doctor of Philosophy at the University of Leicester, November 2010.

A detailed case study of BACP's development as a professional grouping and its attempts to achieve statutory regulation, by a well-informed insider: https://lra. le.ac.uk/bitstream/2381/10261/1/2011aldridgesphd.pdf. For a 30-minute video presentation by Sally Aldridge on this topic, go to: www2.le.ac.uk/offices/red/ researcher-development/DIL-video-archive/css/Counselling-an%20Insecure %20Profession

Bondi, L. (2004) '"A double-edged sword?" The professionalisation of counselling in the United Kingdom', *Health and Place*, 10, 319–328.

Discussion of perceived advantages and disadvantages of professionalisation of counselling, based on interviews with counsellors in Scottish voluntary sector counselling (n: 100).

Centre for Economic Performance Mental Health Policy Group (2006) *The Depression Report: A New Deal for Depression and Anxiety Disorders* (also known as 'the Layard Report'), http://cep.lse.ac.uk/pubs/download/special/ depressionreport.pdf

An influential report which laid the groundwork for the Improving Access to Psychological Therapies (IAPT) programme and the current dominance of CBT in secondary mental health care within the NHS, via the use of NICE evidence-based practice.

Future Foundation Projects (2004) *The Age of Therapy: Exploring Attitudes Towards and Acceptance of Counselling and Psychotherapy in Modern Britain*. London: Future Foundation, www.bacp.co.uk/media/index.php?newsId=309

A key piece of market research, based on telephone interviews (n: 1008), demonstrating significant shifts towards wider social acceptance of counselling in Britain.

Further reading

Aldridge, S. (2014) *A Short Introduction to Counselling*. London: Sage.

A brief, well-informed overview of counselling as a professional occupation and activity.

Cooper, M. (2008) *Essential Research Findings in Counselling and Psychotherapy*. London: Sage.

Useful summary of the evidence for counselling and psychotherapy's efficacy.

Daines, B., Gask, L. and Howe, A. (2007) *Medical and Psychiatric Issues for Counsellors*. London: Sage.

Introduction to the main roles and activities of doctors, psychiatrists and other staff working in medical settings such as the NHS.

Jenkins, P. (2007) *Counselling, Psychotherapy and the Law*. Second edition. London: Sage.

See Chapter 8, pp. 177–193, for a short account of the background and history of the movement towards achieving statutory regulation of therapists.

Reference section for supervisors

The BACP Professional Standards' *Counselling Supervision Training Curriculum* (2014) sets out relevant expectations for supervisors:

Competence 4: Applying Standards:

- knowledge of expected standards of professional conduct;
- knowledge of relevant professional and statutory codes of conduct that set out expected standards for pre- and post-qualification;
- knowledge of standards of clinical practice as defined by both relevant training organisations and local arrangements for clinical governance. (BACP Professional Standards, 2014: 10)

2

Working in different organisational contexts as a counsellor or psychotherapist

Introduction

This chapter looks at the somewhat neglected topic of the organisational context of counselling practice and introduces a model for understanding counselling organisations, based on evaluating their organisational culture. It includes:

- understanding the impact of organisational context on counselling practice;
- exploring the different types of organisational culture;
- working as a counsellor in hybrid or 'mixed' organisational cultures.

Learning context

The BACP *Core Curriculum* (2009) highlights the need for students to be aware of the organisational context of their practice, and this is also emphasised by the *Counselling Supervision Training Curriculum* (BACP Professional Standards, 2014). The BACP *Ethical Framework for the Counselling Professions* (2016) locates the need for organisational understanding mainly in terms of expected *behaviours* related to maintaining professional standards, such as respect, accountability and candour, while underlining the need to access supervision, which is largely independent of formal line management.

BACP *Core Curriculum* (2009)

B9.1.D The social, political and organisational context for therapy:

11. Demonstrate an awareness of power relationships and dynamics within groups and organisations and their potential impact on therapy. (2009: 19)

B6.2 Students must be made aware of the wider political, social, legal and organisational framework for therapeutic practice; to ensure that they are able to work appropriately in different counselling and psychotherapy contexts. (2009: 19).

BACP *Ethical Framework for the Counselling Professions* (2016)

Working to professional standards:

16. We will collaborate with colleagues over our work with specific clients where this is consistent with client consent and will enhance services to the client. (2016: 6)

Respect:

24. We will challenge colleagues and others involved in delivering related services whose views appear to be discriminatory and take action to protect clients if necessary... (2016: 7)

Accountability and candour:

45. We will take responsibility for how we offer our clients opportunities to work towards their desired outcomes and the safety of the services we provide or have responsibility for overseeing. ...

49. We will monitor how clients experience our work together and the effects of the work with them in ways appropriate to the type of service being offered. (2016: 10)

Understanding the impact of organisational context on counselling practice

By definition, all counselling practice takes place in some kind of organisational context, whether it takes the form of counselling in a statutory setting, such as the NHS, or in a voluntary or third sector agency, or in private practice. Curiously, while the *implications* of organisational context are often described in some detail in many accounts of therapy, the wider sense of the organisational background is elsewhere often noticeably absent. Hence 'contextual factors have been largely ignored in counselling theory, research and practice' (McLeod and Machin, 1998: 325). McLeod has maintained a particular interest in this issue over a long period of time in his writing. He goes on to suggest that this neglect may reflect the individualistic focus of most counselling theories (McLeod, 2013: 331). Counsellors are trained to work in the one-to-one, or with couples, or groups. It follows on from this that there is very little writing on applying management and organisational theory to the day-to-day practice of actually *running* counselling organisations (Lago and Kitchin, 1998). This relative neglect of the *theory* of how counselling practice is related to its organisational context is shown in the scarcity of relevant research, models and discussion over the past few decades, at least in the UK (but see Walton (1997, 2010) as a relatively rare exception). This outline therefore draws upon an eclectic range of sources, identified from writing since the 1980s, as well as using more recent sources. Hopefully, this gap in the theory and practice of counselling will be made good in future writing on the topic. In the meantime, the outline discusses some useful models which offer ways of making sense of practice and how organisational setting can radically influence counselling practice, for good or ill.

The organisational context can impact very directly on key features of the therapeutic work in a wide variety of ways. This can range from determining the length of client waiting lists to influencing the goals of therapy and the nature of the process of contracting and defining the limits to confidentiality. Lees (1999) suggests that counsellors actually acquire quite some level of expertise on the organisational background to their practice. They learn how to adapt to the specific requirements imposed by the organisation, whether this is a prison, a university, or a specialist trauma counselling service. However, this knowledge and expertise is developed mainly on a practical, day-to-day survival basis. It is rarely *theorised* in ways which would draw out the more generic principles influencing the relationship between organisational setting and counselling practice, other than in a very pragmatic manner.

> Counsellors, by virtue of the fact that they are usually exposed to the whole range of contextual factors in the organisations in which they work, are able to build up a degree of expertise which arises out of their capacity to understand how the context affects the work. They are, so to speak, experts in working with all the issues that arise from the interface of organisational, social, cultural, political and clinical issues. (Lees, 1999: 17)

Embedding counselling practice in organisations

A good example of how the organisational context can impact directly on counselling practice is shown by the very real challenges faced by counsellors in embedding counselling within schools. Research for the Welsh Assembly by BACP identified no less than 40 separate areas requiring specific attention (Pattison et al., 2009: 170). The vast majority of the requirements relate to *organisational*, rather than to purely *therapeutic*, issues. The latter were nevertheless clearly important and included key aspects of counselling practice, such as:

- *professional* requirements, e.g. the level of the counsellors' training and experience;
- *therapeutic* requirements, e.g. their theoretical orientation, or use of modality, such as group or one-to-one therapy.

In contrast, the vast bulk of *organisational* requirements needed for the successful embedding of the service included a wide range of critical aspects, such as:

- *resourcing*, e.g. funding, access to suitable rooms for counselling;
- *line management*, e.g. the employment of counsellors, their job description, terms and conditions;
- *service delivery*, e.g. the availability of counselling, types of referral system, on- or off-site provision;
- *operational management*, e.g. core policies and procedures, such as for safeguarding, confidentiality and record-keeping;
- *monitoring and evaluation*, e.g. use of appropriate outcome measures, arrangements for reporting back to school, agency and relevant stakeholders.

Relevance of organisational context

The above example shows that this process of embedding counselling practice within an organisation can be quite complex in reality. It also tends to confirm McLeod's earlier point that counselling practice does not occur in a vacuum, but 'always takes place in an organisational and social context' (McLeod, 2013: 523). Hence, 'counselling organisations can exert a strong influence on both their clients *and* their staff. The type of agency and setting, and the way it is organised and managed, can have a significant influence on how effective a counsellor is able to be' (McLeod, 2013: 609). This can include systems for client selection and assessment, waiting lists, the agreed limits to the number of sessions, use of outcome measures, and the physical environment, such as reception, waiting rooms and counselling rooms. The organisation will determine arrangements for funding, fees, charges or voluntary contributions, recording systems and the overall ethos, purpose and style of the counselling provided, depending on the degree of control or autonomy it affords the therapists working for it, on a paid or voluntary basis.

Different types of organisational context

For certain types of organisation, counselling is its *primary* purpose. One example could be a specialist counselling organisation like Relate, which provides relationship counselling. In some organisations, counselling may only be a *secondary*, or *supportive*, part of the organisation's wider purpose, or mission, as for example in the case of counselling in a school context. In addition, organisations can be usefully categorised as to whether they are part of the public or statutory sector, voluntary and third sector, or are part of the private sector.

- **Statutory sector**: Counselling in the statutory sector could include the National Health Service (NHS), Improving Access to Psychological Therapies (IAPT), Child and Adolescent Mental Health Services (CAMHS); education, such as primary and secondary schools, sixth-form colleges, further and high education; and the criminal justice system, such as youth custody and prison settings.
- **Voluntary/third sector**: This covers a wide range of provision, from local voluntary agencies providing counselling services, often church-based in terms of their origins, to established national organisations, such as Women's Aid, National Society for the Prevention of Cruelty to Children (NSPCC) and Victim Support.
- **Private sector**: This includes private practice, whether by individuals or by a group of practitioners, or counselling provision by private agencies on a 'for-profit' basis.

A great deal of counselling is provided by the voluntary or third sector. Handy (1988) distinguishes between different types of voluntary organisation, such as service providers, research and advocacy organisations and self-help organisations such as Alcoholics Anonymous. According to Handy, service-delivery voluntary organisations 'exist to meet a need to provide help to those who need it. They take pride in being professional, effective and low-cost' (1988: 14).

Exercise Evaluating your own experiences of working in organisations

What is your own experience of working in organisations? List some of the organisations (including holiday work, voluntary work and part-time jobs) where you have worked, and rate them in terms of job satisfaction as high, medium or low. Pick one to explore in more detail and identify some of the main factors influencing your choice of rating.

Exploring different types of organisational culture

One author defines culture as 'the personal values and beliefs that people in teams, groups and organisations seem to share' (Kakabadse, 1982: 6). He offers a useful way of making sense of the different cultures that counsellors may come across in their work. These are outlined as involving a focus on *power*, *role* and *task* respectively (Harrison, 1972). The main characteristics of these organisational cultures are briefly set out in Figure 2.1.

The examples in Boxes 2.1–2.3 provide illustrations of the three suggested types of organisational culture, as related to different types of counselling organisation.

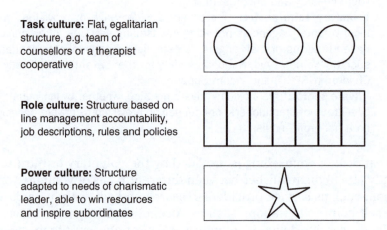

Task culture: Flat, egalitarian structure, e.g. team of counsellors or a therapist cooperative

Role culture: Structure based on line management accountability, job descriptions, rules and policies

Power culture: Structure adapted to needs of charismatic leader, able to win resources and inspire subordinates

Figure 2.1 Contrasting types of organisational culture

Box 2.1 Example of a counselling task culture

We have been able to take the best aspects of our work – essentially summarised as our passion for delivering high-quality counselling tailored to the individual client in an ethical and professional manner – and apply our principles in a method of our choosing, without red tape, unnecessary meetings and restrictions. We are answerable to each other, and we all understand the realities and the practicalities of the job. That is all good.

Every week, we meet to discuss and update each other on our existing contracts, any new referrals, our finances and any other relevant issues. This has always been a meeting of equals. On alternate weeks we make time for peer supervision, which has been both clinically helpful and of enormous benefit in helping each other to feel supported and connected in a profession that can feel very isolating at times. Once a year we have an AGM, which includes associate members too, and a Christmas event. As well as being colleagues for a number of years, we are friends, and it's important to us that we recognize this important aspect of our cooperative. (Gore-Smith, 2015: 31)

Discussion of counselling task culture

The example in Box 2.1 probably represents something of an ideal for many counselling practitioners. It affords individual members a high degree of professional autonomy in their choice of modality, in the type of contract they might negotiate with a client and in their overall approach as a therapist. The example described here also suggests high levels of interpersonal support and, potentially, of the job satisfaction for the participating members. Nonetheless, as with any organisation, ways will need to be found to manage conflict over goals, or over the use of resources, or over group membership. It may be much easier to maintain good working relationships when the organisation is doing well and experiencing growth. However, a real test, for any task-based organisation, may come in trying to resolve any deep-seated conflicts between members. This might arise over a difficult choice, such as a change of direction, or over alternative funding sources, or even the need to 'lose' some participating members, during economic hard times.

Box 2.2 Example of a counselling role culture

A colleague of mine recently told me about a multidisciplinary team meeting that she had attended during the course of her work at a primary care mental health service. The team of mental health workers had been required to increase their caseload and to ask their clients to complete four separate standardised clinical outcome measures each therapeutic session. At the meeting there had been much grumbling and complaining amongst the staff that these additional requirements were onerous, and that the repeated use of clinical measures was disrupting therapeutic work. Their clients were protesting that filling in these forms was taking up precious therapeutic time, and staff did not feel a quantitative measure of such weekly 'progress' could provide any basis for evaluating clinically meaningful change. What had been remarkable, said my colleague, was the way in which during the meeting the manager and clinical leads of the service had eventually concurred with this viewpoint: they agreed that 'everyone knew' these outcome measures were extremely limited and risked being detrimental to client care, but that in order for the service to be funded – in this case to become a site for the Improving Access to Psychological Therapies (IAPT) programme – it was now forced to comply with current NHS governance requirements and demonstrate increased activity targets along with good clinical outcomes. (Rizq, 2012: 7–8)

Discussion of counselling role culture

The example in Box 2.2 is not intended to be representative of all role cultures in emphasising some of the tensions and dissatisfaction recounted here, nor of IAPT programmes in general. No doubt there are many positive features of providing a counselling service within the overall context of a role culture. The benefits could include clear lines of accountability, potential career progression and reference to rule-based protocols for many core aspects of therapy, from record-keeping to risk management. However, the example does capture some of the tensions which may apply for some counsellors when working within a role culture. In such a role culture, it may feel that counsellors' professional autonomy is being restricted by enforced compliance in using prescribed outcome measures. Outcome measures, however valuable, could be experienced by some as representing an *organisational*, but not necessarily a *therapeutic*, priority. Similar kinds of tensions between the professional autonomy seen in task cultures and the need to comply with more formal rules, which are characteristic of role culture, can be seen in counselling teams undergoing major or rapid change. For example, counselling teams in university settings may move to introduce a more uniform system of electronic recording or of risk assessment that can conflict with previous arrangements, which had allowed greater independence to individual practitioners.

Box 2.3   Example of a counselling power culture

Kids Company was always an unusual organisation. It was off by its own in a sector which is commonly collegiate. It made its own rules. So we don't actually know whether it was effective at helping children – though the stories from former service users seem to suggest it had at least some success. ... It's not clear whether it's doing a good job. But that hasn't really affected funding. As with many charities, when it comes to raising money Kids Company's ability to tell a good story has always been more important than its ability to actually do good.

And its leader is a raconteur nonpareil. Camila Batmanghelidjh, a much-larger-than-life figure who founded the charity and dominates its every action and pronouncement, was responsible for setting its standards and was responsible, to its last day, for raising 60 per cent of its revenue. The newspapers claim she 'mesmerised' Cameron, and certainly civil servants seem to have been overruled frequently by politicians keen to be associated with a charismatic character who could make them look good.

But those used to working in the sector will already have spotted the problem here. Founder syndrome. A single individual who retains all decision-making power, who believes their own story, and is integral to the organization's success. The moment that individual is tarnished or has to step aside, the whole structure crumbles. And that is one thing which appears to have happened here.

The other side of the problem is that the charity has invested little in controls. ... It's certainly true that there was no strong scrutiny and control. (Ainsworth, 2015)

Discussion of a counselling power culture

It might be tempting to assume that power cultures cannot exist in a counselling context, given the values of democracy, equality and sensitivity to the needs of others, which are such a strong feature of the counselling community. However, counselling is not immune from the powerful processes which operate within *any* organisation, regardless of whether these are composed of therapists, teachers or police officers. There may be a strong investment in organisations denying that they are based on a power culture, but participants and observers may still identify some of the key features of a power culture at work. These would include the existence of a 'star', or charismatic leader, who has the drive and force of personality to set up an organisation in the first place. Charisma includes the interpersonal skills to lead and motivate others, and the ability to project the organisation successfully to external gatekeepers and to win resources on the necessary scale in order to survive and grow.

Successful charismatic leaders need to innovate, both within the organisation and in relation to the external environment. As a result, rules may sometimes be seen as merely temporary arrangements, to be set aside if preventing organisational growth, or even its very survival. Work relationships may also be based very much on shifting and unreliable alliances, or depend on finding favour in the court of the charismatic leader. The power and status of an individual may rely much more on their personal, or even family, links with the charismatic leader, rather than on their official role, e.g. as accountant, or on their formal line management position, e.g. as head of marketing. Charismatic leadership has undoubted value in responding vigorously to new, previously unrecognised social needs and challenges. However, the organisation may falter if the leader stumbles, or find it hard to consolidate for the longer haul.

Exercise   Evaluating organisational culture

Choose one of the three examples of organisational culture illustrated above. Make a balanced list of the strengths and weaknesses of this type of organisational setting. Evaluate how far this type of organisational culture would meet your own needs and preferences as a developing practitioner.

Overview of organisational cultures in counselling organisations

Kakabadse (1982) provides a useful overview of some major features of different organisations operating across the spectrum, in statutory, voluntary and private sector settings. The suggested ideal-types of task, role and power organisational culture are not exhaustive. In reality, the model will need adapting and teasing out to apply to different types of counselling organisation, which may well not fit neatly into prescribed 'boxes' of this kind. There is also a risk, perhaps, in identifying counselling as essentially constituting a 'task' culture, which does not properly belong in other types of culture, whether pure or, as seen later, as a *mixture* of different cultures.

According to Kakabadse's model, organisational cultures can also be distinguished according to their *structure*. Task cultures may tend to be somewhat 'flatter' and more egalitarian, while role cultures will often be more hierarchical, as being essentially line-management organisations. Power cultures may be more personalised, with a mix of formal line management and what are, in practice, often more powerful *informal* management systems. Task cultures place a high value on professional autonomy and expertise, where counsellors are prized for their experience, skills and their ability to do the job well. Role cultures place a strong value of following *rules*, which have been devised for a reason and serve a number of important purposes. Rules maintain consistency between different practitioners and equity in the treatment of clients. Power cultures, almost by definition, tend to be based on charismatic leadership and decision-making styles. These may appear to be unorthodox at times, but can be justified by 'getting the job done'. Role cultures, in contrast, may tend to deal with uncertainty by trying to reduce the element of risk, or of 'maverick' or unauthorised decision-making, by following set procedures that have been carefully developed over time.

Ethical styles of decision-making may also differ between the different cultures, with task cultures leaning more towards respecting professional autonomy. Here, individual counsellors may balance *outcomes*, e.g. the risk of harm against possible benefits, whereas role cultures possibly may prefer *rule-based* ethics. Power cultures may prefer to rely on using more 'gut' and intuitive styles, which are consistent with their generally more personalised styles of leadership and practice. In terms of warmth and personal support, task cultures may score highly on this feature. For role cultures, support may be linked to continued positive role performance. Power cultures may offer (or even withdraw) intense levels of personal support, depending upon relationships with key 'players', in what might feel at times almost like a medieval court.

Some of these key aspects of the different cultures that may apply to counselling organisations are summarised in Table 2.1.

Table 2.1 Summary of key features of task, role and power cultures within counselling organisations (adapted from Kakabadse, 1982: 15–17)

Organisational aspects	Task culture	Role culture	Power culture
Structure	Egalitarian	Hierarchical	Informal
Core values	Professional autonomy	Rule-following	Personal loyalty
Leadership style	Democratic	Bureaucratic	Charismatic
Decision-making style	Problem-solving	Procedural	Highly personalised
Attitude towards risk	Risk-aware	Risk-averse	Risk-avoidant
Ethical style	Outcome-led	Rule-based	Intuitive
Personal support	Conditional on continued expertise	Conditional on continued role performance	Conditional on personal relationships
Key cultural message	Do your best!	Do your job!	Stick with me!

Exercise   Exploring your own context for counselling practice

Using the summary features in Table 2.1, try to identify some of the main features and messages of your own context for counselling practice, whether for employment or for placement purposes. How far does your organisational context support and promote your learning and professional development? What might need to change?

Task culture in counselling organisations

Task culture can take a number of different forms in counselling organisations. One example has already been given, namely that of a counselling cooperative, where there are high levels of democracy, shared values, practitioner autonomy and, presumably, of resulting job satisfaction. Many counselling organisations in the voluntary or third sector are based on a task culture, where the primary purpose of the organisation is providing a counselling service to clients. These types of organisation include generic counselling services, often originally deriving from faith-based agencies, as well as more specialist counselling services, such as Rape Crisis Centres. While this type of task culture may well need to have some hierarchy and structure in order to function efficiently, at heart it often remains a practitioner-led organisation. Often, key management positions are held by former counsellors, or by counsellors who are formally in a managerial position but who retain a small caseload in order to remain in practice.

Private practice would constitute a classic example of a task culture at work. This will probably read rather strangely to those in private practice. Part of the motivation for opting for private practice may have been to avoid the perceived complications of organisational life. However, any private practice is essentially a small business, and is by definition an organisation of some kind. Private practice offers therapists a high degree of professional and therapeutic autonomy in their work, subject to wider constraints, such as the law of contract and compliance with professional codes of ethics. Nevertheless, this may come at the cost of a degree of separation from other practitioners and the wider professional community, as a predictable feature of this type of organisational context. Clearly, in some instances, 'practising as a therapist can be a somewhat isolating profession and this may particularly be so in private practice' (Kirkbride, 2016: 168).

Combined cultures in counselling organisations

Kakabadse (1982) makes the point that different cultures may operate and apply within the very same organisation. Within hierarchical organisations there may a structure based on a pyramid, where the prevailing culture is strongly determined by the level of authority exercised by individuals (see Figure 2.2).

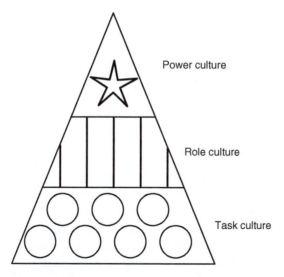

Figure 2.2 Organisational structure, incorporating power, role and task cultures (adapted from Kakabadse, 1982: 109)

In its simplest form, counsellors may operate at the lowest level of the organisation within a *task* culture, where personal and professional relationships depend upon being seen to be doing a good job and keeping to accepted professional and team standards. At the level of middle management, based on a *role* culture, staff may be more focused on maintaining the rules, in order to achieve the goals of the organisation, by checking staff's compliance with policy, managing counsellor time as a scarce resource and monitoring the outcomes achieved. In turn, senior management, at the highest level of the organisation, may be more outward- rather than inward-facing. Managers may be part of a distinctive *power* culture, where the priority is in gaining resources, such as funding and income, and in managing competition by other providers. While at one level this model may appear to be overly schematic, it may also suggest some of the difficulties that counsellors may experience in successfully making a transition from a therapist or supervisor position to a middle or senior manager post.

Organisational culture and the change process

The model of task, role and power culture may also offer some way of understanding *how* counselling organisations may develop over time. New forms of counselling and psychotherapy often begin with a charismatic leader, where experimentation and innovation are key to the emergence of radical news ways of practising. At this early stage, reliance on fixed rules may prove to be premature, and may even stultify the growth of new ideas. Power and the approval of new ideas regarding therapy may often be based on the charismatic authority of a key leader. This seems to have been the case with regard to the development of the psychoanalytic movement, prior to the split between Freud and Jung, where differing models of therapy could no longer be contained within a single organisation. Freud's own view of power, authority and the need for fixed rules is instructive in this respect, as suggested by his biographer, Ernest Jones (1987). The death or departure of a leading charismatic figure in this type of organisation often represents a crisis. The test is whether an organisation based largely around the personality, prestige and personalised authority of a charismatic leader can find a replacement leader. Alternatively, it may be even more challenging, both for the organisation and for its members, to make a successful transition away from the former charismatic power culture towards becoming a more role-based type of organisation (see Box 2.4).

Box 2.4 The early days of the psychoanalytic movement as an example of a power culture

Freud could see little reason for rules in a society, although we got him to tolerate a short list of statutes for the International Psychoanalytical Association. It would happen at times that he would suggest some action which – it would be pointed out – contravened a particular rule or statute. 'Then let us alter it; you can easily put it back again if you want to.' He would often prefer to cut a Gordian knot than to untie it. ... What he was concerned about was that we should retain the freedom to make whatever at any juncture we felt to be the best decision without it being thwarted by a fixed rule. (Jones, 1987: 469)

Working as a counsellor in hybrid or 'mixed' organisational cultures

For many counsellors, their work is provided within an organisation which does not fit any of the pure or ideal-types of model, as suggested by Kakabadse (1982). In some situations, counselling is a subsidiary part of a much wider organisation that may have very different purposes or aims. Examples of this kind of 'hybrid' organisation include counselling services within a largely rule-based culture, such as in a school, a university or a prison setting (see Figure 2.3).

In this type of setting, counselling is a specialist therapeutic activity which runs alongside and is subordinate to other processes, such as the teaching of pupils or students, or the rehabilitation of prisoners. In many cases, the dominant culture of the organisation will be based on relatively fixed roles and rules. Therapy may represent quite a different kind of interpersonal space for both counsellor and client, which appears to be almost at odds with the prevailing organisational culture.

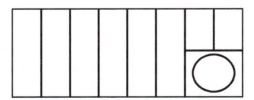

Figure 2.3 Hybrid organisational structure, with dominant role culture and subordinate task culture

> Some clients deal with prison better than others. Counselling sessions can be the only place where they can safely be themselves in a non-judgmental environment. (Hall and Swindells, 2013: 27)

In school-based counselling, as another example of a role-based type of organisational culture, the client may simply appreciate the counsellor offering a very different and certainly more equal type of relationship than may be possible within the more formal constraints of an educational setting:

> I think it would be easier to talk to the counsellor 'cause they are there for you 24–7, but a teacher, she has to care for 30 children in one class. They can't just spend all their time on one. (Fox and Butler, 2007: 104)

Working in role-based organisational cultures

For counsellors used to a more task-based organisational culture, adapting to a more role-based system can prove to be quite challenging. There are a number of strategies that counsellors can develop in order to adapt successfully to the constraints and opportunities offered by role-based or hybrid organisational cultures. These strategies (illustrated below) include:

- providing therapy as a 'protected space' within the organisation;
- developing advocacy for promoting counselling values within the organisation;
- adopting a 'dual focus' that shifts between therapy and wider organisational concerns;
- understanding cultural change processes within counselling organisations;
- working with ethical dilemmas arising from tensions within organisational culture.

Providing therapy as a 'protected space' within the organisation

One (perhaps defensive) strategy may be to offer counselling almost as a therapeutic 'bubble' within the wider host organisation. Rosofsky (2009), working in the distinctive and unusual context of providing therapy in the US managed-care system, provides a striking example of this kind of 'guerilla counselling' (see Box 2.5). The real challenge here may be for the counsellor and the client to establish a separate therapeutic space, with very different boundaries from the external organisation, and to try to maintain these in order to undertake meaningful therapeutic work.

Box 2.5   A psychologist's experiences of providing therapy for older clients in the US residential care system

For my patients, I do my best. When the aide comes in to change the bed, I jabber about the weather. If there's a roommate in the next bed, I'll do a quick assessment of his mental status. If he's too demented to follow the conversation, I'll assume we're in a zone of privacy. (Rosofsky, 2009: 11)

This is not psychotherapy in a designer office with leather chairs, *objets d'art*, and the quiet undertone of a ticking clock. These are field conditions. I'm often moving piled-up clothing or a prosthetic leg to find a place to sit. One of my colleagues abruptly quit after she realised she had been sitting for the past half-hour on a urine-soaked cushion. (Rosofsky, 2009: 12)

Rosofsky (2009) paints a somewhat pessimistic picture of therapy here, as a marginal and perhaps under-valued activity that is seen as being secondary to more important physical health care, in this particular context. In such a setting, a counsellor may well struggle to set up the basic privacy required to undertake meaningful therapeutic work.

Developing advocacy for promoting counselling values within the organisation

Where counselling is seen as being of limited or lesser value than the primary role-based activity of the organisation, such as physical health care, incarceration or education, then there may be tensions around issues of client confidentiality. There may be pressure on the counsellor to share more of the client's sensitive personal information than is consistent with the purposes of therapy. An effective strategy for responding to the particular pressures inherent in adapting to this type of role-based organisation is that of 'embedding' counselling more firmly within the agency in question. Often, counsellors will need to take on the role not just of therapist but also of *advocate* for counselling within the wider host organisation. This may involve relationship-building, information-giving, awareness-training and education for other non-counselling staff on the potential contribution of counselling towards the organisation achieving its wider goals. Cromarty and Richards (2009: 16) give a small, research-based example of this process in exploring how school-based counsellors approach the key issue of maintaining confidentiality, while sharing limited client information with other interested professionals, i.e. teachers, in the school context. This was part of the wider process of embedding counselling more firmly as a valued service within the school.

Adopting a 'dual focus' that shifts between therapy and wider organisational concerns

Another strategy for adapting to the constraints and opportunities provided by working in a dominant role culture is to develop a 'dual focus'. This is the facility of moving from one professional perspective to another without losing sight of the needs of the client or, in this case, the psychiatric patient (see Box 2.6).

Box 2.6 Providing therapy within a psychiatric hospital: Adapting to the medical model

In order to be of service to everybody in a given psychiatric context, the client-centred therapist must work with respect for the medical model of psychiatry, without compromising the philosophy inherent in his work. (Sommerbeck, 2003: 5)

In the medical model of a psychiatric hospital, for example, it is necessary for the client-centred therapist to acknowledge the necessity of psychiatric diagnostics for other professionals and to know about the main psychiatric diagnoses. (Sommerbeck, 2003: 33)

Sommerbeck (2003) writes powerfully about her experience of working as a person-centred therapist in the context of a psychiatric hospital. Here, the dominant role culture can present real challenges for a therapist seeking to work in a client-centred way. Client-centred practice is based on developing a unique therapeutic alliance with each client (or patient), rather than following a role- or rule-based form of practice. Sommerbeck suggests a number of ways in which the therapeutic task culture can be accommodated to the dominant role culture in this situation. First, the therapist needs to work within the established diagnostic language of the psychiatric setting, rather than seeking to challenge its validity on every occasion. She writes persuasively about the therapist as moving between two contrasting models:

> ...the client-centred therapist lives a sort of 'double life' when working in a medical model setting. From the moment a client crosses the doorstep to his consultation room, the therapist sees the world from within the frame of reference of the client. When the therapy session is over, the therapist is back in the world where the dominating frame of reference is that of the medical model. (Sommerbeck, 2003: 38)

Although this is not a concept used by Sommerbeck, this seems close in some ways to the gestalt concept of experiences moving from 'foreground' to 'background' and back again. In person-centred terms, Sommerbeck refers to the concept of the dominant frame of reference in each situation as a useful and productive way of making sense of the expectations to be met variously, both in the therapy room and in the ward round. She argues that the key role of the therapist in this situation is to try to protect the boundaries of the therapeutic process.

Understanding cultural change processes within counselling organisations

Having an understanding of organisational context can help the counsellor to appreciate the possible influences at work when undergoing *change* within an agency. In many cases, this will involve a change or adaptation by task-based cultures, to more role-based ways of working. In the case of voluntary and third sector organisations, this shift towards using more role-based procedures may be a requirement by external funding providers, e.g. compliance with increased use of client outcome measures. However, it may also reflect an adaptation to much wider social shifts in values, affecting *all* counselling organisations, rather than just those in the voluntary or third sector. One example is the shift from a task culture of counsellor record-keeping to one based much more firmly on rules, as required by legislation, in the form of the Data Protection Act 1998. Bedor (2015) provides a useful case study, following the introduction of a more firmly grounded rule-based system of client record-keeping within a local authority occupational health counselling service (see Box 2.7).

> ## Box 2.7 Introducing data protection rule-based client-recording systems into a local authority-based occupational health counselling agency
>
> I have noticed what seems to be the personal nature of note keeping to each practitioner, and how much meaning this has to them, a testament to a firmly protected relationship between therapist client and notes. (Bedor, 2015: 116)
>
> Our current procedure is far from exhaustive and definitive, and will continue to evolve as we become more familiar with the principles, laws and interpretations that inform it. My sense is that our procedure is heavily weighted towards fulfilling our data protection responsibilities, and that this may be at the cost of the therapy. With increasing complexity in our casework, we may choose to retain more case notes, either process or file notes, to keep the consistency and integrity of the therapy intact. (Bedor, 2015: 117)

The shift from autonomous recording practice, based upon the individual counsellor's preference, to a system based on data protection law can best be understood from the framework of a tension between a former task-based culture and the increasing pressure to move to adopt a role- or rule-based procedure. Similar pressures and tensions can be seen in the gathering expectations for assessing, managing and reporting risk to clients and third parties. This might be in the form of reporting current or non-recent child abuse, safeguarding vulnerable adults and client *risk* of suicide. The model also helps provide a way of understanding the different ways in which organisations may think about and make ethical decisions.

Working with ethical dilemmas arising from tensions within organisational culture

Ethical dilemmas reflecting a conflict of ethical principles, such as client autonomy versus avoiding harm, may be experienced very differently by practitioners and their supervisors, according to the organisational context in which they occur. (Ethical dilemmas are covered in more detail in Chapter 6.) Counsellors working in a task culture context, such as in private practice, may find that this affords them a high degree of professional autonomy in making ethical decisions. The private practitioner may be able to exercise greater choice about reporting risky client behaviours, as there is no employing organisation as a key stakeholder in their decision-making in this situation.

Alternatively, rule-following organisations, such as those in the statutory sector, may tend to frame risk issues in a protocol-informed manner, which is consistent with the values of the organisation as a whole. According to Sivis-Cetinkaya, 'counsellors' type of work settings was linked to the nature of ethical dilemmas rated as prevalent by the counsellors' (2015: 478). Hence, he suggests that 'school counsellors are more likely to breach confidentiality in ethically dilemmatic incidents involving risky student behaviours' (2015: 478).

In some hybrid organisations, a very high premium will be placed on following set *rules*, which may even have statutory force, as in a prison setting. There may be explicit rules for counsellors about disclosing client risk of harm to self or others, with very little space for professional autonomy in terms of decision-making. This can present a direct challenge to those counsellors who may be more attuned to a more flexible, negotiated style of ethical decision-making. In this situation, the counsellor may opt for a different approach to ethics, suited to the perceived needs of the individual client but which is contrary to the official rules of the prison as the employing organisation. Of course, this approach is risky, both for the client and counsellor. In the following example, a prisoner was threatening to commit suicide because of serious threats to harm his family. Prison protocol required that the counsellor record any risk of suicide on an ACCT (Assessment, Care in Custody, Teamwork) form.

> [The prisoner] said 'Oh, don't do that, don't put it on a form, I'll definitely commit suicide if you do that.' So the counsellor decided, right, I won't, so they didn't write an ACCT form and said to him 'Let's contract, I won't fill out a form, if you contract not to self-harm'. The client didn't self-harm, and it was great, he did a good piece of work. (Jenkins and Swindells, 2015: 28)

Clearly, with any ethical decision-making, greater counsellor autonomy may also entail greater vulnerability to challenge, or complaint. This underlines the importance of counsellors having access to accurate knowledge about the law, professional guidance and to professional consultative supervision which is independent of line management (see Chapter 7 for further discussion).

Summary

This chapter has presented a model for understanding counselling agencies in terms of their organisational culture. Organisational culture can be based variously on task, role or power, as ideal-types, or as mixed, hybrid versions, which may contain a combination of different competing cultures. Understanding organisational culture can help counsellors to appreciate how organisations may change over time; how counselling can be valued alongside other more primary non-therapeutic activities within organisations, such as in schools, hospitals and prisons; and how counsellors can seek to promote their practice in different organisational settings.

Resources

Research into organisational context

There is limited research into the *organisational context* of counselling, as distinct from research into the therapeutic *outcomes* achieved by specific organisations. One early example of the former is:

McLeod, J. (1994) 'Issues in the organisation of counselling: Learning from the NMGC', *British Journal of Guidance and Counselling*, 22(2), 163–174.

An analysis of the organisational evolution of Relate, the major provider of relationship and marriage counselling, over a period of 60 years.

Bedor, C. (2015) 'Developing agency policy and practice and evaluating organisational policies on confidentiality and record keeping', in T. Bond and B. Mitchels (eds), *Confidentiality and Record Keeping in Counselling and Psychotherapy*. Second edition. London: BACP/Sage. pp. 105–117.

Case study of the process of revising record-keeping practice in a local authority occupational health service, to comply with data protection requirements.

Cromarty, K. and Richards, K. (2009) 'How do secondary school counsellors work with other professionals?', *Counselling and Psychotherapy Research*, 9(3), 182–186.

Small survey (n: 16) of counsellor collaboration with other school professionals, particularly around the issue of maintaining client confidentiality and information-sharing.

Winning, F. (2010) 'Counselling in organisations: What is the experience of the lone counsellor?', *Counselling and Psychotherapy Research*, 10(4), 249–257.

Small survey (n: 9) of lone counsellors experiencing role conflicts around issues of autonomy, confidentiality and professional isolation.

Further reading

De Board, R. (1978) *The Psychoanalysis of Organisations: A Psychoanalytic Approach to Behaviour in Groups and Organisations*. Harmondsworth: Penguin.

Brief summaries of classic psychoanalytic and other writing on groups and organisations, including Freud, Klein, Bion, Lewin, etc.

Daines, B., Gask, L. and Howe, A. (2007) *Medical and Psychiatric Issues for Counsellors*. London: Sage.

Practical introduction to the NHS as a context for counselling practice, making referrals, etc.

Moore, J. and Roberts, R. (eds) (2010) *Counselling and Psychotherapy in Organisational Settings*. Exeter: Learning Matters.

Descriptions of counselling practice in different settings, including a secondary school, a Further Education college, Higher Education, voluntary agency, a residential treatment centre for addictions, an Employment Assistance Programme and a prison.

Sommerbeck, L. (2003) *The Client-Centred Therapist in Psychiatric Contexts: A Therapist's Guide to the Psychiatric Landscape and its Inhabitants*. Ross-on-Wye: PCCS Books.

A therapist's account of adapting person-centred practice to the constraints and opportunities provided by working in a psychiatric hospital.

Reference section for supervisors

The BACP Professional Standards *Counselling Supervision Training Curriculum* sets out a relevant measure in relation to organisational context:

Generic competence – 4 Understanding organisational context and governance:

Working within the supervisee's organisational context and the implications of this for practice, e.g. report writing, contracts and arrangements for governance, *enabling a supervisee to understand how their working context shapes their practice*. (BACP Professional Standards, 2014: 6, emphasis added)

Further reading

Hawkins, P. and Shohet, R. (2012) 'Developing supervision policy and practice in organisations', in *Supervision in the Helping Professions*. Fourth edition. Maidenhead: Open University Press. Chapter 15, pp. 241–249.

Section of an influential training text widely used on supervision courses, locating supervision challenges in their organisational context.

Research

Copeland, S. (2002) 'Professional and ethical dilemmas experienced by counselling supervisors: The impact of organisational context', *Counselling and Psychotherapy Research*, 2(4), 231–238.

Postal survey (n: 218) of counselling supervisors, working both internally and externally in agencies, with problematic issues often related to organisational culture.

3

Working with key client issues in therapeutic practice

Introduction

This chapter will look at a number of key client-related issues that are at the heart of professional counselling practice. These include:

- working with difference and avoiding discrimination in counselling;
- working with risk to self, to the client or to third parties;
- safeguarding adult clients in counselling.

Learning context

The BACP *Core Curriculum* (2009) emphasises the importance of valuing diversity, thorough risk assessment and effective liaison with other services, as does the *Ethical Framework for the Counselling Professions* (BACP, 2016). While the *Core Curriculum* sets out what needs to be formally taught and assessed in the training of counsellors on accredited courses, the *Ethical Framework for the Counselling Professions* details the necessary elements of good professional practice, which flow from the values and principles of respect for clients.

BACP *Core Curriculum* (2009)

9.1.A The professional role and responsibility of the therapist:

12. Manage counselling practice efficiently, including record and note keeping; provision of an appropriate environment; liaison with other services; reviewing of caseloads and evaluation of practice. ...

14. Communicate clearly with clients, colleagues and other professionals both orally and in writing. (2009: 17)

9.1.B Understanding the client:

The practitioner will have relevant knowledge to inform his or her ability to:

1. Devise a strategy for conducting assessment interviews with potential clients.

2. Devise and use a comprehensive risk assessment strategy. ...

6. Demonstrate an awareness of diversity and the rights and responsibilities of all clients, regardless of their gender, age, ethnicity, culture, class, ability, sexuality, religion and belief.

7. Openly and freely discuss sexual matters, when appropriate with a client, whatever the client's sexual orientation or the nature of the client's problem. ...

10. Identify ethical and legal responsibilities with regard to potential risk, including critical decision making with respect to autonomy of the client and potential harm to self or others. (2009: 17)

9.1.C The therapeutic process:

The practitioner will have relevant knowledge to inform his or her ability to:

8. Acknowledge diversity relating to gender, age, ethnicity, culture, ability, religion, spirituality and sexuality as it impacts on the therapeutic relationship or the process of therapy. ...

13. Anticipate the types of 'out of session' communication that clients might use, such as email, letters, text, telephone and visits, and determine an appropriate policy for managing and responding. (2009: 18)

BACP *Ethical Framework for the Counselling Professions* (2016)

Good Practice:

Putting clients first:

7. We will make each client the primary focus of our attention and our work during our sessions together. ...

9. We will give careful consideration to how we manage situations when protecting clients or others from serious harm or when compliance with the law may require overriding a client's explicit wishes or breaching their confidentiality.

10. When the safeguarding of our clients or others from serious harm takes priority over our commitment to putting our clients' wishes and confidentiality first, we will usually consult with any client affected, if this is legally permitted and ethically desirable. We will endeavour to implement any safeguarding responsibilities in ways that respect a client's known wishes, protect their interests, and support them in what follows. (2016: 5)

Working to professional standards:

16. We will collaborate with colleagues over our work with specific clients where this is consistent with client consent and will enhance services to the client.

17. We will work collaboratively with colleagues to improve services and offer mutual support. (2016: 6)

Working with difference and avoiding discrimination in counselling

The need to provide *respect* for the client, whatever their personal characteristics, is at the core of the *Ethical Framework for the Counselling Professions* (BACP, 2016). The counsellor needs to become aware of their own biography, their own developmental influences and their own attitudes, both conscious and unconscious, towards clients who may be experienced as being different, or 'other', to the counsellor. The process of counsellor training requires each of us to undergo personal and professional development activities and specific workshop or CPD training to explore our own attitudes towards others, both clients and colleagues, which may need challenging. The following exercise suggests a number of pointers for self-reflection to underpin this process.

Exercise   Exploring your own experiences and perceptions of difference

Make a list of types of difference, such as race, gender and sexual orientation, which have some personal significance for you. Select one area of perceived difference to work on in more detail. Write brief notes on the following questions:

- When did you first become aware of this difference?
- How did you become aware of this difference?
- What messages did you get about yourself with regard to this area of difference?
- What messages did you get about the 'other'?
- How have your attitudes changed over time?

Counselling and sexual orientation

Rather than explore difference in a generic way, this chapter will instead focus in more detail on one area of perceived difference, namely sexual orientation. This discussion is not intended to equip you to practise in a way geared to acknowledging the specific features of every kind of diversity that you may encounter as a counsellor. The aim here is to explore the past and current history of one specific example of working with diversity, which has had a major effect on perceptions of professional practice in the field of counselling and psychotherapy. For those wanting further information, McLeod (2013: 489–496) provides a sympathetic and informed coverage of some of the main therapeutic issues involved in this area of practice.

Issues of diversity relating to sexuality have clearly been experienced as being highly problematic within the recent history of counselling and within medicine and psychiatry more generally. Counselling and psychotherapy have a somewhat chequered history in relation to responding to certain forms of difference, such as homosexuality. This may have reflected the wider influence of social attitudes hostile to homosexuality, including widespread legal discrimination in the past. In addition, former practices within psychiatry defined homosexuality in terms of diagnostic categories of mental disorder rather than as one form of expression of human sexuality among many. Although homosexual acts between consenting males in private were decriminalised in Britain in 1967, psychiatric treatment for homosexuality continued during the 1970s. This included the use of psychoanalysis in private settings and behavioural aversion therapy, with electric shocks or medication, in the NHS (Smith et al., 2004). In the 1990s, government and media concern over the alleged 'promotion' of homosexuality led to a change in the law, under s.28 of the Local Government Act 1988. This prohibited the promotion of homosexuality in local authority schools as 'a pretended family relationship'. 'Section 28', as it was known, was later repealed in Scotland in 2000 and in England and Wales in 2003.

While mainstream counselling and psychotherapy has moved to embrace inclusive and non-discriminatory practice, there are sectors of the therapeutic community that have continued to see gay, lesbian and bisexuality as remaining outside accepted social or religious norms. (See, for example, the article by Charles Socarides (n.d.), then a leading psychoanalyst and psychiatrist in the USA, in the Further Reading section at the end of this chapter.) What is called 'reparative' or 'conversion' therapy has been developed in the UK and USA as a form of therapy which, it is claimed, will address and reduce same-sex attraction by focusing on potentially unacknowledged past sexual abuse or attachment problems with male parents. In the past, this use of therapy to police clients' sexuality may have had some weak legitimacy, through reference to psychiatric and medical practices, as evidenced by the US *Diagnostic and Statistical Manual of Mental Disorders* (DSM) (see Box 3.1).

Box 3.1 Brief timeline for evolving psychiatric and social perspectives on homosexuality as a mental disorder

1952 DSM-I, the main US psychiatric diagnostic manual, listed homosexuality as a 'sociopathic personality disturbance'.

1957 Wolfenden Report published, concluding that 'homosexuality cannot legitimately be regarded as a disease'.

1967 Sexual Offences Act passed, decriminalising homosexual acts in private between two men aged 21 or above.

1969 Stonewall Riots in New York, with gay people actively resisting police harassment and arrest. Gay Liberation Front is set up in the USA.

1970 Gay Liberation Front established in the UK.

1973 Removal of homosexuality as a 'sexual orientation disturbance' from DSM-II.

1980 Diagnosis of 'ego dystonic homosexuality' is included in DSM-III, relating to a patient's distress caused by 'unwanted homosexual arousal'.

1987 Reference to 'ego dystonic homosexuality' is removed from the revised version of DSM (DSM-III-R) and subsumed under 'sexual disorder not otherwise specified', but includes 'persistent and marked distress about one's sexual orientation'.

'Reparative therapy' claims to be based on research undertaken in 2003 by Dr Robert Spitzer, which appeared to demonstrate a degree of effectiveness for such therapy (Spitzer, 2003). However, Spitzer himself issued a poignant self-critique in 2012, stating that his earlier survey, using a sample of 200 gay and lesbian clients who had undergone 'reparative therapy', was based largely on client self-report to substantiate the positive outcomes claimed (Harris, 2012). The research therefore crucially lacked any external verification of its effectiveness. While Spitzer's retraction was an important admission, we would still judge 'reparative therapy' to be unethical, simply on the grounds of discrimination, even in the unlikely event that it did prove to be effective in 'reversing' homosexuality.

In 2009, Patrick Strudwick went, as a client and as an undercover journalist, to see a senior BACP-accredited counsellor for help with his expressed concerns about his sexual orientation (see Box 3.2). He covertly taped the ensuing two sessions of therapy and later made a formal complaint to BACP.

Box 3.2   A client's experience of undergoing 'conversion therapy' for homosexuality

After asking God to heal me, she opens her eyes. 'I know the boundaries to keep within', she says.

She begins by asking me about my psychological history. I tell her that I was depressed as a teenager because I feared I would face prejudice for the rest of my life.

Can I learn not to feel attraction to men?

'Yes', she replies, 'because that attraction is connected to a deep need that needs to be met and responded to and healed.'

But how do I instead become attracted to women? [The counsellor] explains that it's about 'reprogramming' and going back to my early developmental stages. 'Parts of you have developed but there is a little part of you that has stayed stuck', she says.

Oh, like being retarded?

'It's a bit like that', she agrees. (Strudwick, 2010: 3)

His complaint received wide publicity in the media, given the growing attention then being paid to 'conversion' and 'reparative' therapy. His professional complaint against the therapist in question was upheld, and BACP issued a formal statement of its position on 'reparative therapy', which was followed by a similar statement by the UKCP (see Box 3.3).

Box 3.3 *Statement of Ethical Practice* (BACP, 2012b)

The British Association for Counselling and Psychotherapy (BACP) is dedicated to social diversity, equality and inclusivity of treatment without discrimination of any kind. BACP opposes any psychological treatment such as 'reparative' or 'conversion' therapy which is based upon the assumption that homosexuality is a mental disorder, or based on the premise that the client/patient should change his/her sexuality.

BACP recognises the Pan-American Health Organisation's (2012) recent position statement that practices such as conversion or reparative therapies 'have no medical indication and represent a severe threat to the health and human rights of the affected persons'.

(This statement has since been issued as a Joint Memorandum of Understanding with 13 other organisations and is extended to cover gender identity.)

In terms of the *Ethical Framework for the Counselling Professions* (BACP, 2016), this event and the robust BACP response underline a key point about the need for all therapists to respect their clients' experiences, to value diversity, to develop inclusive practice, to avoid unfair discrimination against clients and to monitor their own possible prejudice and bias against individuals or client groups.

The need for awareness regarding potential discrimination can also be set within the legal framework regarding 'protected characteristics'. Under the Equality Act 2010, there are nine protected characteristics, such as age, disability and sexual orientation, which are legally protected against discrimination when receiving services such as counselling (see Box 3.4).

Box 3.4 Protected characteristics under the Equality Act 2010

1. Age
2. Disability
3. Gender reassignment
4. Marriage and civil partnerships
5. Maternity and pregnancy
6. Race
7. Religion or belief
8. Sex
9. Sexual orientation

The change in social attitudes and in the law in relation to discrimination can be illustrated by an example from 1995, when a transsexual alcohol and HIV counsellor was banned from working in a prison because of concerns about her 'increasingly camp behaviour'. She later lost her case at an employment tribunal for unfair dismissal. It was held that this did not then contravene EC law on the equal treatment of men and women at work (Directive 76/207). As she later reported to the press, 'the law doesn't protect transsexuals in any shape or form' (Dyer, 1995).

More recent changes in the law indicate a significant and more pro-active shift towards protecting the rights of individuals who may be likely to experience discrimination while in receipt of services, whether as a gay couple requesting a room with a double bed, a fostering couple with strong views against homosexuality, a judge with similar views about gay adoption, or a counsellor refusing to provide psychosexual counselling for gay couples (see Box 3.5).

Box 3.5   Cases related to potential discrimination against people with protected characteristics

2011 A Christian couple, who fostered children, lost their claim against a local authority for discrimination on the basis of their views opposing homosexuality.

2011 A gay couple successfully sued B&B owners who had refused them a double bed.

2012 A counsellor was dismissed by Relate for claiming that his beliefs prevented him from providing psychosexual therapy to gay people.

2016 A magistrate who had publicly opposed adoption by same-sex couples was removed from the bench for 'serious professional misconduct'.

These cases underline the distinct shift in attitudes about the legal unacceptability of this kind of discrimination. However, the main point for counsellors is that the exclusion of, and unfair discrimination towards, both clients and other therapists would still be completely unacceptable on *ethical* grounds alone, even if the law did not properly endorse this approach. Indeed, the law requires counsellors *not* to discriminate unfairly against clients or therapists with protected characteristics, but the *Ethical Framework for the Counselling Professions* (BACP, 2016) poses a higher standard, about *valuing diversity*, rather than simply *avoiding* discrimination:

23. We will take the law concerning equality, diversity and inclusion into careful consideration and strive for *a higher standard* than the legal minimum. (BACP, 2016: 7, emphasis added)

Working with risk to self, to the client or to third parties

Working with risk presents a number of challenges to counsellors as it can appear to shift to a more medical model of practice, based on avoidance of harm to the client, and away from a therapeutic model linked to promoting client autonomy. In addition, counsellors are rarely trained in any systematic way to do risk assessment. We often have to rely on our own professional judgement, past experience, and thorough consultation with peers, managers and supervisors. Furthermore, trainee or student counsellors are frequently shielded from overtly 'high risk' clients, where this is known in advance, when starting their practice on placement. Often, clients will be assessed by a more experienced counsellor, either face-to-face, or on the phone, or via self-assessment online, so that clients presenting an appreciable level of risk will be appropriately allocated to a more experienced counsellor. However, this system is not foolproof, and it does happen that relatively novice counsellors face working with high and quite unfamiliar levels of risk in clients. In a sense, all counsellors need to work slightly outside and on the edge of their comfort zone, in order to learn and extend their range of skills. Yet this learning needs to be done with maximum support and containment by the agency, supervisor and course tutors, where available. This will help the student to learn, but also to keep an effective watching brief on the level of risk posed by the client to him- or herself, or to others.

Clients suitable for student and trainee counsellors should be those assessed as having the following characteristics:

- some degree of *'psychological mindedness'*, i.e. a willingness to explore potential links between their own thinking, behaviour and emotions;
- preparedness to accept at least some *degree of responsibility* for their own actions, both current and in the past;
- ability to invest in *a basic level of trust with the counsellor* and in the counselling process;
- *sufficient commitment* to attend counselling with agreed regularity and to observe appropriate boundaries;
- *limited complexity* of initial presenting problems or mental health condition;
- *low perceived risk* of potential harm to self, others, or to the counsellor.

Using the term 'risk' in this context probably begs many questions. When we use the term 'risk', what do we actually mean – risk of *what* happening and to *whom*? This is often subsumed into the phrase that counsellors seem to have acquired, almost unconsciously, and repeat when setting up the contract with the client: 'Whatever you say is confidential, unless we think you are at risk of harm, or someone else is at risk of harm.' Clients rarely challenge this stock phrase or ask for further explanation. Often, the client will just nod, before launching straight into the material that has brought them into counselling in the first place. Ideally, the limits to client confidentiality have been carefully set out and explained in more detail, both beforehand and elsewhere (e.g. in a leaflet, on a poster, or on a website), rather than relying solely on the counsellor's word of mouth in the heat of the first session.

Defining the concept of risk

We need to return to the concept of risk. This can be defined as an adverse or damaging *outcome* to a specific *action or decision*. According to Carson and Bain (2008: 20), 'a risk is made up of two variable elements: outcomes and likelihood'. Both factors can be evaluated in terms of *degree*. A negative *outcome* can be slight, serious or extreme in its impact. The *likelihood* of this happening can be judged to be low, medium or high. At the most basic level, offering or providing a client with a hot drink in a mug might be seen automatically as a caring and empathic action on the part of the counsellor or a receptionist. From a risk point of view, the likelihood may be low, but the outcome might be more serious if an aggrieved and angry client were to throw the mug and its hot contents at the counsellor. This is not to argue against the practice of providing drinks for clients – there may be better arguments to be made against this practice from a strictly therapeutic point of view – but simply to illustrate that even the most simple and everyday interactions probably involve at least some degree of risk. Perhaps a completely risk-free form of counselling is simply not achievable, or even desirable. Nevertheless, some thought may need to go into thinking through what levels of risk to the counsellor, the client or to third parties can be anticipated and are judged to be acceptable. Risk assessment is often assumed to apply mainly to the client, to third parties, such as children, or to other adults who may be harmed by the client's actions.

Risk to the counsellor

Counsellors do not always pay enough attention to the risks which the client may pose towards them, and need to become more risk-aware as a result. Despenser (2007: 15) identifies a number of sources of risk to counsellors:

- the isolation of the setting;
- being alone with a stranger;
- working in an organisation that (for various reasons) ignores or denies the existence of risk;
- when the therapist ignores warning signs, e.g. by denying their own safety needs.

Exercise   Assessing risk to yourself as a counsellor

How aware are you of potential risk to yourself as a practitioner on placement? Make a brief list of risk factors and of corresponding potentially protective factors that you can arrange or can ask to be put in place.

Risk to client

Rogers captures very well the background anxiety experienced by many counsellors, including very experienced practitioners, about the prospect of clients successfully attempting or committing suicide (see Box 3.6). This anxiety is probably even higher for new and beginning counsellors, particularly in the early stages of their career. Given the intensity of the therapeutic process, it is not surprising that client suicide can have a very marked effect on the counsellor. The counsellor may feel responsible for the client's action in taking their own life, or feel guilty for failing to prevent this, or perhaps feel highly anxious about the professional, or even the supposed *legal*, consequences to this outcome.

Box 3.6   Working with the risk of client suicide

If we practise for any length of time the chances are that we will have to deal with a serious attempted suicide or a completed suicide. It is difficult to be prepared for the emotional turmoil that ensues but it helps if it can be seen as something that goes with the territory rather than a personal failure. (Rogers, 2004: 19)

To start with the latter first, the law in the UK does not currently hold professionals personally responsible for the deaths of patients or clients by suicide. This is unlike the legal situation applying to therapists in the USA (Jenkins, 2007a: 77–78). An unexplained death in the UK is normally followed by an inquest, the purpose of which is to establish the cause of death. A counsellor could be called by the coroner to hand over the deceased's records of therapy, or to act as a witness, in order to give evidence regarding their contact with the deceased. This can be a very straightforward, if sometimes nerve-wracking, process. An inquest is not a criminal court and the counsellor is not personally on trial as a defendant. Nor is the counsellor, or agency, likely to be sued for negligence under UK law. The closest development to this has been where several NHS Trusts have been subject to action for breach of human rights law for discharging psychiatric patients into the community who then committed suicide.

This is not to encourage any level of complacency about working with potentially suicidal clients, but simply to put the risks into their proper legal context. If decision-making is driven, at least in part, by an overwhelming fear of the assumed legal consequences, this may tend to cloud rational consideration of the options available to the therapist, the client, their family and to other closely involved support agencies.

Case example of working with a client with depression

The following section includes an outline of working with a client experiencing high levels of depression. It illustrates some of the counselling responses that might be made, in terms of the content of the therapy, record-keeping, contact with the client outside therapy, liaison with other professionals such as the client's GP, risk assessment and the construction of a safety plan.

The counsellor, who has prior experience of counselling clients with high levels of depression, is working in a voluntary agency. Clients self-refer and are not assessed in detail prior to counselling, except in cases where they are likely to be referred to counselling students on placement.

Box 3.7   Internal referral notice to counsellor

Mr A (45) is recently bereaved. His wife died from cancer three months ago. He has been on the waiting list for counselling for six weeks. He is not currently on any medication from his GP. He has given us permission to be contacted by text, or by letter and phone at his home address.

Mr A was contacted by letter by the agency and offered a day-time appointment with a named counsellor, but failed to attend. The counsellor sent a text from the agency's mobile phone system to the client (this was previously agreed with him as an acceptable form of contact outside therapy) querying his non-attendance.

Box 3.8   Text sent to client

(Add to client file)

> Dear Mr A, I am sorry that you were not able to attend your appointment with me, arranged for 10.00am this morning, Tuesday 23rd May. If you would like to re-book another appointment, please contact our reception on (phone number). I look forward to hearing from you. Best wishes, (Name) Counsellor

---

Mr A re-booked and attended the next arranged session, explaining that he was unable to attend the day-time session on that Tuesday because of a sudden and unforeseen work commitment. The counsellor made the following electronic notes of the session for the agency, including pasting in a copy of the text sent, regarding his non-attendance. The text provided a record that the agency had acted responsibly and had made contact with the client in order to offer a further appointment.

Box 3.9   Record of counselling

(Add to client file)

Client: Mr A
Counsellor: (Name)
Date: 6/6/XX

Mr A – bereavement thru wife's death from cancer 3 months ago. Feeling very down at present, not sleeping or eating properly, increased drinking to 20+ units per week, work affected, 'Doesn't see the point in anything any more', very close to wife, has taken her death very hard, little contact with friends and family. Moderate risk of suicide on CORE form. Has some suicidal ideation in terms of 'throwing myself under a train', but no active plans yet to do this.

Countervailing factors include strong Catholic faith and sense that he would be letting everyone down (including his wife) by taking the 'easy way out'. No previous experience of mental health problems or of counselling, not sure of the value of talking to someone, hard to identify his own emotions, more one for 'just getting on with it', some support from GP. Angry with hospital for wife's delayed treatment.

Reasonable therapeutic alliance, but little eye contact made during session. Apologised for missed session, but maybe ambivalent about accepting help, 'You must have others who need it much more than me?'

Discussed checklist for depression symptoms, open to seeing GP re anti-depressants, gave consent for follow-up letter to GP. Completed safety plan (limit drinking, social activity, Samaritans, GP, A&E, contact best mate). Open to initial 6 session contract here.

Action:

1. Gave leaflet on 'Depression and low mood'
2. Mr A to take checklist and see GP re anti-depressants
3. Write to GP re ongoing counselling
4. Safety plan drawn up (see file).
5. Next appointment 10.00am 13/6/XX

Box 3.10   Safety plan

(Add to client file)

Risk:

Very low mood, risk of taking own life/suicide.

Triggers:

Drinking alone, evening time.

Action:

- Cut down on drinking, plan social activity instead
- Call best friend, meet up for support
- Phone Samaritans 116 123
- Contact GP for urgent appointment
- Go to A&E at local hospital, ask for urgent psychiatric assessment

Box 3.11 Letter to GP

(Add to client file)

Agency
Address

GP
Address

Dear Dr [Name],
re: Mr A, [date of birth], [address]

I am writing to you, with Mr A's consent, to inform you that he came to [agency] today, presenting with some symptoms of low mood and some suicidal thoughts. His risk score for suicide was moderate on CORE, with no active plan as yet, and some strong countervailing factors, such as his faith and the adverse effect on others. Mr A completed a safety plan of agencies to contact and action he can take to reduce the risk of suicide.

As you will know, Mr A's wife died of cancer three months ago, which may be the main trigger for his current low mood. He says that his sleep and appetite are badly affected, and he has limited contact with friends and family at present, with some reliance on alcohol as a support. He is open to combining medication with counselling as a means of coping with his current situation. We will be able to offer him six sessions of counselling, which may be extended to a maximum of twelve in total, over the next three months. I will contact you towards the end of counselling to inform you when the counselling is ending, or if Mr A has decided not to attend further.

Please contact me if you need any further information.

Yours sincerely
[Name]
Counsellor

Box 3.12 Risk assessment

(Add to client file)

Risk factors specific to Mr A:

Moderate/severe depression

Feelings of hopelessness ('Doesn't see the point in doing anything any more')

Alcohol abuse (20+ units per week)

Male gender

Other risk factors:

Access to potentially lethal means of self-harm/suicide ('throwing myself under a train')

Possible protective factors:

(Some/limited) social support

Religious beliefs

Risk of suicide:

Moderate

- may increase slightly after starting anti-depressants/counselling
- may decrease with positive impact of anti-depressants after 3–4 weeks, plus engagement with counselling

Box 3.13   Post-it note for supervision

(Destroy after use in supervision; not to be added to permanent client file)

> Possible process/supervision issue?
>
> Depressed man (45)
>
> - hard to connect with?
> - felt 'dismissed' by his attitude?
> - my 'le perfect' driver yet again?

Commentary

The material outlined above shows the progression of contact with a client presenting with depression to a voluntary or third sector coun-selling agency. An alert counsellor may pick up on the first missed session as a possible 'enactment', i.e. the possibility that the client is sending a rather unclear behavioural message about their ambivalence regarding counselling, or conveying their reluctance to accept help. From an agency point of view, tracking the contact with the client, by sending a text or email and copying this into the electronic notes, demonstrates good professional practice. It provides evidence of the agency making every effort to contact and to provide support for the client, even a potentially reluctant one, like Mr A.

The counselling record may seem somewhat bald and terse in its tone, but it does contain the essential facts of the session. This factual record can then be used by the practice manager, supervisor or a colleague in the event of the counsellor being unavailable in a crisis, or because of illness. There is practically no reference to the counsellor's own *process* within the agency record. The counsellor's own process and issues for supervision are instead kept, for short-term use only, on a Post-it note, to be destroyed after discussion in supervision and not to be retained as part of the permanent agency file. This practice is designed to be consistent with the established data protection principle of keeping personal data 'no longer than is necessary'.

There is a very brief acknowledgement of a barely 'good enough' therapeutic alliance, and noting of the client's non-verbal communication, in terms of limited eye contact. The latter might suggest either low self-esteem, which may fit with the client's depressed mood, or perhaps suggest his limited trust in the counsellor, albeit at what is still a relatively early stage of the therapy.

Crucially, it records the client's verbal *consent* to contact the GP, supplementing his earlier written consent in the contract, or working agreement for counselling, by the agency. This is important, in order to justify the counsellor sending the letter to the GP, outlining the current and proposed counselling support and the perceived level of suicide risk. In the absence of the client's verbal (or preferably written) consent, the counsellor, or agency, could contact the GP regarding a heightened risk of suicide on the broad legal grounds of it being 'in the public interest'. However, it is preferable to have obtained clear client consent *before* contacting appropriate third parties, for example at the stage of making the contract or the working agreement to therapy.

Written communication with the client's GP

The letter to the GP is cautious and respectful in tone, and is noticeably careful to avoid straying into the GP's medical and diagnostic territory by using the specific term 'depression'. The letter refers instead to Mr A's 'low mood', with examples of his symptoms, such as sleep and appetite problems. One clear risk is that a letter to the GP may be seen by him or her as simply 'passing the buck', so that clinical responsibility for the client now rests solely with the GP, should the client later attempt suicide. The real purpose of this letter is much more within terms of *sharing* professional responsibility *for* the client *with* the GP, so that the GP is fully aware what, if any, counselling is being provided and – an important factor – when it is likely to end. The letter is therefore part of a planned, collaborative approach to patient and client care. Here, the risks are identified, known about, shared and, hopefully, effectively managed and reduced in the process, not least by encouraging the active involvement of the client.

The risk assessment carried out is informed by solid research evidence, in this case from the Centre for Suicide Research (2013) at Oxford University (see Box 3.14).

Box 3.14   Risk assessment summary of key points (Centre for Suicide Research, 2013: 14)

All patients with depression should be assessed for possible risk of self-harm or suicide. Risk factors for suicide identified through research studies are:

Risk factors specific to depression

- Family history of mental disorder
- History of previous suicide attempts (this includes self-harm)
- Severe depression
- Anxiety
- Feelings of hopelessness
- Personality disorder
- Alcohol abuse and/or drug abuse
- Male gender

Other risk factors for consideration

- Family history of suicide or self-harm
- Physical illness (especially when this is recently diagnosed, chronic and/or painful)
- Exposure to suicidal behaviour of others, either directly or via the media
- Recent discharge from psychiatric in-patient care
- Access to potentially lethal means of self-harm/suicide
- Social support
- Religious belief
- Being responsible for children (especially young children)

(Continued)

(Continued)

In assessing patients' current suicide potential, the following questions can be explored

- Are they feeling hopeless or that life is not worth living?
- Have they made plans to end their life?
- Have they told anyone about it?
- Have they carried out any acts in anticipation of death (e.g. putting their affairs in order)?
- Do they have the means for a suicidal act (do they have access to pills, insecticide, firearms...)?
- Is there any available support (family, friends, carers...)?

Where practical, and with consent, it is generally a good idea to inform and involve family members and close friends or carers. This is particularly important where risk is thought to be high. When a patient is at risk of suicide this information should be recorded in the patient's notes. Where the clinician is working as part of a team it is important to share awareness of risk with other team members. Regular and proactive follow-up is highly recommended.

(http://cebmh.warne.ox.ac.uk/csr/clinicalguide/docs/riskAssessment.pdf. Reproduced with the kind permission of the Centre for Suicide Research, Department of Psychiatry, University of Oxford)

However, a risk assessment without a corresponding safety plan is of limited value. Here, the counsellor and client have negotiated a basic safety plan for triggers and action, to which the client can hopefully turn, outside and between counselling sessions. Similarly, the counsellor's response to the client, their letter to the GP and offer of counselling are also based on research evidence from primary care, namely that 'counselling and medication in combination is more effective than either intervention offered as a single treatment' (Brettle et al., 2008: 212).

Exercise   Evaluating a risk assessment

Refer to the points made in the counsellor's recording in Box 3.12: Risk assessment.

Which risk factors specific to depression apply to Mr A?

What other more generic risk factors could apply?

What are the possible protective factors?

Discuss and compare with suggested risk assessment in Box 3.14: Risk assessment summary of key points.

Safeguarding adult clients in counselling

In addition to risk of suicide, counsellors are increasingly expected to be aware of, and respond appropriately to, safeguarding issues with regard to two main client groups: children and young people, and vulnerable adults. The following section focuses particularly on safeguarding in relation to vulnerable adult clients. Many of the key issues will also be encountered when working with children and young people. (See Resources section for more specific information on training in safeguarding children and young people.)

What is 'safeguarding'?

Safeguarding is essentially about promoting the civil and human rights of clients and others in order that they can be able to live their lives, free from abuse and neglect. Public understanding and research into the dimensions of abuse have grown over the past few decades. There has been increasing investment in terms of legislation and guidance about how best to recognise and seek to prevent abuse to other human beings. While reporting abuse is not necessarily a legal imperative for counsellors, it is becoming an explicit expectation for trainees, volunteers and paid members of staff, and is often written into agency policies and contracts of employment where relevant. The Care Act 2014 has put adult safeguarding on a statutory basis, with a requirement, under section 42, for local authorities to carry out investigations of potential abuse and neglect of adults and to share information as necessary with other agencies, such as the NHS and the police, in order to achieve this goal.

Abuse can take many forms. Department of Health guidance identifies a number of forms of abuse affecting vulnerable adults, many of which will also apply to children and young people, including:

- physical abuse;
- domestic violence;
- sexual abuse;
- psychological abuse;
- financial and material abuse;
- modern slavery;
- discriminatory abuse;
- abuse occurring within institutional settings;
- neglect and acts of omission;
- self-neglect. (Department of Health, 2014: 234)

No list can ever be completely comprehensive. This one could be extended, for example, to cover the risk of radicalisation, under the

Government's Prevent strategy (Her Majesty's Government, 2015a). One of the potentially confusing aspects of safeguarding with regard to adults is in terms of defining who is assessed as being 'vulnerable' to abuse. There are a number of different definitions of 'vulnerable adult' currently in use (see Box 3.15). At one level, there are fairly narrow and precise definitions of what the term 'vulnerable adult' means. At another level, the concept of vulnerability seems more elastic and capable of embracing almost the vast majority of adult clients who might want to see a counsellor for therapy.

Box 3.15 Definitions of a 'vulnerable adult' or an 'adult at risk' (i.e. a person aged 18 or over)

Definitions of a *vulnerable* adult

- [An adult who] has needs for care and support (whether or not the local authority is meeting any of those needs) and;
  - o is experiencing, or at risk of, abuse or neglect; and
  - o a result of those care and support needs is *unable to protect themselves from either the risk of, or the experience of, abuse or neglect*. (Department of Health, 2014: 229, emphasis added)
- [A]n adult requiring registered activities (i.e. residential and health care services): 'if any adult requires them, [this factor] will mean that the adult will be considered vulnerable at that particular time.' (Department of Health, 2011: 5)
- [V]ulnerable adult *witnesses* (under s.16 Youth Justice and Criminal Evidence Act 1999) are adults with a mental disorder, learning disability, or physical disability. (Department of Health, 2014: 248, emphasis added)

Definition of an adult *at risk*

- [An adult] who is in need of care and support regardless of whether they are receiving them, and because of those needs are unable to protect themselves against abuse or neglect. (London Multi-Agency, 2015: 4)
- 5.2 The term 'adult at risk' is used in this policy to replace 'vulnerable adult'. This is because the term 'vulnerable adult' may wrongly imply that some of the fault for the abuse lies with the victim of abuse. We use 'adult at risk' as an exact replacement for 'vulnerable adult' as that phrase is used throughout existing government guidance. (Office of the Public Guardian, 2015: 4)

The definitions in Box 3.15 do not necessarily make any clearer exactly how a counsellor might best identify a vulnerable adult or an adult at risk. Vulnerable adults seem to be defined, variously, in terms of their eligibility for specific services (i.e. registered residential and healthcare provision) or, in the criminal justice system, by having specific characteristics (i.e. a mental disorder, learning disability or physical disability). Perhaps the key common characteristic of a vulnerable adult or of an 'adult at risk' is therefore broadly described as a *potential for being subjected to abuse or neglect*.

While counsellors need to be fully aware of the development of safeguarding policies with regard to vulnerable adults, or adults at risk of harm, we also need to be mindful, as therapists, of the potentially negative and distancing impact of language and labelling on our attitudes and perceptions of clients. Allan suggests a need for caution in adopting the terms used in policy documents in an uncritical manner (see Box 3.16).

Box 3.16 Critiquing the language of 'vulnerability' in official policy documents

The rhetoric is, of course, that these measures protect 'the vulnerable' … I also find such language, with its implication that society is divided into those who are vulnerable and those who are not, distinctly troubling. 'The vulnerable', 'the mentally ill', 'the long-term sick' – they are not separate species. There is no impermeable barrier, dividing the mentally healthy from mentally ill, for example. We all exist at any time somewhere on a spectrum of mental wellbeing, and factors such as housing insecurity, financial hardship and debt, unemployment, loss of support networks and so on, can rapidly propel us along it in a negative direction. (Allan, 2016)

It is worth bearing this corrective in mind, when working to follow safeguarding policies in our everyday counselling practice.

In terms of protecting vulnerable adults, one policy response has been to prohibit inappropriate access to children and vulnerable adults through the Disclosure and Barring Scheme (DBS). The DBS requires individuals applying to work in healthcare and counselling to obtain a certificate demonstrating that a check for relevant criminal convictions has been carried out. Safeguarding is thus designed to protect vulnerable adults from abuse, by prohibiting persons with relevant criminal convictions from gaining access to them, and by sharing information between agencies, in order to take action to protect them and end the abuse.

The case study in Box 3.17 illustrates the kind of situation that can arise when counselling a full-time carer for issues of stress and anxiety.

> ## Box 3.17   Counselling a vulnerable adult at risk of abuse
>
> Mrs D lives with her husband, B. B has a long-term brain injury which affects his mood, behaviour and his ability to manage close family relationships. This has often led to him shouting and hitting out at his wife, who is also his main informal carer. Mrs D told a professional who was involved in supporting her that she was becoming increasingly frightened by B's physical and verbal outbursts and at times feared for her personal safety. (Department of Health, 2014: 246)

Exercise   Exploring risk to a vulnerable adult

Review the information in Box 3.17 relating to counselling a vulnerable adult at risk of abuse. Which parties are at risk in this scenario? What types of potential abuse might be relevant? How might a counsellor who was concerned about potential risk respond?

The client disclosing her experience of being subject to her husband's physical and verbal outbursts is at risk of a number of different types of abuse. These include physical abuse, psychological abuse and domestic violence. The person being cared for may himself be at risk of physical abuse, psychological abuse and domestic violence. This might develop if the carer retaliates in kind. Alternatively, the person being cared for might be at risk of neglect and self-neglect if the carer starts to withdraw from caring for him. This might be due to a change in their relationship or through the carer's fear of being harmed in the process of caring for her husband. Assuming that this disclosure was made in the context of a counselling relationship, the counsellor now has several options. One is to encourage the client to seek help herself, perhaps to avoid a deterioration in the situation. Another is to take action on a safeguarding basis, in order to bring this situation to the attention of the relevant authorities. If the counsellor is working in a voluntary setting or in private practice, then this responsibility is not a statutory one required by law. If the counsellor is working in a statutory setting, e.g. in health or social care, then this will be a duty imposed by statute (the Care Act 2014) on the *agency* concerned, and also a duty imposed on the *counsellor*, under their contract of employment.

The issue of client *consent* to onward disclosure to another agency, such as health care, social care or the police, is crucial here. If the client

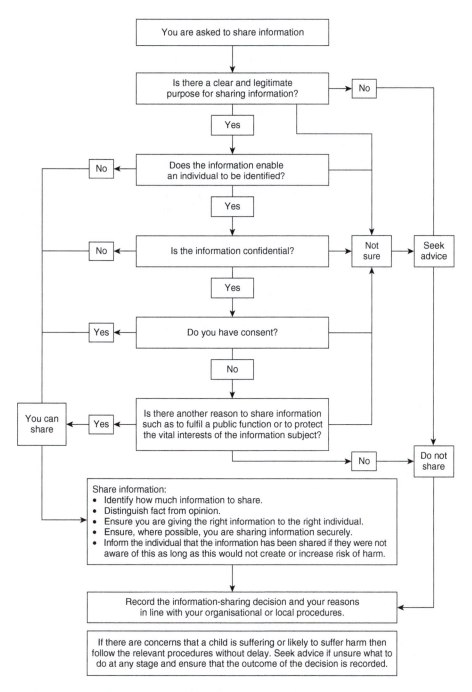

Figure 3.1 Flowchart of when and how to share information
(Her Majesty's Government, 2015b: 12)

gives her consent to the counsellor making the referral, then this permission means that the counsellor is largely protected against any later complaints regarding a potential breach of client confidentiality. However, if the client does *not* give consent to the referral, then the counsellor needs to carefully consider the available options (see Figure 3.1).

Confidential information can be shared with another agency 'in the public interest', i.e. to prevent crime or to prevent harm occurring to an individual. The options for information-sharing are applicable *both* to situations of risk of harm applying to vulnerable adults *and* to children under 18 years. The counsellor urgently needs to obtain accurate, informed advice from their placement or service manager, supervisor or course tutor when facing a complex dilemma, such as the one briefly outlined in Box 3.17. From a therapeutic point of view, the counsellor also needs to consider the potential damage to the counselling relationship when a decision is taken to report potential abuse *without* client consent. While this risk is not necessarily the sole, or even the main, factor to consider, it does need to be borne in mind that reporting risk *without* client consent can break the client's trust in the counsellor, or in the counselling service more generally. Alternatively, the reporting may be experienced by the client as a positive and helpful action. The outcome cannot be predicted with certainty in advance.

Summary

This chapter has focused on a number of key issues relating to professional counselling practice with clients. The concept of respect for clients is of core importance within the *Ethical Framework for the Counselling Professions* (BACP, 2016), and is the subject of detailed and prescriptive coverage within it. As counsellors, we need to become aware of, and engage with, our own histories and attitudes towards others, who we may perceive as being different from ourselves in some significant way. The chapter focused on the problematic history of psychiatry, counselling and psychotherapy towards the issue of sexual orientation. This is evidenced by a key recent case of a complaint regarding the use of 'reparative' or 'conversion' therapy. The case and its outcome have underlined the importance of counsellors avoiding discrimination towards clients and, instead, valuing diversity in all its many forms. The chapter also explored concepts of risk in counselling. It followed, in some detail, an example of the recording of work with a depressed client, presented as being at some significant risk of suicide. Finally, the issue of safeguarding was discussed, primarily in terms of vulnerable adults, or adults at risk, but with important parallels for work with children and young people under the age of 18.

Resources

Online learning session on 'Safeguarding young people and vulnerable young adults'

This is a free, half-hour, interactive session on safeguarding young people within counselling practice, with a video case example, which is part of the Counselling MindEd programme. To register for these resources and to access this session, go to: www.minded.org.uk/course/index.php?categoryid=15

Research

'Reparative therapy'

Spitzer, R. (2003) 'Can some gay men and lesbians change their sexual orientation? 200 participants reporting a change from homosexual to heterosexual orientation', *Archives of Sexual Behaviour*, 32(5), October, 403–417.

This research (n: 200; 143m; 57f) has been widely misused to justify the partial efficacy of 'reparative' or 'conversion' therapy. However, it relies entirely on participant self-report to demonstrate a change, from a predominantly homosexual orientation to a predominantly heterosexual orientation, with no acknowledgement of the social pressures on participants to report this perceived positive outcome. Spitzer later disavowed his own conclusions (Harris, 2012).

Risk to counsellor

Despenser, S. (2005) 'The personal safety of the therapist', *Psychodynamic Practice*, 11(4), 429–446.

Small survey (n: 14) of therapists' problematic attitudes and experiences with regard to personal safety, in private practice and in organisational settings.

Suicide risk to client

Hawton, K., Casanas i Comabella, C., Haw, C. and Saunders, K. (2013) 'Risk factors for suicide in individuals with depression: A systematic review', *Journal of Affective Disorders*, 147, 17–28.

Meta-analyses of international studies of suicide (n: 19), identifying risk factors that include: male gender, family history of psychiatric disorder, previous suicide attempt, more severe depression, hopelessness, and co-morbid disorders, including anxiety, alcohol and drug misuse. Of recorded suicides, 25% were in touch with mental health services and 40% had seen their GP in the previous month. Risk increased just prior to starting medication or psychotherapy and in the first few weeks after discharge from in-patient psychiatric care.

Further reading

Reeves, A. (2010) *Counselling Suicidal Clients*. London: Sage.

An evidence-based and readable coverage of a key topic for counsellors.

Socarides, C. (n.d.) 'The erosion of heterosexuality', www.orthodoxytoday.org/articles/SocaridesErosion.php

Argument against removal of homosexuality as a diagnostic category from DSM-11, as this 'prevented the homosexual from seeking and receiving help'.

Reference section for supervisors

BACP Ethical Framework for the Counselling Professions (2016)

48. We will review in supervision how we work with clients. (2016: 10)

56. Trainee supervision will require the supervisor to ensure that the work satisfies professional standards.

57. When supervising qualified and/or experienced practitioners, the weight of responsibility for ensuring the supervisee's work meets professional standards will primarily rest with the supervisee. (2016: 11)

Training and education

66. Clients will usually be informed when they are receiving their services from a trainee. (2016: 12)

Research into working with difference

Moore, J. and Jenkins, P. (2012) '"Coming out" in therapy? Perceived risks and benefits of self-disclosure of sexual orientation by gay and lesbian therapists to straight clients', *Counselling and Psychotherapy Research*, 12(4), 308–315.

Qualitative exploration (n: 8) reporting high levels of anxiety among gay and lesbian therapists in disclosing their sexual orientation to 'straight' clients, which was experienced by some therapists as being problematic and risky.

Wong, L., Wong, P. and Ishiyama, F. (2013) 'What helps and what hinders in cross-cultural supervision: A critical incident study', *The Counseling Psychologist*, 41(1), 66–85.

US survey (n: 25) indicating positive factors facilitating cross-cultural supervision included the personal attributes of the supervisor, their supervision and multi-cultural competences, mentoring and relationship skills.

4

Working with key professional issues in therapeutic practice

Introduction

This chapter looks at some key professional issues for counsellors and psycho-therapists. Counselling practice is undergoing a period of rapid change and adjust-ment. This is happening in response to the shifts in the organisation and delivery of the talking therapies, initiated, and indeed accelerated, by the Improving Access to Psychological Therapies (IAPT) programme. These professional issues include:

- working as a member of a multi-disciplinary team;
- understanding the shift towards evidence-based practice;
- exploring the 'stepped care' model of service delivery;
- using outcome measures to evaluate counselling.

Learning context

The BACP *Core Curriculum* (2009) emphasises a number of interrelated themes with regard to professional practice. These include working in multi-disciplinary teams and settings and managing the counselling process with regard to note-taking and evalu-ation of practice. The BACP *Ethical Framework for the Counselling Professions* (2016) refers to the role of collaborative work in improving services to clients. The BACP's *An Evidenced Informed Curriculum Framework for Young People (11–18 Years)* (BACP Professional Standards, 2016) is also relevant, referring to the need for counsellors to work within and across agencies.

BACP *Core Curriculum* (2009)

B.6.3 The course must enable students to understand the role boundaries and issues around communication and collaboration within a multidisciplinary setting. (2009: 9)

9.1.A The professional role and responsibility of the therapist:

12. Manage counselling practice efficiently, including record and note keeping; provision of an appropriate environment; liaison with other services; reviewing of caseloads and evaluation of practice. ...

14. Communicate clearly with clients, colleagues and other professionals both orally and in writing. (2009: 14)

9.1.D The social, professional and organisational context for therapy:

12. Work in multidisciplinary teams with other professionals and participate effectively to maximise the therapeutic outcomes as appropriate. (2009: 19)

BACP *Ethical Framework for the Counselling Professions* (2016)

Working to professional standards:

16. We will collaborate with colleagues over our work with specific clients where this is consistent with client consent and will enhance services to the client.

17. We will work collaboratively with colleagues to improve services and offer mutual support. (2016: 6)

BACP Professional Standards *An Evidenced Informed Curriculum Framework for Young People (11–18 Years)* (2016)

Subject Area 20: Working within and across Agencies.

'... work effectively within and across agencies, particularly with regard to confidentiality and consent.' (2016: 33)

Working as a member of a multi-disciplinary team

Counselling is often perceived as essentially a dyadic, or two-way, relationship between the therapist and the client. The organisational context of the therapy is sometimes left rather vague, a factor which is explored in more detail in Chapter 2. However, as distinct from this primary – and understandable – focus on the therapeutic relationship with the *client*, counsellors are increasingly required to work closely with other professionals in a collaborative manner. This type of contact can range from occasional contact by letter, fax or email with a client's GP (with the client's consent), to more focused work, for periods of time, as a member of a team with a specific task (e.g. in providing pre-trial therapy to a young person or to a vulnerable adult), to working in a continuous relationship with other members of a team, which might include *both* counsellors and non-counsellors. These different types of working context can raise complex issues for therapists. In part, it may be due to the fact that counsellors will often have broad experience of working in *groups* throughout their training, but may have less experience of working in *teams*. A team is a specialised form of group, combining a focus on a work-related task, with specific types of process, membership and roles for those belonging to, or joining, the team.

Exercise   Evaluating your own experience of groups and teams

Briefly list the different types of *group* of which you are, or were, a member during your professional training. Now add a list of any *teams* to which you have belonged, e.g. sports teams, work-based teams. What differences, if any, can you identify between a group and a team?

Working in teams

Opportunities, or expectations, for counsellors to work in a team have increased over the past decade. This is partly because of the growing recognition of the valuable role that counsellors can play within health, social care, and other work settings, such as education and the workplace. Another factor is the complexity of many issues affecting society and its members. No single profession, taken on its own, has the capacity to help resolve all the issues facing one person. An example might be working with a young person at risk of self-harm. This may require at least some level of cooperation with other professionals, such as teachers, youth workers and mental health workers.

Confusingly, the language relating to working in teams can vary widely, with 'the terms multiprofessional, interprofessional, multidisciplinary, interdisciplinary, multiagency and interagency being used to describe what appears to be very similar activities' (Thomas et al., 2014: 12). What all these terms have in common is the process of *collaboration* between individuals from different professional backgrounds or from different organisations to achieve *joint tasks or goals*. Some of the situations where counsellors can be expected to work closely with other professionals are shown in Figure 4.1.

There are specific skills needed for effective working in teams, just as there are skills for working in groups. Fortunately, there is some overlap with the one-to-one skills needed for counselling. Groups entail

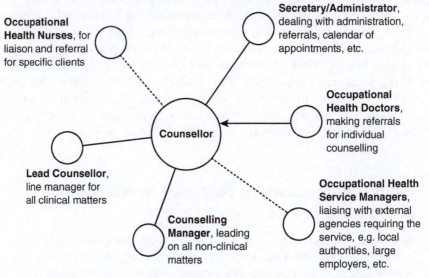

Counsellor working in an occupational health multi-disciplinary team

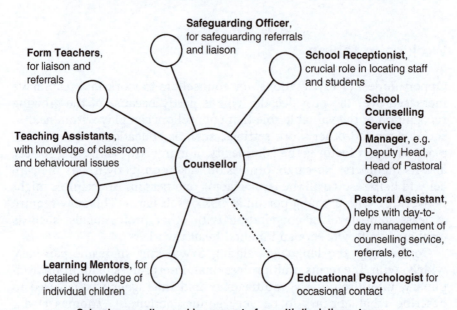

School counsellor working as part of a multi-disciplinary team

Figure 4.1 Examples of counsellors working in multi-disciplinary teams

more complex relationships, because of the wider range of interpersonal connections that any group will generate. Teams are increasingly used to address particular types of issues which require input from more than one professional, or agency. However, there can be real difficulties within teams, as individuals bring quite different expectations and values to the process of working together. Some of the requirements for effective team working are listed in Box 4.1.

Box 4.1   Requirements for effective team work

- Awareness and valuing of other professions' roles and contributions
- Willingness to question own assumptions and practice
- Open, non-defensive communication style
- Commitment to overall policy and team goals
- Trust and mutual respect
- Personal and professional confidence and assertiveness
- High level of interpersonal communication skills
- Reflective learning style

(For further discussion, see Keeping, 2014)

Potential problem areas for counsellors when working in teams

There are some particular problems that can arise for counsellors when working in teams, in addition to any caused by a lack of the desirable attributes listed in Box 4.1. These can arise from professional differences in relation to core aspects of the counsellor's role and practice, with regard to client privacy, confidentiality, record-keeping and clinical supervision.

- **Privacy** refers to information *about the client* attending counselling. In schools, for example, other professionals may be tempted to compromise client confidentiality by claiming the right to know who attends counselling, or through the actual physical location of the counselling room, which makes it easier for third parties (e.g. other pupils, non-counselling staff) to infer that a pupil is attending for counselling.
- **Confidentiality** can be compromised by other professionals, who may be expecting a high level of information-sharing from the counsellor. It can be helpful to separate out different levels of information in order to clarify which types of client information may be shared, and on what basis. For example:

    o *anonymised outline of client issues, attendance*, etc. This information might be appropriately shared with other professionals for the purposes of organisational audit, service evaluation or professional supervision;

    o *information arising from safeguarding concerns* about the client's risk to self or others may be shared either with client consent or on a 'public interest' basis with other professionals, again on a limited 'need to know' basis;

    o more *detailed information on client issues, the narrative of therapy, or the therapeutic alliance, etc*. This would require client consent to be shared with other professionals, again on a limited 'need to know' basis.

- **Record-keeping**: Within multi-disciplinary teams, other professionals may expect a high level of access to client records, assuming that all information that is recorded about a client is therefore accessible, in principle, to other members of the team. Levels of access need to be clarified through a clear team policy on record-keeping. Good practice guidelines in the field of infertility counselling, for example, recommend that counselling records are to be kept separately from the main patient's medical record, as they will often contain highly sensitive personal information (British Infertility Counselling Association, 2012: para 5.4). Alternatively, if counselling records are deemed to be accessible to all other members of the team, then this might mean that the counselling record may need to become much more selective and condensed, in order to retain its purpose as an *aide-mémoire*, but without unnecessarily compromising client confidentiality.

Electronic client records will perhaps be more quick and convenient than paper-based files, in many respects, but they may also pose significant problems for maintaining appropriate levels of client data security. This can be a particular issue for those counsellors who work online with clients, where the actual process of communicating with the client, by email or via online chatrooms, might generate a detailed transcript of the communications by both parties (see Box 4.2).

Box 4.2 Online counselling transcripts and confidentiality issues in the context of safeguarding concerns

The main concern I still have ... is that of confidentiality. There are very many opportunities for a client's transcript to be read by others: if a client doesn't shut the page down properly, or if someone else is present, or if a teacher logs them on and off. Similarly for counsellors: while transcripts are a great learning tool and very useful for safe-guarding in terms of accurate recall of what was said, I do feel that there is a very real risk that a client's confidentiality can be uninten-tionally compromised. ... The problem with having a transcript is that all too often the whole thing becomes visible to managers, admin and supervisors during the process of reporting or making a decision to report. While this may be very reassuring to organisations, I have real concerns that it is too easy to share transcripts under the policy of organisational confidentiality. (Yates, 2014: 37)

- **Supervision**: Finally, multi-agency teams containing workers from other professions, such as medicine, teaching or social work, may need to be informed or reminded of the distinct focus of counselling supervision. Counselling supervision is intended as an aid to thera-peutic work with the client, rather than for the purposes of case man-agement or line management, which is often the norm in many other professions. Referring to the BACP *Ethical Framework for the Counselling Professions* (2016) on this point may help other professionals to appre-ciate the distinct *therapeutic* focus of counselling supervision in this regard. (Supervision is discussed in more detail later in Chapter 7.)

Understanding the shift towards evidence-based practice

Counselling and psychotherapy are undergoing intense change at pres-ent. In the last decade, there has been a marked shift towards producing the evidence that 'therapy works' and is effective in reducing human distress. The growing evidence that counselling is effective, in turn, has unlocked government resources, enabling the funding of counselling provision on a broad scale. This has come at some cost and involved some compromises, however. The shift towards evidence-based prac-tice and towards a 'stepped care' model of assessment and service delivery has been at the cost of a perceived medicalisation of counsel-ling, particularly in the form of the Improving Access to Psychological Therapies (IAPT) programme within the NHS.

The search for clear evidence of the effectiveness of therapy goes back to Freud and the writing of his influential case studies (McLeod, 2013: 90), and to the research carried out by Carl Rogers from the 1940s onwards (McLeod, 2013: 262–3). The research agenda in the UK for counselling has accelerated with the opportunities to provide counselling within diverse settings, such as schools, universities, workplaces and the NHS. Within the NHS, research into the effectiveness of medicine and

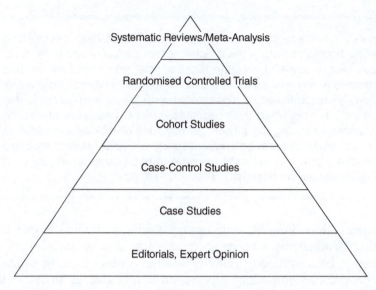

Figure 4.2 Hierarchy of research evidence (adapted from Cooper, 2008: 181)

other treatments is organised on the basis of a hierarchy of evidence. This ranges from the most authoritative evidence, i.e. based on the strongest research, to what are considered to be weaker forms of evidence (see Figure 4.2).

The hierarchy of evidence is firmly based on a medical approach to science. This in turn is derived from a positivist approach to understanding both the natural and the social worlds. It uses techniques of measurement and comparison to establish *causal* mechanisms of change. This approach has been used to evaluate the efficacy of counselling and other therapeutic approaches for psychological problems since the turn of this century.

NICE Guidelines for psychological therapies

Within the NHS, this particular research model dominates the provision of psychological therapies. Relying on diagnosis, specific psychological treatments are recommended – or not – based on the relative strength of their evidence base and, in particular, on the use of evidence derived from randomised controlled trials. The evidence is then used to compile official guidance, under the auspices of the National Institute for Health and Care Excellence (NICE), i.e. the NICE Guidelines. A patient presenting with symptoms of persistent low mood is likely to be diagnosed with depression by their GP and prescribed anti-depressant medication, referred for psychological therapy, or offered a treatment combining *both* medication and therapy. Both treatments, i.e. medication and therapy, are assessed on their available evidence base. A patient asking for a particular type of therapy for depression, e.g. gestalt or transactional analysis, is probably unlikely to receive it, just as a patient asking for a herbal remedy, such as St John's Wort, would probably be politely declined by the GP. This is not to suggest that gestalt, transactional analysis, or St John's Wort are necessarily ineffective in helping a client or patient to overcome their experience of depression. It is simply that there is currently limited evidence for their *efficacy*, according to this medicalised model of evidence-based practice.

The current guidelines for psychological treatments are summarised in Table 4.1 for adults and in Table 4.2 for children aged over 8 years.

Exercise   Reviewing the NICE Guidelines

Quickly review the summaries for the NICE recommendations for adults and for children over 8 years of age and pick out any diagnoses which do *not* recommend CBT. Go online and download at least one set of guidelines for future reference.

What seems immediately apparent is the critical role played by medical diagnosis in two key areas. First, diagnosis is crucial in accurately identifying the client's perceived condition or illness, such as social anxiety or post-traumatic stress disorder. Secondly, diagnosis can be significant, for example, in further distinguishing *between* different types of eating disorder (e.g. anorexia, bulimia or binge eating), or between different types of depression (e.g. mild, moderate, severe or bipolar). This kind of close attention to diagnostic criteria is something about which many counsellors would probably feel uncomfortable, but which is a clear hallmark of medical practice. Following on from this, psychological treatments are recommended (or not) according to the relative strength of their evidence base. It is striking that individual or group CBT, in one form or another, is recommended for nearly every single type of psychological problem listed here, for both adults and children. This is a reflection of the strong and growing evidence base enjoyed by CBT as a therapeutic model, compared with that of other modalities. CBT's dominance of the NICE Guidelines has presented a challenge to other models of therapy to develop their own evidence, based on the use of randomised controlled trials. This has been evident in the case of therapy for depression. According to the relevant NICE Guideline (CG90), counselling should be offered *only* to patients who

Table 4.1 Summary of NICE treatment recommendations for the use of psychological therapies: Adults

Guide line	Year	Diagnostic category	Recommended treatment
CG113	**2011**	**Anxiety (includes panic and generalised anxiety disorder)**	CBT/medication/self-help approaches
CG72	2008	Attention deficit hyperactivity disorder	Medication/CBT
CG185	2014	Bipolar disorder	Medication/electroconvulsive therapy/CBT/interpersonal therapy/family therapy/behavioural couples therapy
CG53	2007	**Chronic fatigue syndrome/myalgic encephalomyelitis**	CBT/graded exercise therapy/activity management/pain management clinic
CG42	2006	Dementia	Structured group cognitive stimulation programme/multi-sensory stimulation/animal-assisted therapy and exercise
CG42	**2006**	**Dementia with depression and anxiety**	CBT/reminiscence therapy/medication
CG90/CG91	2009	Depression: Mild	Self-help approaches/exercise/brief CBT/computerised CBT
CG90/CG91	2009	Depression: Moderate/severe	Group or individual CBT/mindfulness-based CBT/interpersonal psychotherapy/couple-focused therapy/behavioural activation/counselling/psychodynamic therapy/medication
CG90/CG91	**2009**	**Depression: Complex and severe**	CBT *plus* medication/electroconvulsive therapy
CG9	2004	**Eating disorder:** Anorexia nervosa	Cognitive analytic therapy/CBT/interpersonal psychotherapy/focal psychodynamic therapy/family interventions focused on eating disorders
CG9	2004	**Eating disorder:** Bulimia nervosa	Self-help approaches/medication/CBT – bulimia nervosa/interpersonal psychotherapy
CG9	2004	**Eating disorder:** Binge eating disorder	Medication/interpersonal psychotherapy/dialectical behaviour therapy/CBT – binge eating disorder
CG31	2005	**Obsessive compulsive disorder and body dysmorphic disorder**	CBT (group and individual)/exposure and response prevention/medication
CG26	2009	**Post-traumatic stress disorder**	Trauma focused CBT/eye movement desensitisation and reprocessing *or* medication
CG178	**2014**	**Psychosis and schizophrenia**	Medication/family interventions/CBT/arts therapies

Table 4.2 Summary of NICE treatment recommendations for the use of psychological therapies: Children (over 8 years)

Guideline	Year	Diagnostic category	Recommended treatment
CG72	**2008**	**Attention deficit hyperactivity disorder**	Group-based or individual parent training/ education programmes/CBT (individual or group)/ social skills training/medication
CG28	**2015**	**Depression:** Mild	Non-directive supportive therapy/group CBT/ guided self-help
		Depression: Moderate/severe	CBT/interpersonal psychotherapy/family therapy/ psychodynamic psychotherapy/individual child psychotherapy/medication/electroconvulsive therapy (for adolescents with severe depression)
CG185	**2014**	**Bipolar disorder**	CBT/interpersonal therapy/medication
CG9	**2004**	**Eating disorder:** Anorexia nervosa	Family interventions addressing eating disorders
		Eating disorder: Bulimia nervosa	CBT – Bulimia nervosa
		Eating disorder: Binge eating disorder	CBT – Binge eating disorder
CG31	**2005**	**Obsessive compulsive disorder and body dysmorphic disorder**	Guided self-help/CBT/exposure and response prevention/medication
CG26	**2009**	**Post-traumatic stress disorder**	Trauma-focused CBT

have first declined an anti-depressant, CBT, interpersonal therapy (IPT), behavioural activation and behavioural couples therapy. It recommends:

- counselling for people with persistent subthreshold symptoms or mild to moderate depression
- short-term psychodynamic psychotherapy for people with mild to moderate depression.

Discuss with the person the uncertainty of the effectiveness of counselling and psychodynamic psychotherapy in treating depression. (NICE, 2009: para 1.5.1.14)

The NICE Guidelines have contributed, at least in the short term, to the relative decline – if not eclipse – of counselling as an evidence-based modality within the NHS. This has been challenged by efforts by BACP to develop and promote an evidence-based model of person-centred counselling that has a proven record of efficacy in relation to depression, namely Counselling for Depression (Sanders and Hill, 2014). While this shift towards evidence-based practice is largely welcomed, as providing an opportunity for counselling and psychotherapy to prove their worth, it has also contributed to the relative marginalisation of counselling within IAPT and the NHS. The turn to an evidence-based practice that is set firmly within a medical paradigm or perspective is closely linked to the concept of 'stepped care', which is the preferred healthcare model for delivery of the talking therapies.

Exploring the 'stepped care' model of service delivery

The concept of stepped care can be traced back to notion of 'triage', i.e. separating emergency incident patients into priority categories: those requiring immediate care, palliative care, or (in extreme cases) 'no treatment'. It can also be linked to medical ethics and to the Latin injunction for doctors and health workers of *primum non nocere*, or 'First, do no harm'. The key principle employed here is that of using scarce medical resources in the most effective manner, given that, as GPs are repeatedly informed, 'common things are common'. Medical interventions inevitably carry side-effects, some of which may be damaging to the patient's health. Interventions should therefore be minimally intrusive and should be increased mainly where previous interventions have proved to be slow to take effect or have been shown to be ineffective. Such interventions are also based on a hierarchy of skill and training. Routine treatments can be provided by appropriately trained and qualified medical aides or by nursing staff, while progressively more skilled or demanding interventions are provided by more highly trained or qualified healthcare practitioners.

Stepped care and assessment of need

The stepped care model of service delivery immediately presents a number of problems for therapists concerning the issue of assessment and the provision of therapy. Many therapists, once fully trained and qualified, are understandably keen to exercise their own professional judgement. Counsellors can exercise their own skill and knowledge in deciding, together with the client, what the agreed issues and goals of therapy are to be, and how to work on them in a joint and appropriate manner. This kind of approach emphasises the importance of high levels of professional autonomy, subject of course to supervision. It probably finds its most direct illustration in private practice settings. Working in an organisational setting, there may be practical constraints on the autonomy enjoyed by the counsellor. For example, an agency might prescribe a maximum number of sessions, or determine the range of client issues considered appropriate for counsellors to work with. Alternatively, in many settings, a preliminary assessment is carried out by an experienced practitioner, before referral to another counsellor, usually within the same agency, for ongoing work. This model is common in some psychodynamic agencies and in many placement settings. Clients are assessed for their perceived level of risk and also their suitability, in terms of complexity and co-morbidity of the client's issues, for student or trainee counsellors to work with.

The stepped care approach is based on the medical model of care briefly outlined above. It provides a direct challenge both to the counsellor's own direct assessment of client need and to their ability to decide on the amount and type of therapy to be provided. It also breaks down the generic skill-set of therapists into 'low intensity' interventions, which can be delivered effectively by staff with appropriate training such as Psychological Wellbeing Practitioners, and 'high intensity' interventions, requiring highly skilled practitioners with more specialist or extensive training and qualifications. Some of the main features of the stepped care model for the treatment of depression are illustrated in Table 4.3.

It is tempting to see the stepped care model as being confined largely to the NHS and IAPT, as representing very specific medical or organisational settings. In practice, there are growing pressures on *all* counselling agencies to gatekeep and manage client demand and to allocate scarce and expensive resources, such as counsellor time. It may mean that this model will increasingly become the template for delivering counselling in settings outside the NHS, such as the third sector

Table 4.3   Development of IAPT stepped care model

	Who is responsible for care?	What is the focus?	What do they do?
Step 5	In-patient care, crisis teams	Risk to life, severe self-neglect	Medication, combined treatments, electro-convulsive therapy
Step 4	Mental health specialists, including crisis teams	Treatment-resistant, recurrent, atypical and psychotic depression and those at significant risk	Medication, complex psychological intervention, combined treatments
Step 3	Primary care team, primary care mental health worker	Moderate or severe depression	Medication, psychological interventions, social support
Step 2	Primary care team, primary care mental health worker	Mild depression	Watchful waiting, guided study, computerised CBT, exercise, psychological intervention
Step 1	GP, practice nurse	Recognition	Assessment

Source: Cohen, 2008: 9

and beyond (Craig, 2017). This also appears to be the case with counselling in the university context (see Box 4.3). Cowley and Groves present the model of counselling developed at Cardiff University as 'a forward-thinking stepped care service for students, offering choice' (2016: 113).

Box 4.3   Cardiff University Model of stepped care for counselling

The Cardiff University Model represents the introduction of a stepped care model to the process of counselling in Higher Education settings. It also demonstrates the application of some of the core underlying principles discussed above. For example, these principles include the use of a comprehensive assessment of client need, via a 90-minute therapeutic consultation, plus minimal intervention, geared to meeting the perceived level of a client's need and risk. There is a reliance too on systematic outcome measures to evaluate the overall effectiveness of the model in practice. The model seems to shift away quite decisively from more traditional 'entitlement' models of counselling provision within university settings. The more traditional model of counselling in HE currently seems to be struggling to cope effectively with rising student and staff demand, and with the growing number of clients presenting with more complex mental health problems.

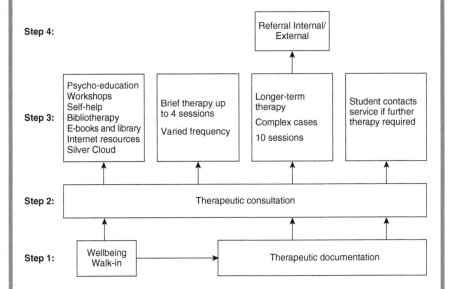

Figure 4.3 Stepped care model applied to counselling in Higher Education (adapted from Cowley and Groves, 2016: 115)

The Cardiff Model retains an element of client choice in that there are multiple points of entry to the service, such as self-referral, drop-in and via the Wellbeing Walk-in service. There are also several ways for clients to seek and obtain appropriate help from the service, including the use of psycho-educational tools such as Silver Cloud, short-term focused therapy, longer-term therapy and re-entry into the counselling service after a gap to consolidate any changes that have been made. Overall, the Cardiff Model is an example of a more systemic approach to re-organising counselling provision in an era of scarce resources and pressure to demonstrate effectiveness in providing a high-quality service. Voluntary and third sector counselling organisations are clearly subject to the same economic and professional pressures as are universities in this respect, so it is likely that the stepped care model may become more influential outside the NHS in the medium-term future as the process of 'IAPT-isation' gathers pace.

Using outcome measures to evaluate counselling

The use of NICE Guidelines and of the stepped care model has been closely linked with another innovation in the provision of counselling services. This is the increasing use of outcome measures to evaluate the *efficacy* of counselling services. Previously, agencies have often tried to devise their own outcome measures, as, for example, in Higher Education or in school-based counselling. Alternatively, therapists might use specific measures for a particular client condition, such as the Beck Depression Inventory. There has been a shift towards more generic outcome measures, such as Client Outcomes in Routine Evaluation (CORE). Using more generic measures permits client data to be pooled and thus compared with other services. It also confirms the quality of the data obtained because it is a validated measure, rather than one which has been designed solely by the agency itself, for largely in-house purposes. The use of a validated outcome measure is increasingly required for funding purposes. This is in order to demonstrate the actual *efficacy* of counselling as an intervention, i.e. that it *works* in reducing distress, rather than simply to indicate often simply high levels of client *satisfaction*, i.e. clients reporting a positive experience of accessing and undertaking counselling.

CORE consists of a 34-item self-report questionnaire, which is typically given out to clients at the beginning and end of counselling to chart their progress over time. The questions cover four domains, relating to the past week. These are the client's subjective sense of wellbeing, experience of problems and symptoms, life functioning, and risk to self or others. 'Subjective sense of wellbeing' includes the degree to which the client feels good about him- or herself, or feels overwhelmed by problems such as crying a lot, or feels optimistic about the future. Problems and symptoms include levels of anxiety, depression, trauma and physical problems such as difficulties in sleeping or physical aches and pains. The client's general level of functioning includes how happy they feel about being able to achieve things, how close relationships are experienced in terms of warmth or isolation, and in terms of feeling irritated, or even humiliated, in their interactions with others. Risk is explored in terms of risk to self (e.g. self-harm, suicidal thoughts) and risk towards others. A section from a CORE questionnaire is shown in Figure 4.4.

CORE makes a distinction between the general population (i.e. a non-clinical/non-psychiatric population) and a clinical population (i.e. one with significant recorded levels of psychological distress). There are slight differences in calculating scores for male and female clients, to take account of relevant clinical gender differences. CORE can be completed by clients in a traditional paper-based format or on a

Over the last week	Not at all	Only occasionally	Sometimes	Often	Most or all the time	OFFICE USE ONLY
1 I have felt terribly alone and isolated	0	1	2	3	4	F
2 I have felt tense, anxious or nervous	0	1	2	3	4	P
3 I have felt I have someone to turn to for support when needed	4	3	2	1	0	F
4 I have felt OK about myself	4	3	2	1	0	W
5 I have felt totally lacking in energy and enthusiasm	0	1	2	3	4	P

Figure 4.4   Section from CORE questionnaire

Section of the CORE-OM reproduced with permission from the CORE System Trust: https://www.coresystemtrust.org.uk/home/copyright-licensing/

PC, which permits easier translation to a graph or bar chart format for interpretation. Depending on ability and familiarity with the measure, completing CORE can take around 10 minutes on first encounter, or around 5 minutes on subsequent use. There are also versions of CORE which are briefer, for screening purposes (CORE-5 and CORE-10), or which have been adapted for specific audiences (e.g. CORE LD for clients with learning difficulties and CORE YP for young people).

Using CORE, or another appropriate outcome measure, is increasingly seen as a hallmark of good professional practice in that it opens the counselling practice of individuals up to wider scrutiny and accountability. It enables both therapist and client to 'track' client change, improvement and deterioration over time, including session-by-session change, if necessary. The example of a client CORE chart in Figure 4.5 shows a fairly typical process of improvement over a short period of time, in coming down from a high level of anxiety to a more bearable level of anxiety and distress.

In contrast, the example in Figure 4.6 shows a sustained and continuing high level of distress and a medium-to-moderate level of risk for a client with moderate depression over a medium-term period of counselling. The few 'dips' in the relatively high levels of distress and risk were reported by the client as being due to feeling more relaxed while on holiday before returning to a stressful work and home situation.

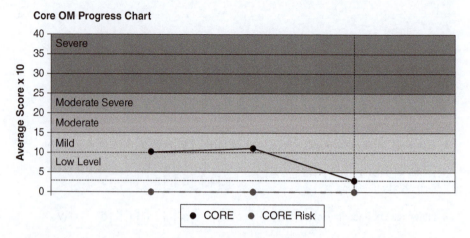

Figure 4.5 CORE chart scores for a short-term counselling intervention

Reproduced with permission of CORE IMS.

In Figure 4.6, the persisting higher-level scores for distress and risk may suggest that the client is not responding to the use of anti-depressants, either the level prescribed by their GP or the specific type of anti-depressant, or even to the counselling itself. It may be appropriate for the client to be referred back to their GP, with their consent, for a review of their anti-depressant medication or for referral for a type of counselling specifically geared to working with moderate or treatment-resistant depression.

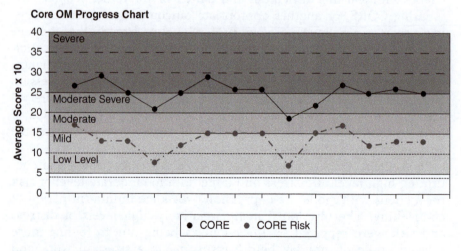

Figure 4.6 CORE chart scores for a longer-term counselling intervention

Reproduced with permission of CORE IMS.

Some therapists are very sceptical about the value of collecting out-come data in this way, or tend to see the process as interfering with the therapeutic relationship between client and therapist. Streatfield (2012), as a supporter of the value of CORE, presents an alternative view in Box 4.4.

Box 4.4   Positive features of using outcome measures within therapy

Therapists who integrate outcome measures into their everyday prac-tice do so because they have found ways to make them relevant. They see outcome measures complement clinical judgement, rather than replace it, and that clients respond well to being able to track their own progress. This positive attitude is likely to be conveyed to the client who then also sees the value of the measures, the results they show, and the curious conversations they generate. Collecting outcome measures is seen as a normal, helpful and integral part of the therapy. (Streatfield, 2012: 31)

CORE has also contributed to the continuing debate over the relative efficacy of different models of counselling. This debate has tended to be dominated by the large amount of data endorsing CBT. Non-CBT modalities have tended to undertake fewer randomised controlled trials than CBT. This has meant that non-CBT approaches are much less likely to feature in the NICE Guidelines, at least until relatively recently. Randomised controlled trials and meta-analyses of RCTs underpin what is termed 'evidence-based practice', on a medical model. In other words, a particular medication, such as statins for high blood pressure, is prescribed by a GP on the basis of a close examina-tion of the relevant data from laboratory and experimental trials. While the analogy is contested by some, cognitive behavioural therapy may be recommended by the same GP for a patient showing signs and symptoms of acute anxiety or panic attacks.

Given their relative lack of RCTs and meta-analyses, other counsel-ling modalities have relied on evidence drawn from practice, or 'practice-based evidence', to argue the case for their effectiveness. This evidence is drawn from practice in the 'real world', with clients who may have multiple problems rather than having a single diagno-sis, as is often the case with clients carefully selected for experimental trials. Some of the differences between evidence-based practice, or efficacy studies, and practice-based evidence, or effectiveness studies, are outlined in Table 4.4.

Table 4.4 Comparison of evidence-based practice and practice-based evidence models of research

	Evidence-based practice: *Efficacy* **studies**	**Practice-based evidence:** *Effectiveness* **studies**
Research setting	Controlled conditions	'Real world' conditions
Therapist variables	Manualised therapy to reduce therapist variations from model	Degree of practitioner autonomy permitted
Patient variables	Single diagnosis as basis for client participation in study	Frequent complex, or co-morbid, diagnosis
Model of research	Randomised controlled trials	Naturalistic service evaluation
Level of internal validity	High	Low
Degree of generalisability	Low	High
Primary reference group	Research community, government policy makers	Service providers, audit managers, practitioners, funding agencies, client and advocacy groups

Source: adapted from Hill et al., 2008: 18

In the short term, effectiveness studies have provided a way to argue the continuing relevance of non-CBT modalities to counselling practice. Research was undertaken by Gibbard and Hanley (2008) over a five-year period of CORE outcomes achieved by a team of counsellors working in primary care. This showed that the majority of clients (n: 697) used 6–8 sessions, while 67% of participants showed reliable improvement, according to CORE scores, and 90% found counselling helpful. Although this form of practice-based research does not carry the same weight as randomised controlled trials, it does go some way in underlining the continuing relevance of other modalities in the debate and of the need for client choice of therapies besides CBT. To redress the balance, a number of randomised controlled trials have been undertaken, particularly in school settings, to demonstrate the efficacy of modalities other than CBT (Pybis et al., 2015).

Summary

This chapter has looked at some of the current developments relating to professional practice in counselling and psychotherapy. This included the increasing involvement of counsellors working in multi-disciplinary teams. Working in multi-disciplinary teams can present challenges to therapists with regard to issues such as client privacy, confidentiality of client material and orientation to a therapeutic, rather than a line-management, model of supervision. New 'stepped care' models of counselling service delivery, such as IAPT, are based on a medical model of diagnosis and evidence-based practice, as represented in the NICE Guidelines. Counsellors are increasingly expected to use relevant outcome measures, such as CORE, to evaluate their practice and, on occasion, to provide useful practice-based evidence of their effectiveness.

Resources

Research

Multi-disciplinary team working

Cameron, A., Lart, R., Bostock, L. and Coomber, C. (2012) *Factors that Promote and Hinder Joint and Integrated Working between Health and Social Care Services.* SCIE Research Briefing No. 41. London: Social Care Institute for Excellence.

Systematic review of organisational, professional, cultural and contextual issues impacting on multi-agency teams in health and social care.

NICE Guidelines and 'Counselling for Depression'

Hill, A. and Elliott, R. (2014) 'Evidence-based practice and person-centred and experiential therapies', in P. Sanders and A. Hill, *Counselling for Depression: A Person-Centred and Experiential Approach to Practice.* London: Sage. Chapter 2, pp. 5–20.

Detailed review of evidence used for NICE Guidelines, contrasted with evidence from randomised controlled trials and meta-analyses, based on person-centred and experiential approaches to Counselling for Depression.

Counselling in primary care

Hill, A., Brettle, A., Hulme, C. and Jenkins, P. (2008) *Counselling in Primary Care: A Systematic Review of the Evidence.* Lutterworth: BACP.

A systematic review of research studies (n: 41) into counselling in primary care, pre-IAPT, demonstrating that counselling is as effective as CBT with typical primary care populations and more effective than routine primary care with regard to short-term mental health outcomes.

Further reading

Cowley, J. and Groves, V. (2016) 'The Cardiff model of short-term engagement', in D. Mair (ed.), *Short-Term Counselling in Higher Education: Context, Theory and Practice.* London: Routledge. pp. 108–126.

Case study describing the origins and development of Cardiff University's stepped care model for student counselling.

Reference section for supervisors

Supervision training is now strongly influenced by the competence approach. Competences have been developed, both for counsellors and for similar practitioners, such as Psychological Well-being Practitioners (PWPs) working in the context of IAPT. For IAPT supervisors, a set of CBT competences has been developed. Further modality-based supervisory competences could follow for other approaches, e.g. person-centred, integrative and psychodynamic models.

Taylor, K., Gordon, K., Grist, S. and Olding, C. (2012) 'Developing supervisory competence: Preliminary data on the impact of CBT supervision training', *Cognitive Behaviour Therapist*, 5(4), 83–92.

Small repeated measures, self-report survey (n: 28) of positive outcomes for CBT supervisors in developing relevant competences after completing a five-day training programme.

Turpin, G. and Wheeler, S. (2011) *IAPT Supervision Guidance*. London: IAPT/NHS.

Supervision requirements for staff involved in IAPT, ranging from high-intensity therapists to low-intensity therapists, trainees and Psychological Well-being Practitioners (www.iapt.nhs.uk/silo/files/iapt-supervision-guidance-revised-march-2011.pdf).

5

Understanding the legal context of professional practice

Introduction

Professional practice is partly defined by our profession's overall relationship to the law, as in whether or not we are subject to statutory regulation. For many counsellors, the law can be experienced as a challenging and unfamiliar area of practice, characterised by inflexible rules and unforgiving complexity. This chapter aims to provide an introduction to the key areas of the law which are necessary for engaging confidently with the legal context of our work. It covers:

* defining the law and relevant legal frameworks for practice;
* understanding the professional, legal and ethical aspects of confidentiality;
* applying data protection principles to counselling records;
* using contracts with clients.

Learning context

The legal context for professional counselling practice is set out in two key documents, the BACP *Core Curriculum* (2009) and the *Ethical Framework for the Counselling Professions* (2016). Counsellors are required to develop an understanding of the law and how it relates to their practice with clients, with particular regard to issues such as informed consent, diversity, confidentiality, record-keeping and contracting.

BACP *Core Curriculum* (2009)

9.1.A.12: The Professional Role and Responsibility of the Therapist: Manage counselling practice efficiently, including record and note keeping. ...

9.1.B.10: Understanding the client: Identify legal and ethical responsibilities with regard to potential risk, including critical decision making with respect to autonomy of the client and potential harm to self or others.

9.1.C: The therapeutic process: Demonstrate awareness of theoretical and research literature regarding the provision of a secure frame for therapy, including physical environment, contractual arrangements and ethics.

9.1.D: The social, professional and organisational context for therapy: Demonstrate an understanding of the relevant legislation that affects the practice of counselling and psychotherapy. (2009: 17)

BACP *Ethical Framework for the Counselling Professions* (2016)

Our commitment to clients:

Work to professional standards by:

(e) keeping accurate and appropriate records. (2016: 1)

Values: Our fundamental values include a commitment to:

Protecting the safety of clients. (2016: 2)

Putting clients first:

(9) We will give careful consideration to how we manage situations when protecting clients or others from serious harm or when compliance with the law may require overriding a client's explicit wishes or breaching their confidentiality.

(10) When the safeguarding of our clients or others from serious harm takes priority over our commitment to putting our client's wishes and confidentiality first, we will usually consult with any client affected, if this is legally permitted and ethically desirable. We will endeavour to implement any safeguarding responsibilities in ways that respect a client's known wishes, protect their interests, and support them in what follows. (2016: 5)

Working to professional standards:

(14) We will keep skills and knowledge up to date by:

(f) keeping up to date with the law, regulations and any other requirements, including guidance from this Association, relevant to our work.

(15) We will keep accurate records that are appropriate to the service being provided. (2016: 6)

Respect:

(23) We will take the law concerning equality, diversity and inclusion into careful consideration and strive for a higher standard than the legal minimum. ...

(25) We will protect the confidentiality and privacy of clients by:

(a) actively protecting information about clients from unauthorised access or disclosure.

(b) informing clients about any reasonably foreseeable limitations of privacy or confidentiality in advance of our work together. ...

(27) We will work with our clients on the basis of their informed consent and agreement. (2016: 7)

(28) Careful consideration will be given to working with children and young people that:

(a) takes account of their capacity to give informed consent, whether it is appropriate to seek the consent of others who have parental responsibility for the young person, and their best interests. ...

(29) We will give careful consideration to obtaining and respecting the consent of vulnerable adult clients, wherever they have the capacity to give consent, or involving anyone who provides care for these clients when appropriate. (2016: 8)

Integrity:

(42) We will give conscientious consideration to the law and any legal requirements concerning our work and take responsibility for how they are implemented. (2016: 9)

Defining the law and relevant legal frameworks for practice

This chapter will look at the law and the ways in which it can influence, for good or ill, our work as therapists. Unusually for a professional group, the law is not covered in detail in most therapy training courses. This stands in sharp contrast to training for other professional groups, such as nurses and social workers, where it is considered to be an essential component of training for their future practice (Griffith and Tengnah, 2010; Johns, 2010).

There are a number of reasons why the law is often not considered to be central to therapeutic work with clients. Counselling and psychotherapy are not regulated professions. They have a long history of developing in private practice and in the voluntary or third sector, rather than in the statutory sector, such as in schools and in the NHS, at least until the last decade or so. Many therapists do seem to feel anxious and under-confident when dealing with legal issues affecting their practice, such as responding to court or client demands to disclose records of therapy. McLeod expresses a widely-held view that the law is somehow external to the therapeutic process. He suggests that, for some counsellors, 'the intrusion of legal considerations can in some cases interfere with the creation of a productive therapeutic relationship' (2013: 539). He does go on to acknowledge, however, that 'the relationship between the therapeutic professions and the law seems to be growing in importance' (McLeod, 2013: 539).

If it is true that the law is having an increasing influence on therapeutic work, then this would partly justify including it as a key component of this book. There are, in fact, good reasons why any discussion of professional practice needs to address the law. It can be useful for counsellors by:

- setting counselling within a wider social frame;
- specifying the nature of counsellor liability;
- clarifying boundaries for counsellor/client behaviour;
- denoting clients' rights. (Jenkins, 1996: 452)

These themes can be used to explore legal issues occurring in everyday counselling practice, as the following exercise and discussion demonstrate.

Exercise   Case study: Exploring law and counselling practice

Nasreen is a qualified counsellor, working for a third sector agency which provides therapy for a broad range of clients. In the first session, she forgets to explain the agency's policy on confidentiality to the client. Her client is an adult, Roger, who discloses a history of mental health problems to her, including having thoughts of serious self-harm. Nasreen realises her error immediately after ending the session with her new client. She is left in a dilemma as to how to handle the information she has just received from the client about his risk of self-harm. She decides to leave this issue until her next supervision session, which is in a week's time.

Write down some of the ways in which the law might be relevant to Nasreen's practice in this situation.

(For discussion see below.)

Discussion of case study: Law and counselling practice

Setting counselling in a wider social frame

Nasreen and her client, Roger, are not meeting in a social vacuum, as isolated individuals. Nasreen is an employee of the counselling agency, and subject to its policies through her contract of employment and according to employment law. The agency and Nasreen are both subject to the law on confidentiality and data protection. Nasreen has failed to set out the limits to confidentiality which apply to the client's disclosures about mental health and the related risks of self-harm. Roger is therefore unable to give his informed consent to his taking part in the therapy.

Specifying the nature of counsellor liability

Nasreen is employed by the counselling agency, which carries vicarious liability for her errors and omissions. If she had been seeing the client in private practice, then she would carry personal liability for her own practice. In the event of a serious complaint by the client, the nature of this liability (i.e. whether it was judged to be a case of the counsellor having vicarious, or personal, liability) would determine whether the client would bring a legal action against the *employing agency* or against *her*, as a private practitioner.

Clarifying boundaries for counsellor/client behaviour

The law on confidentiality requires that the client's material be kept private and protected from unauthorised disclosure, with certain exceptions. The same law also requires her to pass on certain types of information (e.g. regarding terrorism). The law enables her to pass on information 'in the public interest', where the client, or others, may be at risk of harm. The law on contract may be relevant too in this scenario, if the client is paying either the agency or the counsellor for the counselling provided. The law of contract sets a minimum standard of quality and provides a means of redress for both parties in the event of major disagreement.

Denoting clients' rights

The client has a right to confidentiality. He could take legal action for an unjustified breach of confidentiality if the counsellor passed on his personal information to third parties (e.g. to a partner or to an employer) without his consent. This type of legal action is possible, but perhaps less likely to succeed, if the third party was his general practitioner. In addition, in case of major dissatisfaction, the client has the right to take legal action for breach of contract against the agency, or against the counsellor if he/she is in private practice. The client also has the right to sue the agency or therapist for professional negligence, if he were to suffer a 'psychiatric injury' as a direct result of the therapy provided.

Understanding the law

Understanding and valuing the law is clearly seen as important by BACP. Some of its key expectations regarding the law are set out in the BACP *Core Curriculum for Accredited Courses* (2009) and in the *Ethical Framework for the Counselling Professions* (2016) (see Box 5.1).

Box 5.1   Summary of BACP ethical requirements regarding the law

- [G]iving conscientious consideration to the law and legal requirements (para 42); including those applying to supervisors (para 60);
- [K]eeping up to date with the law (para 14f);
- [C]arefully considering situations where compliance with the law requires overriding their wishes or breaching confidentiality (para 9);
- [S]triving for a higher standard than the legal minimum regarding equality, diversity and inclusion (para 23);
- [N]otifying BACP of any criminal charges or civil claims, bankruptcy, or insolvency measures brought against us (para 43). (BACP, 2016)

So what do we mean by 'the law'? Essentially, the law consists of a set of rules which govern behaviour in a given society, sometimes defined as a jurisdiction. These rules have force in that they are applied by institutions, such as the police, courts, judges and, ultimately, the prison system. Applying these rules sets in train certain consequences. Breaking the law regarding drinking and driving, for example, can result in a court appearance, possibly leading to a fine or disqualification from driving.

Differences between legal jurisdictions in the UK

Within the United Kingdom, there are a number of different societies, or jurisdictions, each with their own legal system, i.e. England, Wales, Scotland and Northern Ireland. Most of the specific examples of the law in this chapter will be drawn from England and Wales, but reference will also be made to Scotland and Northern Ireland from time to time. Generally speaking, there are broad legal principles which apply throughout the UK, although they may take slightly different forms. For example, professional negligence is sometimes described as 'tort' law in England (from the French or Norman word for 'a wrong'), whereas it is referred to as a 'delict' in Scotland.

In a way, the example of drink-driving given on the previous page might be seen as slightly misleading regarding the law. It uses an example of the law relating to a *criminal* offence. There is a major distinction we need to make at this point between the *criminal* law and the *civil* law. The criminal law concerns rules that have been devised by society to protect individuals and property from harm, such as theft, fraud and assault. Most readers will be familiar with the basic principles of criminal law, if only from watching films and TV programmes. Under the criminal law, an individual is assumed to be innocent until proven guilty. If charged with breaking the law, a criminal prosecution is brought by the Crown Prosecution Service. The case has to be proven 'beyond reasonable doubt', i.e. no reasonable person would doubt that the accused had, in fact, committed the theft, or assault, on the basis of the evidence presented to the court. If found 'not guilty', the accused is released as a free person. If found 'guilty', the accused receives a criminal conviction. The punishment can be a fine or a sentence to community service or incarceration in prison.

Readers might rightly be wondering how this is relevant to becoming a counsellor or psychotherapist. Criminal law of the kind described above is probably of limited relevance to most therapists, unless they are working within the criminal justice system, such as in a prison setting, for example. Criminal law stands in sharp contrast with the system of civil law, which is the branch of law that is of most immediate relevance to counsellors.

So what is civil law? Civil law provides a means of regulating social relationships and resolving contested issues or disputes in a peaceful manner, such as via divorce proceedings. It does this by imposing injunctions, or by resolving business disputes, etc. Under civil law, an individual can bring a case against another party, for example for breach of a contract to install a new kitchen. The parties are referred to as the plaintiff and the defendant, and the case is decided 'on the balance of probabilities', rather than 'beyond reasonable doubt', as in a criminal case. This is a much lower threshold for proof compared to the criminal law. The legal term 'on the balance of probabilities' means 'it is more probable than not' that the new kitchen was not installed properly. The court finds in favour of one party or the other. The outcome may involve an order for compensation, a fine or another court decision.

Exercise Exploring your attitude towards the law

Take a moment to reflect on your own personal attitude towards the law. Note down in one column any strong feelings about the law and consider how these might influence your practice as a counsellor. In a second column, identify what steps you can take in response to the feelings you have identified, e.g. reducing anxiety by identifying gaps in your current level of knowledge or confidence regarding the law.

Sources of guidance on the law

Finding out about the law tends to be seen by many counsellors as either scary, or boring. This need not be the case. The law provides an essential boundary for our practice as therapists. In many ways, the law is very protective of our professional practice, with regard to key aspects such as confidentiality.

It would be worth building up your knowledge and awareness of the law by looking at some of the further reading suggested at the end of this chapter. Beyond this, you could build up a resource file of relevant material, either in a ring binder or folder, or by downloading and saving relevant material to a storage device for future reference.

Information about the law comes in a number of different formats, such as:

- Acts of Parliament (see www.gov.uk) for the Children Act 1989, Data Protection Act 1998, etc.;
- Statutory Codes of Practice (see www.doh.gov.uk for the Code for the Mental Health Act 1983);
- statutory guidance (see, for example, *Working Together to Safeguard Children* (Department for Education, 2015));
- case law (e.g. see www.BAILI.org.uk for the Naomi Campbell case in 2003, discussed on p. 112);
- articles in the professional press, such as *Therapy Today*;
- information sheets on specific topics produced by BACP (www.bacp.co.uk).

Most of the law that impacts on counselling and psychotherapy will be drawn from civil rather than criminal law. Within the field of civil law, there are a number of key areas that directly influence therapeutic practice. These include the law relating to:

- confidentiality;
- data protection and recording;
- contracting with clients.

Understanding the professional, legal and ethical aspects of confidentiality

Lawyers tend to refer to 'the law of confidence', whereas therapists might use the term 'the law of confidentiality' instead, but these essentially refer to the same concept. Confidentiality is a key value for therapists. Right from the beginning of our training, the very first 'ground rules' posted up on the flipchart on almost any course will inevitably include some reference to 'confidentiality'. But what does this mean in practice?

Confidentiality refers to the keeping of the client's personal information – as derived from the counselling process – private, secure and contained. Maintaining client confidentiality is both an ethical obligation under the BACP *Ethical Framework for the Counselling Professions* (2016) and a legal requirement. The law requires us as counsellors to keep client information protected and safe, where confidentiality would be a 'reasonable expectation' on the client's part. Within counselling and psychotherapy, confidentiality can refer to three different levels of information relating to clients: their identity, the content of therapy and the fact of their attending therapy.

- **The identity of the client**: Therapists need to protect the client's identity from disclosure as far as is possible. This can be achieved by using a number of different means, for example:
  - using only a client's first name (or agreed name) when greeting them in a busy reception area;
  - separating the client's name, address and contact details from the content of therapy in records;
  - using only the client's first name (or a code, such as Mr S) for use in supervision;
  - clarifying safe and appropriate means for communicating with the client outside therapy, e.g. texting to an agreed phone number or emailing an agreed address to inform them of any changes to planned times or dates of sessions.

- **The content of therapy**: Therapists need to strike a balance between being able to record key details of therapeutic material for later use in supervision, their own training, if relevant, and for agency purposes, and by maintaining safeguards on the disclosure of such content by:

     o   keeping written and electronic records secure and safe from access by other therapists who do not need to access them, by using a locked filing cabinet or strong passwords in electronic recording systems;

     o   avoiding discussion of client material, or the client's reasons for coming to counselling, in front of other counsellors or administrative staff who do not need to know this;

     o   avoiding disclosure of client material to other third parties unless you have client consent to pass this information on, e.g. writing to a GP to make a referral for medical treatment of depression.

- **The fact of attending therapy**: This is really about a client's right to *privacy* rather than to confidentiality as such. Case law confirms that attending therapy is a privacy right, comparable to accessing medical treatment. An example is the Naomi Campbell case in 2003. The courts held that her attending a therapy session, with Narcotics Anonymous, was a strictly private matter (Jenkins, 2007a: 110–11). It should, therefore, not have been reported by the press. Attending therapy remains a *private* matter *unless* the client gives their consent to others being informed of this. Counsellors need to protect the client's privacy by:

     o   taking care in terms of the physical siting and location of counselling services (e.g. in workplaces and schools) in order to limit the chances of others being able to deduce that a client is attending therapy simply by being seen to go into a certain room or to a particular corridor;

     o   limiting disclosure of information about clients' attendance at therapy to third parties, such as administrators in schools, colleges and workplaces, who request information for non-therapeutic reasons (e.g. health and safety, funding of special support services, occupational health, etc.).

Confidentiality in counselling training

Confidentiality is a key value within counselling training. A value can be defined as an attitude or a willingness to act in a certain way. Values are defined in the BACP *Ethical Framework for the Counselling Professions* as 'a useful way of expressing general ethical commitments that underpin the purpose and goals of our actions' (2016: 2). In counselling training, we learn, or re-learn, how to securely hold private information disclosed to us by, or about, others, and how others hold the personal information that we may disclose about ourselves. This is not an easy process as, almost inevitably, some mistakes will be made. It may be tempting to assume that information disclosed in one setting, e.g. in a counselling skills practice session, can be relayed to others in another setting, such as a personal development group. Trainers and students need to set, agree and maintain clear boundaries about how personal information is to be held, or shared, within the learning community. This process can be aided by negotiating disclosure of personal material within the large group, and course community meetings and in personal development groups. Rules about sharing disclosures need to be agreed about skills work, e.g. in relation to reporting back to the large group, or using recordings of skills for course assessment purposes. Similarly, there should be clear expectations about confidentiality in supervision, on placement work with clients and, perhaps more surprisingly, in our own personal life, particularly in using social media (see the next exercise and the discussion that follows).

Exercise   Responding to potential challenges to confidentiality

Consider your responses to the following scenarios.

1. You discover that a student on your course is complaining on social media of being 'victimised' by tutors because she has failed her assignment.
2. You feel very reluctant to get consent from your only satisfactory medium-term client for use in your Case Study assignment because you think they will probably refuse. What are your options?
3. Your line manager on placement (a non-counsellor) insists that you hand over all your written records on clients for monitoring, as they 'belong to the agency'.
4. Your supervisor (external to your placement agency) asks that you use the client's full name and address (in the privacy of supervision sessions), so they can get a more accurate 'picture' of them in their mind in your supervision discussion.
5. Your client appears to be suicidal but insists that you keep this a 'secret' between the two of you, or else they will act on their self-destructive impulses to show you that they are serious about this.
6. Solicitors are demanding access to the client records at your NHS placement. No one at your placement has yet realised that you made a digital recording of your last session with the client to take to supervision.
7. The secondary school where you are on placement insist that all counselling of pupils must be done in a classroom with a glass panel in the door, next to a busy corridor for 'safeguarding reasons'.

(For discussion of responses, see below.)

Discussion: Responses to scenarios

1. This is a potential serious breach of the confidentiality agreement for the course and of the ethical requirement of respect for the tutor as a professional colleague. The student making allegations on social media should raise their concerns within the course itself, initially via informal means and then, if necessary, via the course complaints procedures.

2. Your options are very limited here. In ethical terms, you need to obtain the client's (preferably written) consent for you to write about their material in the form of a Case Study. If consent is refused, or is not possible, because the client is no longer contactable or has moved away or has died, then it may be possible to write your Case Study without client consent, but only by taking extreme care to avoid the client being identified, e.g. by changing key demographic features and therapeutic material.

3. This situation needs clarification from the placement agency. In legal terms, counselling records are under the control of the agency. However, it should be clarified in the placement contract what elements of the counselling recording are for training purposes, and may therefore be retained by you as a student, and which are to be managed by the agency. Agency policy may, in fact, require that counselling records be managed, or accessed, by certain authorised non-counsellors, such as administrative staff or data protection officers. However, the counselling material is still confidential to the agency and must be protected from any unauthorised disclosure. It may be possible, for example, for managers to 'audit' counselling records for client attendance or outcomes without needing to have access to the client's identity.

4. This seems to be an untenable position for the supervisor to adopt. Disclosing the client's identity and their therapeutic material in supervision in this way makes the client easily identifiable. You would need to obtain client consent for this arrangement or to consider changing your supervisor.

5. You would need to return to the original agreement for confidentiality, made at the contracting stage of therapy. The client may have given advance consent for you to contact a third party, such as their GP, in the event of their feeling suicidal. Even if this consent was missing, or had been withdrawn, then the risk of client suicide could justify a breach of confidentiality, on the legal grounds of it being 'in the public interest', in order to avoid the risk of harm or death to the client, or to others.

6. You would need to take advice from the placement manager on this issue. The courts are able to demand disclosure of any relevant material under a court order, so this court order would potentially include your digital recording of the client session, even though this

was made for course training purposes, rather than as an intended part of the agency record system. You could also obtain legal advice under the terms of your own professional indemnity insurance cover via the latter's legal helpline.

7. This requirement is in potential breach of the child's right to privacy, under existing case law (e.g. the Naomi Campbell case, discussed on p. 112). A balance needs to be struck here between the school's safe-guarding duties and the child's right to privacy. The limits to privacy in the counselling set-up may have the effect of severely limiting the value of the counselling if the child is uncomfortable and anxious about being seen in the counselling room. It may also undermine the reputation of the counselling service as a whole, in the eyes of other pupils and by staff as a properly *confidential* service.

Ethical and legal aspects of confidentiality

The preceding section has set out some of the main professional aspects of confidentiality that counsellors need to be aware of and to apply in their practice. There are also ethical principles which relate to the need for balancing trust and client safety within the framework of confidentiality (see Box 5.2).

Box 5.2   Ethical principles and confidentiality: Summary of key points

- [I]nforming clients beforehand of foreseeable limitations to confidentiality or privacy. (para 25b)
- [P]rotecting client safety (Ethics, para 2); and considering how to manage situations when protecting clients or others from serious harm. (para 9)
- [C]onsulting with clients when safeguarding them or others from serious harm. (para 10)
- [P]rotecting client information from unauthorised access or disclosure. (para 25a) (BACP, 2016)

The legal requirements for maintaining client confidentiality as far as possible are discussed below, in relation to the range of situations where counsellors may be obliged to pass on client information without consent, if necessary. These situations usually involve a perceived degree of risk to the client, or to others. In these situations, disclosure of client information to others may be obligatory, contractual or discretionary, depending on certain factors, such as the nature of the legal obligation on the counsellor and the format of agency policy for such disclosure.

Legal context of confidentiality

The law is generally very protective of confidentiality. The law will assume that personal material which is disclosed to another person should be respected as confidential. Confidentiality applies where this is seen as a reasonable expectation on the part of the person disclosing. It would apply in a doctor–patient relationship or in a therapist–client relationship.

Adults and young people aged 16 or 17 are entitled to confidentiality by law. Case law in England and Wales, in the form of the *Gillick* principle, has extended this right of confidentiality to those young people aged under 16 who are able to demonstrate 'sufficient understanding', i.e. having a broadly adult level of understanding and reasoning. Confidentiality may be spelled out in a contract between counsellor and client, either as a contract by a counsellor working in private practice or as part of the 'working agreement' made between counsellor and client (Jenkins, 2006). This might permit the therapist to contact the client's GP, for instance, in case of risk of self-harm to the client. Confidentiality might also be spelled out in terms of the counsellor's contract of employment, so that any breaches of confidentiality will be considered as a disciplinary issue.

Confidentiality is protected by statute, i.e. Acts of Parliament. Under section 60 of the Data Protection Act 1998, unauthorised disclosure of client information (or 'personal data') is potentially a criminal offence.

Under Article 8 of the Human Rights Act 1998, the client also has a right to respect for their privacy, such as the fact of their attending therapy, as in the Naomi Campbell case referred to on p. 112.

However, confidentiality is not an *absolute* right for the client. There are situations where the counsellor *must* break confidentiality or face legal consequences themselves. There are situations where the counsellor *may* be obliged to break client confidentiality under the terms of their employment contract, or by the terms of the agency's policy, which they have agreed to follow. Finally, there are also situations where the counsellor may have a degree of *choice*, at least in narrowly legal terms, on whether or not to break client confidentiality. Of course, the counsellor must also consider the ethical aspects of maintaining or breaking confidentiality as well as the law itself.

The counsellor needs to carefully consider the issues involved in breaking client confidentiality and discuss these with their supervisor, practice manager or an experienced practitioner, or a professional advice helpline.

These contrasting situations will be considered below in terms of whether disclosure of client information to a third party without consent is obligatory or discretionary.

Statutory obligations on counsellors to break confidentiality

The existing statutory obligations on counsellors to break client confidentiality are limited. They consist of the following:

Terrorism: s. 19, Terrorism Act 2000

Counsellors must report all information about terrorism. They must also not inform the client that they are doing so, in order to avoid 'tipping the client off' and enabling them to leave the UK, for example.

Drug money laundering: s. 52, Drug Trafficking Act 1994

This legal duty is widely misunderstood. This requires counsellors to report drug money laundering, i.e. a *financial* offence, again, *without* informing the client that they are doing so.

Potential contractual obligations on counsellors to break confidentiality

There are a number of situations where counsellors *may* be obliged by their contract of employment, or by their agency policy, to report certain types of potential harm to the client or to vulnerable third parties. These include:

Child abuse

- The duty lies on the local authority, under s. 47, Children Act 1989, to investigate situations where a child under the age of 18 is at risk of 'significant harm'.
- There may be a potential conflict here with the *Gillick* principle, i.e. a duty of confidentiality towards a young person under 16, where the young person discloses past abuse but does not want it to be reported to social services or to the police.
- It is important for counsellors to be aware of contact details for their local safeguarding team and to be up to date with relevant child abuse reporting guidelines, such as *Working Together to Safeguard Children* (Department for Education, 2015).

Suicide/self-harm

- There is no absolute requirement in law to report risk of suicide by an adult client, but this may be a limitation to client confidentiality set by an agency policy, particularly within NHS settings.

Risk to third party

- Counsellors have a right (but not necessarily a legal *duty*) to report 'serious crime', with the exception of terrorism and drug money laundering, as outlined above.

Discretionary breaches of confidentiality by counsellors

Although this may seem slightly contradictory to the previous paragraph, counsellors can choose to break client confidentiality in order to report risk to the client or to third parties, even if they are not legally required to do so. The legal defence for doing so would be that it was considered to be 'in the public interest', i.e. for the welfare of the client or a third party, or in order to avoid harm.

Reporting crime

- Under s. 115, Crime and Disorder Act 1998.
- In the public interest (see Box 5.3).

Applying data protection principles to counselling records

Counselling recording and the keeping of records on work with clients is governed primarily by the Data Protection Act 1998. Unfortunately, this Act needs careful translation in order to be properly understood and applied by counsellors. Even the guide of the Information Commissioner's Office admits that 'The legislation itself is complex and, in places, hard to understand' (Information Commissioner's Office, 2009: 2). The keeping of 'personal data' is intentionally defined in very wide terms in order to avoid creating any loopholes in the law. Personal data refer to information kept on an identifiable living individual. They include coded information, where a client's ID may be kept separately from their records of therapy. However, they exclude anonymised data, where the client's ID is not recorded. The

Act covers manual (or handwritten) recording as well as computerised and digital data processing, such as audio and video recordings of sessions. Information about the client's physical, mental or sexual health is termed 'sensitive personal data' and requires additional safeguards and care in handling. Clients will also have the right to access their own counselling records in many cases.

Counsellors, as data processors, need to obtain the client's consent for processing and recording data. This will often be obtained by the agency at assessment. Explicit consent is required for the processing of 'sensitive personal data', as referred to above. Explicit consent is to become the new standard for all data processing from 2017, under the updated requirements of the General Data Protection Regulation (Information Commissioner's Office, 2016).

The Data Protection Act 1998 restates the existing protections on client confidentiality outlined in the previous section. Personal data cannot be disclosed unless the client gives their consent; or unless disclosure is required by a statutory duty (e.g. in reporting terrorism, or by a court order); or unless disclosure is made 'in the public interest' (e.g. for the prevention of crime); or unless disclosure is authorised by statutory provisions concerning tax, justice or national security. It can be challenging to understand *all* aspects of data protection law (see Box 5.3).

Record-keeping and data protection in counselling practice

Record-keeping is a central part of counselling training and professional practice. There are a number of key aspects to consider. Record-keeping will be part of the training course requirements and will be required by the placement agency. There are professional and ethical considerations as well as legal considerations, such as those arising from data protection law. The principles of the Data Protection Act 1998 are fairly straightforward and easy to apply in practice (see Box 5.3).

Box 5.3   Resources for practice

Key phone numbers

Crimestoppers: 0800 555 111

Samaritans: 116 123

NSPCC: 0808 800 5000

(Continued)

(Continued)

Childline: 0800 1111

Terrorism hotline: 0800 789321

Data protection: Sources of help and advice

BACP Information Office: 0870 443 5252

Compliance Officer, Health, Information Commissioner: 01625 545745

www.ico.gov.uk

Professional Indemnity Insurance Helpline

Principles of the Data Protection Act 1998

Personal data are to be:

- processed fairly and lawfully;
- obtained only for one or more specified lawful purposes;
- adequate, relevant and not excessive for their purpose;
- accurate and kept up to date;
- kept no longer than is necessary;
- processed in accordance with the rights of data subjects;
- protected against unauthorised use or loss;
- not transferred outside the European Economic Area unless subject to similar levels of data protection.

Fortunately, it is possible to comply with data protection by using fairly simple means, such as by password-protecting electronic documents (see Box 5.4).

Box 5.4   Protecting client data

Advice from the Information Commissioner's Office on protecting client data

1. Tell people what you are doing with their data.
2. Make sure you are adequately trained.
3. Use strong passwords.
4. Encrypt all portable devices.
5. Only keep people's information as long as necessary.

(Adapted from the Information Commissioner's Office, 2012)

How to password-protect a Word document
(Word 2010 version)

1. Open document in Word.
2. Go to **File**, click on **Information**, then click on **Protect document**.
3. Select **Encrypt with Password**.
4. Enter chosen password.
5. Re-enter chosen password when prompted, then click **OK**.
6. Save document in usual way.
7. If sending the password-protected document as an attachment, send password via a separate email to correct address of recipient and request acknowledgement of its safe receipt.

Examples of action taken against counsellors, or counselling agencies, by the Information Commissioner's Office (ICO) on breaches of data protection law are, fortunately, fairly rare. The following case study, however, illustrates some of the problems which can arise in providing web-based access to counselling services, in this case in relation to pregnancy advice (see the next exercise and the discussion that follows).

Exercise   Case study: Exploring ICO action against a pregnancy advice and counselling agency

A pregnancy advice agency provided a website for callers, enabling them to request a call-back for counselling and pregnancy-related advice by submitting their contact details online. However, the call-back details of 9,900 callers were retained unnecessarily for more than five years by the website. These data were then seriously compromised by a malicious hacker who threatened to publish callers' personal details online. 'Some of the call back details were from individuals whose ethnicity and social background could have led to physical harm or even death if the information had been disclosed by the hacker' (Information Commissioner's Office, 2014). The hacker was arrested by the police the day after the illegal breach of the website, thus preventing the threatened online disclosure of the callers' personal data.

Task: Compare the above scenario with the key principles of the Data Protection Act 1998 and identify any principles which, in your opinion, may have been breached by this website.

(For discussion, see below.)

Discussion of case study: ICO action against a pregnancy advice and counselling agency

The two data protection principles breached in this example are that personal data are to be:

- kept no longer than is necessary;
- protected against unauthorised use or loss.

The ICO found that the agency had retained the call-back data for five years longer than was necessary for its purposes. It had also failed to take appropriate security measures to protect the data of callers, in the context of 'the extremely personal and sensitive services provided'. Unauthorised disclosure of the data by malicious hacking had the potential to cause substantial distress and substantial damage, such as physical harm or even death. The ICO imposed a fine of £200,000 on the agency, via its statutory powers, under section 55 of the Data Protection Act 1998.

Recording of client work on placement

The basic principles of recording client work are that counselling records should be factual, timely, accurate and secure. There are a number of different purposes for professional recording for counsellors. These can include producing a record of client work for the agency and as evidence of your developing skills in reflective practice for training course purposes. Your course requirements may include the keeping of a practice portfolio, comprising a record of your client work, i.e. the total number of client hours, with dates of attendance or non-attendance, an overall summary of client hours, and similar information on your supervision sessions, both individual and group.

Box 5.5 provides a suggested format for keeping your records. It can be adapted according to the needs of your training course and the placement agency.

Box 5.5   Template for record-keeping on placement

(This can be roughly a side of A4. Not every prompt will be used in every recording. Try to vary the style and content of your recording in order to cover previously unaddressed themes or areas.)

1 Client details (anonymised)/date of session: (NB: To be retained as part of the agency record.)

Client code/identifier:_____

Date, session number (e.g. Client A, Session 3); duration of sessions (if shortened); note of cancellations, DNAs, emails, texts, letters: _____

_____

2 Content of session: (NB: To be retained as part of the agency record.)

(Use self-prompts or note down key words soon after the end of the session.)

Reason for/source of referral: _____

Brief client demographic details: _____

Account of session:

- beginning/contact/contracting
- issues raised by client
- observed non-verbal communication
- responses by yourself
- risk issues (raised by client or perceived by you)
- ending of session/future work/referral

Brief summary of key issues: _____

_____

3 Process issues from session: (NB: *Not* to be retained as part of the agency record, but to be added to your practice portfolio.)

Your own reflection on session:

- relationship issues (e.g. dependency, conflict)
- own personal issues, skills used (or attempted)
- client's process, stage of therapeutic development
- relevant theory (e.g. perceived conditions of worth, introjects, defences)

4 Issues for supervision/action/agency: (NB: *Not* to be retained as part of the agency record, but to be added to your practice portfolio.)

Issues for supervision:

- any emotional support you may need
- personal/professional learning points
- professional guidance (e.g. risk issues)
- own learning or CPD needs (e.g. relevant articles or books, BACP guidance)
- issues to take back to placement agency or course (e.g. training needs, policies)

Using contracts with clients

The third aspect of the law relating to counselling practice is that of contracting with clients. Agreeing a contract to work together defines counselling as being distinct from using counselling skills in other roles, such as a teacher, nurse or social worker. Within counselling and psychotherapy there is an explicit contract, or 'working agreement', to provide therapy, within the agreed roles of counsellor and client. Negotiating the contract underlines the voluntary nature of the agreement and supports the autonomy of the client in choosing to work with the therapist, or not, as the case may be. Culley and Bond (2011) suggest that there are two separate elements to this contract. First, an 'agreement for the type of help you are offering', and secondly, clarifying 'the focus, content and direction of your work together' (2011: 74).

Contracting is seen as a hallmark of good practice in the BACP *Ethical Framework for the Counselling Professions* (2016), for sound ethical, professional and therapeutic reasons (see Box 5.6).

Box 5.6   Ethical principles and contracting

32. We will give careful consideration to how we reach agreement with clients and contract with them about the terms on which our services will be provided. Attention will be given to:

a. reaching an agreement or contract respecting the client's expressed needs and choices

b. communicating terms and conditions understandable to the client and appropriate to the context

c. stating foreseeable limitations to the client's confidentiality or privacy

d. providing the client with a record, or access to a record, of what has been agreed

e. keeping a record of what has been agreed and of any changes or clarifications when they occur. (BACP, 2016: 8)

Some aspects of the contract may be carried out by the agency, rather than by the counsellor face to face. The policies regarding confidentiality, record-keeping, etc. can be conveyed to clients via a leaflet or communicated via a website. The counsellor's role may be to confirm these aspects rather than have to introduce them for the first time. Not every contract will necessarily carry the status of a legally binding agreement or contract, particularly where the client does not pay a fee to the counsellor or agency for the counselling provided, as in the NHS, for example (Jenkins, 2007a: 27–31).

Making a contract or a working agreement with the client can also meet the requirement of obtaining the client's *informed consent* to the therapy. Informed consent means that the client is able to *understand* the information about the therapy on offer, *believes* it, can *retain* it and is able to make a *reasoned choice* between alternatives. In turn, being able to exercise informed consent, e.g. about the type of therapy on offer – such as person-centred counselling, as compared with cognitive behavioural therapy – first requires that the client has *capacity*. 'Capacity' is a legal term that refers to the ability of the client to *understand* the information being put to him or her by the counsellor. This ability might be limited or impaired by a number of factors, such as the effect of alcohol, drugs, learning disability or age, in the case of a younger, pre-adolescent client, who might be unable to demonstrate 'sufficient understanding' to satisfy the criteria for *Gillick* (see Jenkins, 2015c). Assuming that the client does have capacity and is able give their informed consent to therapy, then the counselling can proceed, perhaps on the basis of the model contract outlined for client work. See Box 5.7 for the elements to be considered in a model contract for therapy.

Box 5.7   Elements of a model contract, or working agreement, for therapy

- Cost of sessions (if applicable)
- Duration and frequency of sessions
- Arrangements and charges (if relevant) for cancellation or holiday periods
- Main characteristics of therapy to be provided
- Total number of sessions and arrangements for review
- Limits to confidentiality
- Arrangements for termination of therapy
- Cover or substitution of therapist in case of illness
- Complaints procedure
- Date and signature of both parties
- Record-keeping and data protection compliance

(Adapted from Jenkins, 2007a: 30)

The case study exercise below illustrates some of the features of good practice in applying the law to everyday counselling practice.

Exercise   Exploring law and counselling practice

Compare and contrast this second version of Nasreen's practice with the first version. What does she do differently? What might be the ethical, professional and legal reasons for her practice in this second version of the session?

Case study: Law and counselling practice (Version 2)

Nasreen is a qualified counsellor working for a third sector agency which provides therapy for a broad range of clients. In the first session with a new client, she explains and clarifies the nature of confidentiality to the client, particularly in relation to the agency's policy of contacting a client's GP in the case of risk to self or others, with the client's consent if possible, but *without* their consent in an emergency. Her client is an adult, Roger, who discloses a history of mental health problems to her, including having thoughts of serious self-harm. Nasreen checks with Roger that he understands what counselling will involve from him and what it can offer, and that he is willing to try it, as a contracted, therapeutic relationship. She briefly outlines her preferred integrative style as a counsellor, and suggests that they review their work during each session and at the end of the initial planned six sessions provided by the agency. She explains that she will keep brief written records for the agency, which are retained for three years, and that Roger can apply for access to these records under data protection law. Both Nasreen and Roger sign and date the pro-forma working agreement provided by the agency and each keeps a copy for future reference.

Summary

This chapter has outlined the importance for counsellors of developing an informed understanding of the law as a key element of professional practice for counsellors and psychotherapists. The areas of civil law that have most relevance for counsellors include confidentiality, record-keeping and data protection, and contracting. Confidentiality is not an absolute obligation under the law, but certain requirements are necesssary to break confidentiality, such as terrorism, drug-money laundering and other exceptions, which may be set out in an agency's policy. Record-keeping is governed by complex data protection law, requiring that personal data are kept securely, for a specific purpose, and are kept no longer than is necessary. Contracting is one of the main ways in which counsellors can convey the boundaries and purpose of therapy to clients and ensure their active participation in counselling on the basis of their informed consent.

Resources

DVD training resources

There is a 40-minute outline of the law relating to counselling and psychotherapy in the UK on the DVD *Therapists and Professional Negligence: A Duty of Care?*, which is obtainable from: www.counsellingdvds.uk

There is a five-minute clip from this DVD available at: https//sites.google.com/site/counsellingdvds/therapists-professional-negligence-a-duty-care

Web resources

There is a video presentation, *Records as Evidence*, produced for the Psychologists Protection Society, on counselling confidentiality and record-keeping, which is available at: http://youtu.be/x7C_aPo8a1w

Research

There is limited peer-reviewed research into the law and counselling and psycho-therapy published in the UK. Some examples include:

Jenkins, P. (2003) 'Therapist responses to requests for disclosure of therapeutic records: An introductory study', *Counselling and Psychotherapy Research*, 3(3), 232–238. DOI: http://dx.doi.org/10.1080/14733140312331384402

This is an early exploration of this issue, based on a questionnaire survey pub-lished in the BACP journal (n: 77), combined with a follow-up sample (n: 38). The research preceded major changes in professional indemnity insurance cover for counsellors with regard to requests for disclosure of records.

Jenkins, P. and Potter, S. (2007) 'No more "personal notes"? Data protection policy and practice in Higher Education counselling services in the UK', *British Journal of Guidance and Counselling*, 35(1), 131–146. DOI: http://dx.doi.org/10.1080/03069880701219849

Electronic questionnaire survey (n: 50) of university and college counselling ser-vices, identifying a key shift in record-keeping towards more factual and fewer process-types of record-keeping.

Jenkins, P. and Palmer, J. (2012) '"At risk of harm?" An exploratory study of school counsellors in the UK, their perceptions of confidentiality, information shar-ing and risk management', *British Journal of Guidance and Counselling*, 40(5), 545–559. DOI: http://dx.doi.org/10.1080/03069885.2012.718732

Questionnaire survey of school-based counsellors (n: 13), combined with follow-up interviews (n: 6), exploring perceptions of risk and of their assumed legal duty to report instances of child abuse.

Further reading

The following provide brief, and hopefully user-friendly, outlines of the law in relation to counselling and psychotherapy:

Jenkins, P. (2015) 'Client confidentiality and data protection', in R. Tribe and J. Morrissey (eds), *Handbook of Professional Practice for Psychologists, Counsellors and Psychotherapists*. Second edition. London: Routledge. pp. 47–57.
Jenkins, P. (2015) 'The legal context of therapy', in R. Tribe and J. Morrissey (eds), *Handbook of Professional Practice for Psychologists, Counsellors and Psychotherapists*. Second edition. London: Routledge. pp. 58–69.
Jenkins, P. (2017) 'Therapy and the law', in C. Feltham, T. Hanley and L. Winter (eds), *The Sage Handbook of Counselling and Psychotherapy*. Fourth edition. London: Sage (forthcoming).

The law relating to work with children and young people is more complex than that relating to adults. For a brief summary and discussion, see:

Jenkins, P. (2015) 'Law and policy', in S. Pattison, M. Robson and A. Beynon (eds), *The Handbook of Counselling Children and Young People*. London: Sage/BACP. pp. 259–276.

For more detailed discussion of the law in relation to therapy, see also:

Bond, T. and Mitchels, B. (2015) *Confidentiality and Record Keeping in Counselling and Psychotherapy*. Second edition. London: Sage/BACP.
Jenkins, P. (2007) *Counselling, Psychotherapy and the Law*. Second edition. London: Sage.
Mitchels, B. and Bond, T. (2010) *Essential Law for Counsellors and Psychotherapists*. London: Sage/BACP.

Reference section for supervisors

Supervision:

(60) Supervisors will conscientiously consider the application of the law concerning supervision to their role and responsibilities. (BACP, 2016: 12)

This chapter contains general information which will be relevant to supervisors, both as the first point of contact with supervisees (who may be seeking clarification about the role of the law in counselling), and with regard to their own supervision practice. The more specific legal responsibilities of *supervisors* are outlined in:

Jenkins, P. (2001) 'Supervisory responsibility and the law', in S. Wheeler and D. King (eds), *Supervising Counsellors: Issues of Responsibility*. London: Sage. pp. 22–40.

Jenkins, P. (2007) 'Supervision in the dock? Supervision and the law', in K. Tudor and M. Worrall (eds), *Freedom to Practise: Volume 2: Developing Person-Centred Approaches to Supervision*. Ross-on-Wye: PCCS Books. pp. 176–194.

Jenkins, P. (2016) 'Chestnuts roasting on an open fire: Supervisor liability revisited', *Contemporary Psychotherapy,* 8(2), www.contemporarypsychotherapy.org/volume-8-no-2-winter-2016/chestnuts-roasting-on-an-open-fire-supervisor-liability-revisited/

There is a video resource by Peter Jenkins, *Supervisors: A New Duty of Care?*, which is available at: https://www.onlinevents.co.uk/category/practitioners/peter-jenkins/

6

Working ethically as a counsellor or psychotherapist

Introduction

This chapter looks at the role and definition of ethics in counselling and psycho-therapy, in promoting the welfare of clients and maintaining professional stand-ards on the part of therapists. It considers the shift from codes of ethics to more flexible ethical frameworks. The main focus of the chapter concerns:

*   applying ethics to therapeutic practice;
*   exploring ethical principles and different approaches to ethics;
*   identifying and responding to ethical issues.

Learning context

The BACP *Core Curriculum* (2009) takes a broad-ranging view of ethics and its relation-ship to therapeutic practice, while the BACP *Ethical Framework for the Counselling Professions* (2016) provides detailed coverage of ethics, briefly summarised here and then explored in more detail. This chapter explores the background to current debates on counselling ethics, in order to place the *Ethical Framework* in a wider context.

BACP *Core Curriculum* (2009)

9.1.A: The professional role and responsibility of the therapist:

7. Understand the values underpinning the profession, as exemplified in the *Ethical Framework for the Counselling Professions*.

9.1.B: Understanding the client:

10. Identify ethical and legal responsibilities with regard to potential risk, including critical decision making with respect to autonomy of the client and potential harm to self or others. (2009: 17)

9.1.C: The therapeutic process:

6. Demonstrate awareness of theoretical and research literature regarding the provision of a secure frame for therapy, including physical environment, contractual arrangements and ethics. ...

9.1.D: The social, professional and organisational context for therapy:

The practitioner will have relevant knowledge to inform his or her ability to:

2. Show a critical awareness of the history of ideas, the cultural context and social and political theories that inform and influence the practice of counselling and psychotherapy.

3. Identify and critique the philosophical assumptions underpinning the practice of counselling and psychotherapy.

8. Demonstrate a clear commitment to best practice and work within an ethical framework for professional practice. (2009: 18)

BACP *Ethical Framework for the Counselling Professions* (2016)

Ethics:

Our ethics are based on values, principles and personal moral qualities that inform and underpin the interpretation and application of our commitment to clients and good practice. (2016: 2)

Applying ethics to therapeutic practice

Counselling and psychotherapy are intrinsically linked to ethical behaviour on the part of the therapist. For counselling to be able to take place, the client needs to feel safe enough to be able to disclose and share deeply personal and often shaming material, which may never have been shared before with another person. Almost by definition, the client is vulnerable, simply by virtue of entering into this relationship with the therapist. The client may be distressed, and concerned about aspects of their current or past behaviour, or through being unsure of how to live their life. The client's vulnerability points to the corresponding need for the therapist to act in ways that do not take advantage of this incongruence or vulnerability. The counsellor needs to act to support and empower the client in coping with their situation, and to facilitate them in finding meaningful ways of moving on from their distress.

Any discussion about ethics immediately runs into a number of difficulties. It is easy to see ethics as a rather dry subject. It may seem to have an earnest and rather worthy feel to it. It can also seem somehow divorced from real life and from the actual practice of counselling. This view is understandable but really misses the key importance of ethics for therapists. Ethics help us to make difficult choices together with, or on behalf of, our clients. Ethics is about working with real-life dilemmas, rather than engaging in abstract and rather academic discussion about philosophical ideas, important though the latter may be.

So, what do we mean by ethics? Ethics can be defined as 'a generic term for various ways of understanding and examining the moral life' (Beauchamp and Childress, 2008: 1). Ethics can help shed light on what is seen to be right or wrong, correct or inappropriate, as a course of action. These ethical decisions might be based on a range of influences. As a therapist, your sense of what is the right course of action may be strongly influenced by a number of factors (see exercise on exploring the origins and sources of your own personal sense of ethics). These factors could include your:

- personal values;
- family upbringing;
- religious faith or worldview;
- understanding of the law;
- agency policy (if relevant);
- philosophical stance;
- prior professional role or training (as a nurse, social worker, etc.);
- professional code of conduct;
- experience of working with dilemmas, or difficult moral issues, in your own personal or professional life.

Exercise   Exploring the origins and sources of your own personal sense of ethics

Look at the list of possible influences on your own ethical stance. Take a moment to reflect on the sources of your own ethics as a therapist. What are the main influences on you regarding your own ethical stance? What aspects have had the least influence and why?

Codes of ethics

One of the main ways in which therapists have sought to guide each other in working with clients has been through the development of codes of ethics. A code of ethics is seen as a hallmark of established professions, such as law and medicine. Professional associations, such as BACP and UKCP, have developed and refined their codes of ethics over time, setting out the expected standards of behaviour for therapists to follow. A code of ethics can also become an important reference point for clients. They may be unfamiliar with therapy and may be unsure of what to expect from their therapist. As a client, is it acceptable to have to pay for missed sessions? What if the therapist seems very keen to offer a hug at the end of every session? What if client and therapist disagree about the need to end the therapy?

A code of ethics can assist clients and therapists in setting out the minimum expectations for the counselling relationship. These may then be further clarified in a contract or working agreement for therapy, and by policy documents provided by the counselling agency, if available, about confidentiality, record-keeping, etc.

Nonetheless, there are a number of limitations to codes of ethics. Any code, however detailed and comprehensive, is unlikely to be able to anticipate every possible circumstance that might arise within therapy. Given that therapy is based on a relationship and that each client has unique characteristics, it may be important to build in a degree of flexibility. This will allow for exceptional circumstances and for a degree of professional autonomy and choice on the part of therapist and client. As counsellors have expanded into a broad range of work situations, such as the workplace, schools, prisons, etc., it has emerged that codes which make sense in one situation may have much less relevance in another. For example, a rule about therapists avoiding dual relationships with clients may be easy to observe within larger agencies, or working in urban environments. But it may be much harder to maintain where a counsellor is working in an organisation in which he/she is also expected to provide training to employees in stress management or in listening skills. These training groups may inevitably contain former clients, from time to time.

Ethical frameworks

There has been a shift within BACP since 2000, away from prescriptive codes of ethics for therapists and towards adopting the *Ethical Framework for the Counselling Professions* (2016), which provides a basic set of rules and guidance. This *Framework* can be adapted in a more flexible way to accommodate different counsellor roles and work situations. However, this can come at the cost of changing counsellors' perceptions about the nature of their professional accountability. While there is some security in following very specific rules, there may be more uncertainty, and even a degree of anxiety, about working within a more flexible framework. Here, therapists may have to choose between competing ethical values and principles and to be accountable for their decisions via a professional complaints procedure.

The adoption by BACP of the *Ethical Framework for Good Practice in Counselling and Psychotherapy* in 2002 marked a decisive change in the way that the discussion of ethics was to be carried on by therapists within the organisation. This stance also had implications for its relationship to other organisations, such as UKCP and BPS, and also in relation to clients and to the wider general public. Earlier versions of the BAC *Code* contained both prescriptive requirements ('counsellors *must* do this') and more general advisory statements ('counsellors *should* do this'). For example, the BAC *Code of Ethics* (1992) included statements such as:

2.2.6 Counsellors must not exploit their clients...

This would be an example of a prescriptive statement or rule. In contrast, the majority of statements within the *Code* included the word *'should'*, suggesting an advisory stance, which was less absolute in tone, such as:

2.2.18 Counsellors should not counsel when their functioning is impaired...

The BACP *Ethical Framework for the Counselling Professions* (2016) represented a move away from a set of general statements of minimal professional behaviour towards a more flexible, problem-solving model. This shift allowed a greater diversity of ethical stances. In terms of its structure, the *Framework* includes both a commitment to put clients first and a statement of ethics, including values, ethical principles and the personal moral qualities required to put these into practice. The commitment to good practice runs as a thread through the *Ethical Framework for the Counselling Professions*, so that good practice is seen as being inseparable from ethics. This commitment includes putting the client first, working to professional standards, demonstrating respect and building appropriate relationships by showing integrity, accountability and candour in practice with clients. Good practice also includes consideration of factors such as research, training, education, self-care and responding to ethical dilemmas.

Values

Key aspects of good practice are looked at throughout this book. Focusing for the moment on ethics, the *Ethical Framework for the Counselling*

Professions (BACP, 2016) explores the relevance of values, principles and personal moral qualities. A value can be defined as an orientation or a predisposition to act in a certain way. For example, a person might actively prefer to keep the secrets of others rather than being inclined to share them freely with others. The statement of values includes the following:

- Respecting human rights and dignity
- Alleviating symptoms of personal distress and suffering
- Enhancing people's wellbeing and capabilities
- Increasing personal resilience and effectiveness
- Facilitating a sense of self that is meaningful to the person(s) concerned within their personal and cultural context
- Appreciating the variety of human experience and culture
- Protecting the safety of clients
- Ensuring the integrity of practitioner–client relationships
- Enhancing the quality of professional knowledge and its application
- Striving for the fair and adequate provision of services. (BACP, 2016: 2)

The term 'value', therefore, suggests a tendency to act or behave in a certain way rather than simply holding a belief about what is ethically desirable.

Exercise   Exploring your own values and ethics

Take one example of a value from the *Ethical Framework for the Counselling Professions* (BACP, 2016) that has particular resonance or meaning for you. How can you illustrate your active commitment to this value with regard to counselling practice? Can you improve on what you have achieved in this respect so far?

Ethical principles are perhaps the staple of any code of ethics and practice or ethical framework. The standard statement of ethical principles derives from a biomedical background and is applied, by extension, to a wide range of caring professions (Beauchamp and Childress, 2008). Over time justice and, perhaps more controversially, self-respect (what can be termed self-care) have been added to the original core biomedical ethical principles of trustworthiness, autonomy, beneficence (welfare) and non-maleficence (avoidance of harm). These principles are briefly defined below:

Trustworthiness: honouring the trust placed in the practitioner.

Autonomy: respect for the client's right to be self-governing.

Beneficence: a commitment to promoting the client's wellbeing.

Non-maleficence: a commitment to avoiding harm to the client.

Justice: the fair and impartial treatment of all clients and the provision of adequate services.

Self-respect: fostering the practitioner's self-knowledge, integrity and care for self. (BACP, 2016: 2)

Exercise   Identifying ethical issues in counselling practice

Read through the trigger scenarios below. Which ethical principles seem to be most directly challenged here?

Ethical issues: Trigger scenarios

1. A friend, who is currently in therapy, confides to you that they have begun to meet their therapist in between counselling sessions because they seem to be 'getting on so well'. They clearly have a lot in common, as both are going through a divorce. Your friend says this social arrangement to meet outside and in addition to the therapy makes them feel 'very special'.
2. A client is convinced that he can recognise himself in one of the brief case studies in a professional journal article on 'insecure attachment' that has recently been published by his therapist.
3. You counsel staff within a large organisation, largely on issues relating to workplace stress. One of your clients discloses that their increasingly desperate financial situation has led them to make (very occasional) inflated claims for their travelling expenses.
4. A counselling colleague seems to be under increasing stress following a recent close bereavement. They have not found a replacement supervisor since their last supervisor retired three months ago.
5. An experienced colleague has set up in private practice as a 'trauma therapist', but to your knowledge has no formal qualification or specific experience in this field. She explains her decision as being a response to increasing client requests for her to offer more trauma-focused counselling in her work.
6. Your line manager offers to act as your supervisor while you are training as a counsellor, to save you the expense of paying privately for supervision elsewhere.

(For discussion of these scenarios, see below.)

Discussion of trigger scenarios and ethical decision-making

Some potential key ethical principles are suggested for each scenario, but others may be equally or more significant in your view.

1. **Non-maleficence/avoidance of harm**: This issue raises issues about a potential breach of therapeutic boundaries by the counsellor, in appearing to develop a social (or friendship) relationship with a current client. If unresolved, this may require a formal report or complaint on your part to the counsellor's professional association.

2. **Trustworthiness/Autonomy**: This situation raises issues about a potential breach of trust by the therapist. The client needs to give consent for the publication of written case studies. However, the client may be mistaken about this case study involving him. Even so, the therapeutic alliance may have been strongly challenged here and the level of trust may have been damaged as a result. One initial response would be for the therapist and client to discuss the anxieties aroused by this situation in order to try to find some resolution of this issue.

3. **Justice**: From an ethical point of view, as a counsellor, you may need to consider the interests and welfare of your employing organisation in this situation, as well as those of your client. There may be set agency rules to follow regarding reporting financial malpractice, of which both counsellor and client should have been made aware at the initial contracting stage. There may also be a risk of treating one client more favourably than another if no action is taken to report the potential malpractice in this case but the rule is then enforced for other clients.

4. **Self-respect**: This scenario raises ethical concerns about your colleague's professional judgement, their fitness to practise and their compliance with professional requirements for supervision. It may require you to offer a (hopefully supportive) challenge to your colleague, but if your colleague does not respond, you may also need to consider more formal action by informing their professional association.

5. **Beneficence**: This issue raises issues about professional competence. You need to consider whether your colleague has the necessary qualifications and experience to provide a specialist trauma service to clients, together with the potential for them to cause harm to future clients, and whether you have a professional obligation to raise your concerns with the therapist in question and/or with your professional association.

6. **Self-respect**: This dilemma raises issues about developing a potentially unhelpful dual relationship, where your line manager is also your supervisor for the duration of your training. It may be helpful here to refer to the external policies of your professional association or the training agency, which stress the value of independent supervision. This is distinct from line management. Supervision is to aid the process of you reflecting on and learning from your counselling practice.

Personal moral qualities

It is important for counsellors to possess personal moral qualities if they are to be able to implement the requirements of the *Ethical Framework for the Counselling Professions* (BACP, 2016) in practice. It is not simply a case of this representing a 'counsel of perfection' or of just simply 'following the rules'. It is more about taking stock of how you make difficult decisions in your life, how you behave towards others and how you recognise where you could have behaved differently. These personal moral qualities are defined as:

- Care
- Diligence
- Courage
- Empathy
- Identity
- Humility
- Integrity
- Resilience
- Respect. (BACP, 2016: 3)

Exercise   Identifying personally relevant moral qualities

Looking at the list of personal moral qualities above, select two and show, with examples, how you have put these into practice in your own personal or professional life. Now pick two that you have struggled to find examples of in your practice, or have even failed to fully grasp their relevance to your counselling work. Work on these more problematic qualities and try to find ways in which you can integrate them more fully into your understanding and appreciation of ethics and counselling practice.

Exploring ethical principles and different approaches to ethics

Codes of ethics are not fixed but constantly evolve, over time, in response to changing contexts of practice, contemporary issues such as scandals in health and social care, and moves towards statutory regulation. Codes also vary according to their orientation towards various schools of philosophy. The inclusion of ethical principles, for example, can be linked to an approach to ethics that is related to the importance of following *ethical rules*. This philosophical approach is termed *deontological*

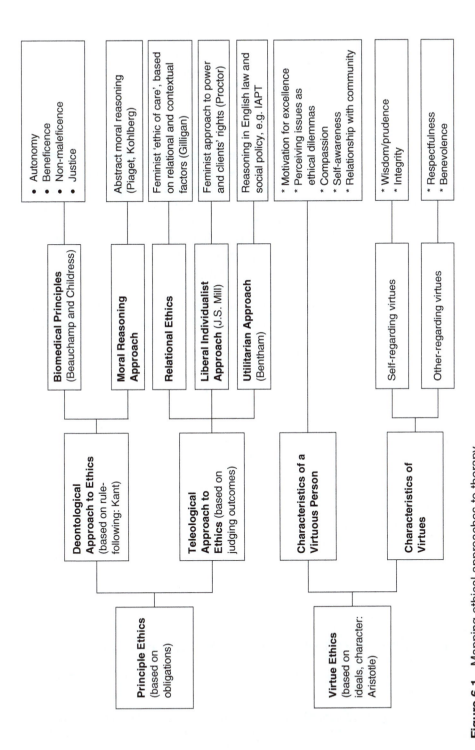

Figure 6.1 Mapping ethical approaches to therapy

Source: adapted from Meara et al., 1996; Jenkins, 2007a: 13

(i.e. rule-following) and is associated with the work of Kant (see Box 6.1). One hypothetical example of such a rule might take the form of '*All client safeguarding concerns must* be reported, without exception'.

An alternative approach is based on evaluating ethical decision-making in terms of the *outcome* achieved. This is a more pragmatic approach, described as *teleological*. This might take the form of a statement that 'Risk-taking in counselling practice can be justified *if* it achieves a positive change desired by the client'. This philosophical approach is consistent with some aspects of utilitarianism, i.e. achieving 'the greatest good for the greatest number', developed by Bentham. This approach to ethics has had a major, continuing influence upon the use of moral reasoning within the English legal system. Arguably, it has had a hand in the development of government indices of national wellbeing and in promoting wider public access to counselling via the Improving Access to Psychological Therapies (IAPT) programme (see Figure 6.1).

The 'Virtues' approach to ethics is closely linked to the concept of personal moral qualities, which is akin to the notion that ethics is something that is more about *being*, than *doing*. The concept of Virtues is associated with classical philosophy developed by Aristotle and has undergone something of a revival recently within modern ethical discourse.

The feminist movement has developed a forceful critique of the role of power and the abuse of power within the therapeutic process. It has challenged the dominance of male theorists within the profession, and argued for a more relational approach to ethics, rather than one which is largely derived from abstract moral principles. Within this model, therapy is closely linked to a process of empowerment (e.g. for the victims and survivors of sexual abuse), both within and outside therapy. This latter approach is also linked to the more recent development of *relational* ethics, where ethical issues are considered in the context of the intense therapeutic alliance that may develop between therapist and client, and the narrative that unfolds within this process, encompassing complex ethical choices and decisions. Identifying the ethical principles which underpin particular responses to difficult challenges in therapy can be useful in clarifying our own ethical stance and style. The following exercise and discussion explores ethical principles in practice.

Exercise   Exploring ethical principles in practice

Try to identify the ethical concepts and principles expressed in the following statements.

1. Breaking client confidentiality depends on a number of factors, such as whether it keeps the client safe from harm, the impact it has on

the therapeutic alliance, and the counsellor's judgement of the level of risk.

2. Therapists should consistently seek to model high standards of ethical behaviour, both in their professional work and in their personal life.

3. Counsellors must always put safeguarding issues first, by reporting suspected abuse to the appropriate authorities without delay, in order to protect vulnerable clients from harm or abuse.

4. Therapists who do not appropriately challenge their clients' gender-based beliefs are guilty of colluding with sexism and oppression in society.

5. A key part of the counsellor's role is to develop the client's awareness of their potential for informed existential choice, i.e. a more fulfilling way of living and being in the world.

6. The client's (and therapist's) actions within counselling can only be judged in the context of their own past or current situation. For example, a client who is seriously self-harming may need a therapist who operates within more flexible boundaries, by providing their home mobile number to such clients, for use in emergencies.

(For discussion of these principles, see below.)

Discussion: Exploring ethical principles in practice

1. This statement is consistent with an outcomes (or *teleological*) approach to working with ethical dilemmas. In terms of philosophy, an outcomes approach can be linked to the work of Bentham ('the greatest good of the greatest number') and Mill (protecting the rights of the individual, except where this infringes the rights of others). According to this approach, there are no absolute rules to apply in considering whether or not to break client confidentiality. The test of whether this is a sound decision will emerge from what actually happens as a result, e.g. a client being kept safe from further abuse, or a client building much greater trust in the counselling process by maintaining confidentiality.

2. The emphasis on the counsellor's personal qualities (integrity, trustworthiness, etc.) in this statement suggests a model based on the importance of personal virtues and character, which is linked to the Virtue ethics of Aristotle.

3. This statement suggests a rule-following (or *deontological*) approach to resolving ethical dilemmas. As a model, it places a high value on the therapist following certain key rules or requirements, which are based on ethical principles, such as promoting welfare, avoiding harm, etc. The model is linked to the philosophical work of Kant.

4. This statement is consistent with feminist approaches, which are sensitised to issues of power, abuse and oppression, and which may be replicated within therapy. This model is particularly aware of

the potential for the power relationships within therapy to replay old, and potentially abusive, patterns of behaviour.

5. At the level of content, this statement seems to prioritise the role of therapy as facilitating the client's potential for exercising autonomy. It is consistent with a rule-following approach (see discussion in point 3 above). However, at the level of therapeutic process, the client may experience the counsellor as being quite paternalistic.

6. This statement might fit best with an approach based on relational ethics, where the responses to therapeutic dilemmas are worked out through negotiation rather than by referring largely to pre-scribed codes of behaviour or agency rules. Ethical choices are driven by the perceived needs of the precise context and situation. Ethics, as applied to practice, may therefore need to be highly per-sonalised and tailored to a client's specific situation, rather than be easily generalised to all clients or to all similar dilemmas.

Key figures and movements in the development of professional ethics

The *Ethical Framework for the Counselling Professions* (BACP, 2016) com-bines elements of the different approaches to ethics, such as rule-following, outcomes, and Virtues approaches. This contrasts with previous BACP *Codes*, which appeared to prioritise autonomy as a key ethical principle (BAC, 1992: 2.2.3). The *Ethical Framework for the Counselling Professions* has moved away from this stance, in part because it no longer follows a primarily rule-following approach, and also because autonomy, as a ther-apeutic goal, may overly reflect Western social and political values. Arguably, it is less relevant for those clients and therapists working in more multi-cultural contexts, where community, cultural and religious factors may figure more strongly in social life. In order to develop an understanding of these competing narratives in ethical discourse and language, it can be helpful to know the origins of particular ethical ideas (see Box 6.1).

Box 6.1   Key figures and movements in the development of professional ethics

Aristotle: Aristotle (384–322 BC) focused on the need for individuals to become ethical beings by actively practising ethics and by demonstrating virtue in their personal and civic relationships with others.

Bentham: Jeremy Bentham (1748–1832) developed utilitarian philosophy, which is often summarised in terms of trying to achieve 'the greatest good of the greatest number'. This model has been hugely influential in terms of UK social policy and the legal system.

Feminism: Contemporary researchers such as Carol Gilligan have criticised the masculine bias in much academic writing on ethics in relying largely on male samples and ignoring the distinctive, relational nature of much real-life ethical decision-making by women, as part of an 'ethic of care'. Gillian Proctor has also written about the neglected dimension of power within therapy.

Kant: Immanuel Kant (1724–1804) argued that ethical decision-making in one specific context, based on principles or rules, can be potentially generalisable to other situations in the form of a 'categorical imperative'.

Mill: John Stuart Mill (1806–1873) developed an approach to philosophy that emphasised the importance of individual rights, which society should only limit where protection of the rights of others becomes necessary.

Relational ethics: Recent discussion of ethics has tended to move away from formal, logical approaches associated with membership of specific schools of philosophy, to situate ethics within relationships between individuals, where situational factors – rather than rule-following – take on a greater significance, particularly within therapy.

Utilitarianism: This has been one of the dominant schools of ethics and philosophy within the UK, exemplified in the work of writers on ethics as varied as Bentham and Mill. It argues that the goal of ethical decision-making, for example in the law or in medicine, should be to achieve 'the greatest good for the greatest number'. This pragmatic approach has been applied more recently to justify the use of cognitive behaviour therapy within the IAPT programme.

(See Further Reading section at the end of this chapter for more on these and other writers.)

Ethics, complaints and disciplinary sanctions

For many people, the concept of ethics is immediately associated with the notion of breaches of the code, complaints procedures and resulting sanctions and disciplinary action. While this should not be the primary reason for considering and following the *Ethical Framework for the Counselling Professions* (BACP, 2016), it is important to be aware of how the complaints procedure can operate. The complaints procedure distinguishes between *professional misconduct*, which involves a therapist making a mistake of some kind, and *professional malpractice*, which is seen to involve exploitation or abuse of the client in some form. Professional misconduct may involve errors of judgement on the part of the therapist, such as inappropriate self-disclosure to the client, poor record-keeping or by showing a lack of respect towards clients and colleagues. The principle behind the complaints procedure is that mistakes and errors of judgement can be rectified. If the complaint is upheld, sanctions imposed by the professional association often involve an educative process, such as the therapist undergoing further training, self-reflection, supervision or some specific continuing professional development activity. The therapist subject to the complaint needs to show evidence of mitigation, i.e. recognition and acknowledgement of their error and a willingness to change, in order to improve their standard of practice.

Professional misconduct is potentially something that could happen to any therapist. This perhaps explains the frisson of concern which many feel on turning to the complaints section of their professional journal. Professional misconduct is quite distinct from professional malpractice, which is defined as practice which falls below the level of 'reasonable care and skill'. This is a legal standard applying in consumer law. It will involve more serious lapses in practice, such as developing an unjustifiably high level of dependency on the part of clients, mishandling the ending of therapy, or working to inadequate or inconsistent boundaries with clients. Again, this may require reparative work by the therapist or it can result in the suspension of the therapist from membership of their professional organisation. The category of 'bringing the profession into disrepute', through what is termed 'disgraceful behaviour', often involves a breach of sexual boundaries by the therapist. It will normally result in the therapist's expulsion from their professional association (Khele et al., 2008; Symons et al., 2011). Complaints against members are briefly publicised in the journal *Therapy Today*, but the fuller account of the proceedings and outcome of the complaint are only available on the BACP website.

Identifying and responding to ethical issues

One of the key challenges in developing a stronger sense of professional ethics as a counsellor is that it may not always be immediately obvious that an ethical issue has arisen. Sometimes ethical dilemmas will only become apparent when pointed out by a colleague or supervisor, or when they jump out of a moment of quiet reflection. What may seem on the surface to be routine or ordinary to counsellors, such as a change to using electronic recording, or a change in the way that the reception of clients is organised, may raise unexpected ethical dilemmas. Part of the characteristics of a 'virtuous' person involves a facility to identify such changes in policy or procedure, or a reappraisal of existing ways of working, as involving an *ethical* dimension – which then needs to be properly addressed.

Ethical standards are primarily intended to protect the interests of clients, and thus rest to some extent on the perceptions and experiences of clients. However, it does not follow that the client's experience is the sole criterion for assessing unethical practice on the part of the counsellor. It will be one factor to be considered, along with others, in making a judgement about whether the therapist was acting in an appropriate way.

In Box 6.2, a client describes two very contrasting approaches by her therapists in their manner of setting out the therapeutic contract. An exercise and discussion based on her experience follows.

Box 6.2   A client's experiences of different types of therapeutic relationship

When I first went to my analyst, I was surprised by his formality. I mentioned, hesitantly, during our second session that he didn't smile very often, thinking, foolishly, that he would smile. He didn't, and gave no response. At the end of the session he said he thought I 'could do with some therapy' and that he would need to write to my GP to tell him he was seeing me. I was surprised and felt rather embarrassed. I wondered what dire neuroses he had sniffed out during the two sessions we had had, and felt a sense of foreboding. It seemed, in retrospect, to set the tone.

Two years later, I went to a very different kind of practitioner in order to look at the traumatic feelings which my first experience of therapy had left me with. She did smile and, when we spoke about the task ahead of us, she said she saw it as a journey, and that she wanted me to know that it was one she was very much looking forward to making with me. The analogy of a journey was no more familiar to me at the time than the techniques of psychoanalysis, but the phrases 'I want you to know', 'looking forward to' and the word 'with' meant a lot to me. Again, it helped to set the tone. (Sands, 2000: 9)

Exercise   Exploring a client's experiences of different types of therapeutic relationship

Having read this client's account of two types of therapy, what ethical issues, if any, does it raise for you?

Discussion: A client's experiences of the therapeutic relationship

From the account in Box 6.2, the client appears to have been very unsettled by the response (or perceived *lack of response*) of her first therapist. She is subsequently reassured by the more evident and warmly empathic response of her second therapist. However, this does not necessarily mean that the first therapist was unethical, or even unskilled, in his approach. Assuming that the first therapist was using a psychoanalytic or psychodynamic model, it is remarkable how much potentially valuable therapeutic material is generated (and recorded) by the client, about her unfulfilled expectations of this therapeutic encounter. Rather than this being an ethical issue, it may be more accurate to explore this in terms of the degree of 'fit', or compatibility, between client and therapist style, or their therapeutic model. There are also potential issues of gender to consider – perhaps the client was able to relate more strongly to a therapist of the same gender than to a male, regardless of their therapeutic style.

From an ethical point of view, differences of therapist style may be addressed, but may not easily or always be resolved, by a process of explicit contracting. From a psychodynamic perspective, the client's powerful responses to therapy and to the therapist are likely to be unconscious in nature. From this point of view, there are limits to how far the client can give meaningful, informed consent to a process which may be working *outside* the realm of their conscious awareness and choice. This is not to give therapists a licence to work in ways that are completely unaccountable to clients and colleagues, but simply to acknowledge some of the problems in establishing a good therapeutic alliance. These responses may be experienced by the client as being very problematic, distressing and challenging, but do not necessarily represent a breach of ethical norms on the part of the therapist.

Box 6.3, and the exercise and discussion that follow, present a different scenario. They look at a client's experience of therapist rules that prohibit post-therapy relationships with former clients.

Box 6.3 A client's experience of therapist rules that prohibit post-therapy relationships with former clients

I knew that Elizabeth [the therapist] and I had a creative, caring connection that had been distorted. I knew there was something wrong with a system of treatment that notices greater potential for harm than healing in authentic relationships between healers and those who seek their help and fails to notice as *harmful* those rules and boundaries that block authenticity. I did not know why I was in such horrendous pain. In the days and weeks immediately following the end of therapy, I thought I was going mad. I was in tears much of the time. Often I would awake sobbing in the morning. (Heyward, 1994: 113–114, original emphasis)

The experience with Elizabeth sharpened my perception of how uncritically the concept of boundaries is being used today amongst many women therapists, especially those working with survivors of childhood sexual abuse. Furthermore, those most involved in efforts to curb sexual abuse by therapists and clergy often tend to absolutize boundaries as walls that discourage intimacy of any sort between professionals and those with whom we work. (Heyward, 1994: 186)

Exercise   Exploring a client's experience of therapist rules on post-therapy relationships

Having read the client's account of her distress at living through the ending of her therapy and the personal impact of the therapist maintaining a boundary about no post-therapy contact with former clients, what ethical issues, if any, does this raise for you?

Discussion: A client's experience of therapist rules on post-therapy relationships

The situation represented in Box 6.3 is again told from the client's point of view, and describes the overwhelming distress that she experienced at the prospect of ending of contact with her therapist, Elizabeth. The client clearly felt continuing acute emotional pain at being denied the possibility of renewing the contact with her on different, and possibly more equal, terms. The irony is that the boundaries set in place to protect the client from potential harm and exploitation are experienced, in this case, by the client as being bureaucratic, unfeeling and unnecessarily defensive in nature. What the client may be looking for is not necessarily having a continuing post-therapy relationship, but at least to have the *possibility* of one?

From the point of view of feminist or relational ethics, can post-therapy contact between client and therapist be justifiable, depending upon the precise nature of the therapeutic work undertaken, the degree of recovery achieved by the client, or the length of time ensuing since the formal ending of therapy? Alternatively, again from a feminist or relational point of view, is there a very real danger of post-therapy contact, no matter how well intentioned on both sides, replaying some of the dynamics of the client's previously abusive experiences? If ethical boundaries are set and agreed by therapists, this will inevitably set at least some limitations to client autonomy, however strongly contested this may be, and however painful this may be for the client to experience. On this occasion, with this particular therapist, 'no' clearly meant 'no', despite the client's very real sense of distress and abandonment. In this situation, the counsellor may have seen no post-therapy contact as a significant boundary to maintain. In other cases, it may be that the proposed boundary seems less absolute and more negotiable to the client, as for example in a request for the limited use of touch within the therapy (see Box 6.4 and the exercise and discussion that follow).

Box 6.4   A therapist's ethical and therapeutic dilemma about holding a client's hand

At the start of the operation Mrs. B.'s mother had been holding her hands, and she remembered the terror upon finding her mother's hands slipping away as she fainted and disappeared. She now thought she had been trying to re-find her mother's hands ever since.

Ms B. began to stress the importance of physical contact for her. She said she was unable to lie down on the couch again unless she knew that she could if necessary hold my hand, in order to get through this re-living of the operation experience. Would I allow that or would I refuse? If I refused she wasn't sure she could continue with her analysis. (Casement, 1990: 157–158)

Exercise   Exploring a therapist's ethical and therapeutic dilemma about holding a client's hand

Having read the therapist's dilemma regarding the client's expressed need for physical contact, in order to resolve a major childhood trauma, what ethical issues do you identify for the client and for the therapist?

Discussion: A therapist's ethical and therapeutic dilemma about holding a client's hand

In exploring the ethical issues involved in this client's apparently simple request, it may be helpful initially to look at it from a *rule-following* approach (e.g. 'No, or minimal, unavoidable physical contact with clients') or an *outcomes* approach ('Hand-holding can be justified if it has a positive therapeutic outcome for the client in resolving their childhood trauma'). In this scenario, it is worth remembering that the client is asking not to hold hands, but that 'she could if necessary hold my hand'. Even this might raise an acute ethical dilemma for some therapists. How ethical is it for a therapist to agree reluctantly to the possibility of hand-holding, but then, perhaps, to fervently hope that this does not prove necessary, or to hold hands in a half-hearted and rather unconvincing manner?

For therapists to experience this situation as a dilemma might depend upon whether they took a *rule-following* or an *outcomes* approach to their therapy. As a dilemma, this situation might also vary according to their modality. The injunction or rule against the therapeutic use of touch may be stronger in the psychodynamic or psychoanalytic tradition than in others, such as the person-centred approach. Patrick Casement, the therapist in this situation, considered the possible meanings and therapeutic consequences of agreeing to the client's request for the *possibility* of holding hands. He decided against it, on grounds drawn entirely from within psychoanalytic theory (Casement, 1990: 158–167), but later recorded a positive therapeutic outcome for the client regarding this difficult therapeutic and ethical decision.

From an ethical point of view, the client's request for direct physical contact, in the form of holding the therapist's hand, might need to be something which is explicitly discussed in the contracting (or re-contracting) stage. From an ethical point of view, physical contact might be considered to be a possible breach of boundaries, which could have unintended consequences in potentially eroticising the therapeutic alliance on one, or both, sides. Alternatively it could be argued, perhaps just as strongly, that the use of touch is not an ethical issue *per se* in therapy. This could apply on the condition that it is negotiated, consensual and can be justified in the context of the therapeutic work. However, if the therapeutic use of touch can be justified in principle in this way, this can open the door to other potential types of physical contact and to much more extensive use of touch within therapy (see Box 6.5 and the following exercise and discussion about 'Sally's' case).

Box 6.5   The case of 'Sally'

During most of these lengthy sessions there came a point when Sally summoned up the courage to remove some of her clothing and on a few occasions she chose to be completely naked for periods of time. This exposure of her physical being never became easy for her but as the weeks passed there were certainly times when it seemed she was

(Continued)

(Continued)

able to accept herself and relax completely in my presence. This was the prelude to astounding journeys into her past which she made word-lessly but often with great emotion. For my part, I discovered, with her help, that my principal task was to massage with great gentleness her stomach, her shoulders and sometimes her buttocks. It was also impor-tant for her to be held, sometimes for long periods. (Thorne, 1987: 62)

More surprising, perhaps, was my own willingness to trust those intuitive promptings which enabled me to encourage Sally to undress or, on occa-sions, to initiate a particular form of physical contact, whether it was sim-ply holding hands or, as in the final stage, joining in a naked embrace. Clearly it would be ridiculous to suggest that such behaviour could or should be repeated in other therapeutic encounters. (Thorne, 1987: 68)

One further point which needs to be noted is that the work with Sally took place between 1979 and 1983, that is, before the 1984 BAC Code of Ethics which first prohibited sexual activity with clients. (Thorne, 1993: 113)

Exercise   Exploring the case of 'Sally'

Having read the case of 'Sally', which is the therapist's account of the use of physical contact between client and therapist, what ethical issues, if any, does this raise for you?

Discussion: The case of 'Sally'

The case of 'Sally' remains one of the most controversial of all case records of therapy, and continues to be still strongly contested many years after its original publication. In terms of ethics, Brian Thorne appears to justify his approach in terms of exceptionalism. In other words, he has pointed out that the therapy did not involve sexual activity as such and also that it took place prior to the BAC ban on sexual activ-ity with a client, so it therefore did not contravene the code of ethics in force at that time. In addition, he argues that this approach should not be followed with other clients, or by other therapists, but appears to claim that this was a highly exceptional set of circumstances, evoking a specific set of responses from him as a therapist.

Arguably, the original publication of the case history and, moreover, the ensuing intense controversy have contributed to significant changes in BACP ethical statements. This process of clarification has included:

prohibiting sexual contact with current clients (BAC, 1984), widening this to include sexual exploitation (BAC, 1990), and introducing an interim measure of a 12-week 'cooling off' period for therapists before initiating a sexual relationship with a former client (BAC, 1992). The BACP *Ethical Framework for Good Practice in Counselling and Psychotherapy* (2002) defined and clarified the nature of 'sexual relations', and the BACP further extended its remit in 2016 to include a ban on 'behaving sexually' towards third parties connected to the client. (The evolution of BACP ethical perspectives on sexual activity with clients is reviewed in Box 6.6.)

Box 6.6   Evolution of BACP ethical perspectives on sexual activity with clients

Engaging in sexual activity with a client whilst also engaging in a therapeutic relationship is unethical. (BAC, 1984: 2.7)

Counsellors must not exploit their clients financially, sexually, emotionally or in any other way. Engaging in sexual activity with the client is unethical. (BAC, 1990: B2.2.6)

Counsellors must not exploit clients financially, sexually, emotionally or in any other way. Engaging in sexual activity with current clients within 12 weeks of the end of the counselling relationship is unethical. If the counselling relationship has been over an extended period of time or been working in-depth, a much longer 'cooling off' period is required and a lifetime prohibition on a future sexual relationship with the client may be more appropriate. (BAC, 1992: B2.2.6)

Counsellors remain accountable for relationships with former clients and must exercise caution over entering into friendships, business relationships, sexual relationships, training and other relationships. Any changes in relationship must be discussed in counselling supervision. (BAC, 1992: 2.3.1)

Practitioners must not abuse their client's trust in order to gain sexual, emotional, financial or any other kind of personal advantage. Sexual relations with clients are prohibited. 'Sexual relations' include intercourse, any other type of sexual activity or sexualised behaviour. Practitioners should think carefully about and exercise considerable caution before entering into personal or business relationship with former clients and should expect to be professionally accountable if the relationship becomes detrimental to the client or the standing of the profession. (BACP, 2002: 7)

33. We will not have sexual relationships with or behave sexually towards our clients, supervisees or trainees.

(Continued)

(Continued)

34. We will avoid having sexual relationships with or behaving sexually towards people whom we know to be close to our clients in order to avoid undermining our clients' trust in us. ...

36. We will not exploit or abuse our clients in any way: financially, emotionally, physically, sexually or spiritually. (BACP, 2016: 9)

Summary

This chapter has explored the importance of ethics in counselling and psychotherapy, exemplified in the shift from codes of ethics to ethical frameworks. The BACP *Ethical Framework for the Counselling Professions* (2016) combines values, personal moral qualities and ethical principles, and is based on a firm commitment to the client. Differing approaches to ethics can result in quite different patterns of decision-making by therapists, as illustrated by the case examples drawn from the counselling literature. Breaches of ethical requirements can lead to complaints and disciplinary action. Codes evolve over time in response to changing perceptions of problematic behaviour by therapists, as illustrated in the changes in ethical rules concerning sexual relationships between counsellors and clients.

Resources

Web resources

There are supporting documents on the BACP *Ethical Framework for the Counselling Professions* on the BACP website (www.bacp.org.uk) and also in the e-book version of Tim Bond's *Standards and Ethics for Counselling in Action* (Fourth edition, 2015), referred to below.

For a web interview with Carol Gilligan on 'Changing the Voice of the Conversation', see: www.youtube.com/watch?v=AXMtB7AU9B8

The Temenos online archive of interviews offers free registration and online access for counselling students: www.onlinevents.co.uk/category/portfolio/

Research

There is a limited amount of empirical research into ethics in relation to counselling and psychotherapy in the UK, although there is much more extensive research into the ethical and professional behaviour of therapists and related professions in the USA.

Lindsay, G. and Clarkson, P. (1999) 'Ethical dilemmas of psychotherapists', *The Psychologist*, 12(4), 182–185; and in Clarkson, P. (2000) *Ethics: Working with Ethical and Moral Dilemmas in Psychotherapy*. London: Whurr. pp. 1–16.

An early survey of UKCP psychotherapists' dilemmas (n: 213), covering confidentiality, dual relationships and colleagues' conduct.

Peer-reviewed research journal papers include:

Brown, A. (2006) '"In my agency it's very clear – but I can't tell you what it is": Work settings and ethical challenges', *Counselling and Psychotherapy Research*, 6(2), 100–107.

Exploration of a wide range of counsellors' experiences of ethical dilemmas (n: 20).

Khele, S., Symons, C. and Wheeler, S. (2008) 'An analysis of complaints to the British Association for Counselling and Psychotherapy, 1996–2006', *Counselling and Psychotherapy Research*, 8(2), 124–132.

Audit of complaints to BACP (n: 84), finding that a disproportionate number of complaints were brought against accredited members or male members, mostly by persons involved in counselling rather than by clients.

Symons, C., Khele, S., Rogers, J., Turner, J. and Wheeler, S. (2011) 'An analysis of the British Association for Counselling and Psychotherapy's Article 4.6 cases, 1998–2007', *Counselling and Psychotherapy Research*, 11(4), 257–265.

Audit of complaints to BACP of serious misconduct (n: 91), with similar findings to Khele et al. (2008) above.

See also:

Halter, M., Brown, M. and Stone, J. (2007) *Sexual Boundary Violations by Health Professionals – An Overview of the Published Empirical Literature*. London: Council for Healthcare Regulatory Excellence, www.professionalstandards.org.uk/docs/default-source/publications/research-paper/sexual-boundary-violations-2007.pdf?sfvrsn=4

Further reading

Bond, T. (2015) *Standards and Ethics for Counselling in Action*. Fourth edition. London: Sage.
Carroll, M. and Shaw, E. (2013) 'Relational ethics', in *Ethical Maturity in the Helping Professions: Making Difficult Life and Work Decisions*. London: Jessica Kingsley. Chapter 6, pp. 101–120.
Gilligan, C. (1982) *In a Different Voice: Psychological Theory and Women's Development*. Cambridge, MA: MIT Press.
Howard, A. (2000) *Philosophy for Counselling and Psychotherapy: Pythagoras to Postmodernism*. London: Macmillan.

Jenkins, P. (2015) 'What is wrong with the BACP Ethical Framework?', *Contemporary Psychotherapy*, 7(2), www.contemporarypsychotherapy.org/volume-7-no-2-winter-2015/what-is-wrong-with-the-ethical-framework

McLeod, J. (2013) 'Virtues, values and ethics in counselling practice', in *An Introduction to Counselling*. Fifth edition. Maidenhead: Open University Press. Chapter 22, pp. 507–543.

Proctor, G. (2014) *Values and Ethics in Counselling and Psychotherapy*. London: Sage.

Vesey, G. and Foulkes, P. (1999) *Dictionary of Philosophy*. Leicester: HarperCollins.

Reference section for supervisors

The BACP *Ethical Framework for the Counselling Professions* (2016) has a specific section on the ethical responsibilities of supervisors, which retains the traditional stance of prioritising the need to protect the welfare of the client:

> 11. We share a responsibility with all other members of our profession for the safety and wellbeing of all clients and their protection from exploitation or unsafe practice. We will also take action to prevent harm caused by practitioners to any client... (2016: 6)

> Supervision:

> 50. Supervision provides practitioners with regular and ongoing opportunities to reflect in depth about all aspects of their practice in order to work as effectively, safely and ethically as possible. (2016: 11)

Further reading

Traynor, B. (2007) 'Supervising a therapist through a complaint', in K. Tudor and M. Worrall (eds), *Freedom to Practise: Volume 2: Developing Person-Centred Approaches to Supervision*. Ross-on-Wye: PCCS Books. pp. 154–168.

Web resources

Temenos online archive of interviews offers free registration and online access for counselling students: www.onlinevents.co.uk/category/portfolio/

There is a video resource by Peter Jenkins, *Supervisors: A New Duty of Care?*, which is available at: www.onlinevents.co.uk/category/practitioners/peter-jenkins/

7

Surviving and thriving as a counsellor or psychotherapist

Introduction

This chapter looks at the process of working as a counselling student, from placement up to qualification and the point of registration with BACP. The areas covered include:

- developing self-awareness and self-care;
- making use of supervision;
- preparing for placement;
- qualifying and registering as a counsellor.

Learning context

The BACP *Core Curriculum* (2009) sets out the detailed requirements for students on BACP-accredited counselling courses, with regard to developing reflexivity and self-awareness, the precise standards for supervision of client work, and expectations of appropriate placements as learning opportunities for students. The BACP *Ethical Framework for the Counselling Professions* (2016) clearly sets out the contours and purpose of supervision and the importance of counsellor self-respect and self-care in maintaining the counsellor's competence to practise effectively.

BACP *Core Curriculum* (2009)

Self-awareness and self-care:

9.1.A The professional role and responsibility of the therapist:

The practitioner will have relevant knowledge to inform his or her ability to:

1. Show a commitment to personal and professional development, including self-awareness and an awareness of fitness to practise in relation to clients.
2. Reflect on personal development, including ways in which life experiences affect self and relationships with peers, clients and other professionals.
3. Demonstrate the psychological and emotional robustness necessary to work with intense feelings and uncertainties.
4. Engage in rigorous self-examination, monitoring thoughts, feelings, physical sensations and behaviour in the therapeutic relationship.
5. Recognise personal and professional limitations and identify ways of addressing these. ...

17. Regularly evaluate and review personal development and progress, making links with theoretical knowledge and the counselling process. (2009: 17)

BACP *Ethical Framework for the Counselling Professions* (2016)

Self-respect:

Fostering the practitioner's self-knowledge, integrity and care for self. (2016: 2)

Working to professional standards:

18. We will maintain our own physical and psychological health at a level that enables us to work effectively with our clients. (2016: 6)

Care of self as a practitioner:

75. We will take responsibility for our own wellbeing as essential to sustaining good practice by:

a. taking precautions to protect our own physical safety
b. monitoring our own psychological and physical health
c. seeking professional support and services as the need arises
d. keeping a healthy balance between our work and other aspects of life. (2016: 13)

Developing self-awareness and self-care

Counsellor training necessarily involves us in looking closely at ourselves, our personal and family histories, our ethnicity, values and class position, and our strengths and prejudices. This can be a bruising process, when, on receiving some accurate (if still empathic) feedback from an observant other, our long-cherished positive beliefs about ourselves can be all too easily deflated. Counselling training provides many avenues for developing a heightened awareness of ourselves in relation to others. This is so that we can gradually piece together a more accurate picture of how clients and colleagues might experience us and how we can better experience our own minute-by-minute responses in the counselling room. Courses will usually have personal development groups, which are led by external facilitators. They will also have frequent self-awareness exercises, geared to providing and asking for reciprocal feedback from our peers. Some courses have a mandatory requirement for undergoing a set amount of personal therapy. This can be useful as a means of reflecting on major life events and changes. It may simply be valuable in providing emotional support for the periodic turmoil caused by undertaking the training course itself. Certain assignments will invite reflection on your experience of the course, in the form of personal learning statements. These are often drawn from your own personal journal, and are reflections that are frequently shared with other members of the group for invited feedback. The following exercise gives a flavour of the kind of reflective process which is encouraged.

Exercise   Exploring your personal learning review

Reflect on the following questions, which are typical of the personal learning review process.

- What have you learned about yourself over the course so far? How has this learning impacted upon you?
- What blocks have you noticed in your own personal development?
- What have you learned about your developing practice as a counsellor? Can you define your practice in a couple of sentences?
- What are the weaknesses in your practice that you wish to work on? How might you do this?
- How has counsellor training affected your relationships at home, in work and with friends and family?
- Overall, what would you say is the biggest change in relation to you that you and others have noticed? How far is this a positive change?
- What goals do you have for your future personal and professional development?

(Mark your position on the line according to how far you agree with one or other of the statements below)

What are you generally like as a person on the course?

I often communicate the core conditions, in practice, 1-1 and group situations. I have stable emotional health. I am able to cope with normal life events and stresses.	I often fail to communicate the core conditions in practice, 1-1 and group situations. My emotional wellbeing is unstable and/or unpredictable.

----------------------------------------*--------------------*--------------------*--------------------*

How in touch are you with your own feelings?

My verbal and non-verbal communication is congruent over time. I can recognise my own feelings and express them with ease.	My verbal and non-verbal communication is frequently misaligned. I cannot recognise or express my feelings very much.

----------------------------------------*--------------------*--------------------*--------------------*

How much personal change have you made on the course?

I can show how I have made changes, in becoming more self-aware, and in improving personal and professional responses to others.	I have been 'stuck' in personal terms during the course and cannot shift from well-worn routines of feeling and/or behaving.

----------------------------------------*--------------------*--------------------*--------------------*

How far can you reflect on yourself and accept feedback from others?

I can show how I have accepted feedback from others, reflected on my behaviour, and can change my behaviour.	I am defensive and fight back against critical feedback. I am not prepared or able to change my behaviour.

----------------------------------------*--------------------*--------------------*--------------------*

How far do you take responsibility for your personal development?

I take charge of my own personal development and use course opportunities well. I accept the need for support or therapy when so advised.	I disown responsibility for my personal development and reject any need for support or therapy. My problems are caused by others.

----------------------------------------*--------------------*--------------------*--------------------*

How do I feel about personal issues perhaps needing work in the future?

I can recognise or agree with others that I may have major unresolved issues needing work now, or after the course ends.	I reject feedback that I have major unresolved issues needing work, either now or after the course ends.

----------------------------------------*--------------------*--------------------*--------------------*

Figure 7.1 Exercise assessing personal development

Personal development is notoriously difficult to assess accurately, as it is very subjective in nature. An alternative exercise is provided in Figure 7.1. It offers some fairly searching questions about your level of congruence, emotional stability and the degree to which you are able to take responsibility for your own wellbeing. This exercise is specifically designed to be completed as a self-report. Ideally, it should then be shared with a trusted peer who knows you well but who will also sensitively challenge your own self-perceptions, if need be.

Reviewing personal development

Counselling training invites you to reflect on your own personal development at regular intervals, often in a format linked to the keeping of a personal journal, such as the example shown in Box 7.1. This example, from a counselling student's personal development statement, makes some strikingly unusual and creative parallels between personal development and another, seemingly unrelated, dimension of physical self-care.

Box 7.1   Review of personal development

This is a short account of the ways in which my practice and study of karate contributes to my self-awareness, and the ways in which that self-awareness can be applied to counselling practice. The first important application of karate to counselling practice is the adoption of a reflective approach. A constant awareness of what you are doing and why is a key aspect of the practice of karate; this is a very similar idea to the concept of mindfulness in counselling. As a counsellor, I am constantly reflecting on my work with clients, how the process of therapy works and what I can do to help my clients achieve the best possible outcomes in their lives. I am thinking and reflecting all the time. This is an exhausting, but fruitful, way to practise and live, which I have learned in part through my karate practice.

One of my former instructors had a favourite, probably apocryphal, karate-related anecdote which has stayed with me, and has been especially helpful in my development as a counsellor. He recalled a question being put to a renowned Japanese instructor, asking him which were the three most important aspects of karate. The master replied, 'Basics, basics and basics'. I find this especially useful in grounding myself through the often bewildering journey of counselling training. Every time I feel lost in abstract theoretical concepts, or in the detail of a client's story in a session, I remind myself to focus on the absolute core of the therapeutic process – listening, establishing rapport and trust, and providing a solid, safe relationship for the client to be themselves.

(Continued)

(Continued)

Another way in which the practice of karate has contributed to my counselling practice is its emphasis on the process of continuous learning, and a continuous process of becoming. This has been especially relevant to me in considering my role as a trainee counsellor. Towards the beginning of my second year, I felt a strong sense of apprehension about qualifying as a counsellor. My fear was that qualification would bring with it expectations (both from myself and others) of a level of competence I would not be capable of achieving. I clung to my 'trainee' status internally as a kind of shield against the expectation of omnipotence in the counselling room, and feared losing that shield. I found it helpful to bear in mind my learning from karate, which is that every practitioner, no matter how experienced, is a student.

A final point. In karate a practitioner can never be the finished article: there is always more to learn. This illustrates perfectly to me the parallel philosophies of karate and counselling: karate teaches humility, sincerity and a continuous endeavour for self-improvement. These principles form part of the *dojo kun*, or guidelines for student conduct, principles echoed by the BACP *Ethical Framework for the Counselling Professions*. This commitment to learning and self-improvement, which I have adopted in my own counselling practice, is perfectly summed up by a saying I heard from one of my karate instructors:

If you think you're doing it perfectly, you aren't.

Tom Brooks

Promoting self-care

Self-care is strongly connected with the process of developing greater self-awareness. It can be a challenging, if sometimes overlooked, aspect of learning to become a therapist. The whole process of undergoing counselling training can be a very taxing one. It is financially expensive, given the costs of supervision, travel, course fees, personal therapy, a decent tablet or laptop and essential textbooks. The focus of counselling is apparently on helping others, namely the clients. It is tempting, therefore, to overlook the *personal* cost, in purely emotional terms, of taking on this life-changing set of demands in the form of counselling training, which may seem never-ending at some points. Respected forms of counselling training will place a heavy and continuing emphasis on personal development and the associated need for taking care of oneself. The alternative is trying to be completely selfless and risking the experience of burnout, when energies are depleted. The lessons learned in training can be helpful in the longer term. All counsellors will inevitably face major life-changes, personal losses and disappointments. Learning the need for self-care at the stage of training can make it easier, hopefully, to spot signs of rising stress levels in our own lives. This can prompt us to take early remedial action. It might take the form of changing our daily routine to build in some exercise or personal reflection, to take on personal therapy, to develop new outside interests, to arrange a break or a holiday, finances permitting, or to cut down, temporarily or permanently, on our client work.

However, anecdotal evidence tends to suggest that counsellors are better in seeking to care for *others*, rather than care for themselves. This intuitive message is borne out by a small piece of qualitative research carried out by Brownlee (2016), which found that some counsellors were very reticent about accepting, in *practice* rather than just in theory, the need for addressing their own self-care (see Box 7.2).

Box 7.2   Counsellors on self-care and internalised messages

'I have a very strong sense that I'm meant to look after other people. … I feel guilty about doing self-care. … It's not OK for me to stop doing – I've got to carry on.'

'Looking back, I've always been the one who looks after everyone. … Everybody else always had to come first, apart from me. So that's what I learned growing up; that's what you do.' (Brownlee, 2016: 17)

Failure to practise self-care runs the risk that we will become emotionally depleted, or gradually become distanced from our clients, colleagues and our own inner emotional landscape. Many of the warning signs of this process are essentially the same as the generic indicators of work-based stress. They can include fatigue, irritability and sleep problems. However, some warning signs may be more closely related to the distinctly *interpersonal* nature of therapeutic work and may include an increasing rate of errors in our work with clients, persistent thoughts about clients and their problems, or just an increased degree of cynicism about the value of counselling and of counselling organisations. In severe cases, counsellors may be affected by intrusive imagery of their clients' traumatic experiences. These may lead to an increased risk of what is known as secondary traumatisation, 'compassion fatigue', or even professional burnout (American Psychological Association, 2016).

So how do we protect ourselves as counsellors from potential damage? The American Psychological Association suggests the following measures:

- Pay attention to balance in work, rest and play. Make personal and professional self-care a priority. Attend to your physical and spiritual well being, as well as your emotional and physical health. ...
- Develop reasonable and realistic expectations about workload, responsibilities and capabilities. (American Psychological Association, 2016: 3)

Brownlee (2016) distinguishes between *professional* and *personal* self-care activities. Professional self-care includes many of the activities that are associated with counsellor training, such as supervision, tutorials and personal therapy (see Table 7.1). All of these may be experienced as potential *additional* sources of pressure. However, they also involve a close, intimate relationship with a skilled and empathic listener, who is able to pick up on surface as well as more underlying and perhaps unrecognised feelings.

Brownlee (2016) also identifies some of the common aspects of taking care of one's self, in both the physical and psychological domains (see Table 7.2).

Many of these will already be well known to us as counsellors, in working with clients and perhaps sharing information about the benefits of exercise on mood and wellbeing. The challenge may be for us to overcome our own introjects ('Be perfect! Work harder!') and to apply some of this learning to our own situation and not just keep it for clients.

Table 7.1 Professional self-care activities

Professional self-care activities
Supervision
Group supervision
Peer support
Tutorials
Conferences and workshops
Personal therapy
Personal development groups
Check-ins
Skills groups
Journal writing

Source: adapted from Brownlee, 2016: 16

Table 7.2 Personal self-care

Physical self-care activities	Psychological self-care activities
Healthy diet	Seeing friends and family
Exercising	Spending time alone
Being outdoors	Watching TV/films
	Reading and writing
	Mindfulness exercises
	Music

Source: adapted from Brownlee, 2016: 16

Exercise   Reviewing your own self-care

Review the suggested aspects of professional and personal self-care discussed above. How can you improve your own levels of self-care? Make a plan for things you can do in the next week to improve your own work–life balance.

Making use of supervision

Supervision is a well-established feature of counselling practice, for both trainee and more experienced practitioners. Unlike other forms of supervision, for example in social work or nursing, therapeutic supervision is not primarily concerned with case management or line management accountability. The main focus of supervision in counselling and psychotherapy is *therapeutic*, in supporting the therapist to work to the best of their ability with the client. The BACP *Core Curriculum* (2009) and the *Ethical Framework for the Counselling Professions* (2016) set out the main expectations and requirements for therapeutic supervision as follows.

BACP *Core Curriculum* (2009)

9.1.A The professional role and responsibility of the therapist.

8. Demonstrate the capacity for reflexivity as applied in therapeutic practice.

9. Understand the importance of supervision, contract for supervision and use it to develop professional and development needs. (2009: 17)

BACP *Ethical Framework for the Counselling Professions* (2016)

Supervision:

48. We will review in supervision how we work with clients. ...

50. Supervision is essential to how practitioners sustain good practice throughout their working life. Supervision provides practitioners with regular and ongoing opportunities to reflect in depth about all aspects of their practice in order to work as effectively, safely and ethically as possible. Supervision also sustains the personal resourcefulness required to undertake the work.

51. Good supervision is much more than case management. It includes working in depth on the relationship between practitioner and client in order to work towards desired outcomes and positive effects. This requires adequate levels of privacy, safety and containment for the supervisee to undertake this work. Therefore a substantial part or preferably all of supervision needs to be independent of line management.

52. Supervision requires additional skills and knowledge to those used for providing services directly to clients. Therefore supervisors require adequate levels of expertise acquired through training and/or experience. Supervisors will also ensure that they work with appropriate professional support and their own supervision.

53. All supervisors will model high levels of good practice for the work they supervise, particularly with regard to expected levels of competence and professionalism, relationship building, the management of personal boundaries, any dual relationships, conflicts of interest and avoiding exploitation.

54. All communications concerning clients made in the context of supervision will be consistent with confidentiality agreements with the clients concerned and compatible with any applicable agency policy.

55. Careful consideration will be given to the undertaking of key responsibilities for clients and how these responsibilities are allocated between the supervisor, supervisee and any line manager or others with responsibilities for the service provided. Consideration needs to be given to how any of these arrangements and responsibilities will be communicated to clients in ways that are supportive of and appropriate to the work being undertaken. These arrangements will usually be reviewed at least once a year, or more frequently if required.

56. Trainee supervision will require the supervisor to ensure that the work satisfies professional standards.

57. When supervising qualified and/or experienced practitioners, the weight of responsibility for ensuring that the supervisee's work meets professional standards will primarily rest with the supervisee.

58. Supervisors and supervisees will periodically review how responsibility for how work with clients is implemented in practice and how any difficulties or concerns are being addressed.

59. The application of this *Ethical Framework for the Counselling Professions* to the work with clients will be reviewed in supervision regularly and not less than once a year.

60. Supervisors will conscientiously consider the application of the law concerning supervision to their role and responsibilities.

61. We also recommend supervision to anyone providing therapeutically-based services, working in roles that require regularly giving or receiving emotionally challenging communications, or engaging in relationally complex and challenging roles. ...

66. Clients will usually be informed when they are receiving their services from a trainee. (2016: 10–12)

Supervision can present many challenges to trainee and newly qualified counsellors. This can start with the seemingly overwhelming task of actually *choosing* a suitable supervisor. It is followed by the challenging process of building the levels of trust needed to open up and explore aspects of one's practice which may seem raw, painful, or just 'not yet competent'. In Box 7.3, one student counsellor, now qualified, reflects on her positive experience of developing the right sort of relationship within the process of supervision, which enabled her to grow in confidence as a practitioner.

Box 7.3   Experience of supervision in practice

I value honesty and expect it from myself and my supervisor. The supervisory relationship has honesty and from the start I have been able to bring anything to supervision. Knowing that transparency enables understanding from a supervisory viewpoint and enables my growth and personal development (also both sides of the supervisory/trainee counsellor therapeutic relationship benefit), i.e. by me being open to discussing spirituality and letting my supervisor know I see it as a part of me, counselling and a life purpose to serve. Through open communication, I encourage my supervisor to speak more freely about religion and spirituality in order to connect and grow.

Supervision feels like a supportive environment in which I can be myself and share what may seem an embarrassing or silly thing which I know could bring a valuable insight into becoming a better counsellor. It also enables me to feel I am working to best practice and have the safety of my clients and self in check.

Helen Wilkinson

Helen Wilkinson very clearly conveys the sense of needing to build and share high levels of trust and honesty within the supervisory process in order to feel safe enough to learn. She also writes of needing to overcome her own concerns of being embarrassed, or of 'feeling silly', in raising those issues in supervision that might seem obvious to a supervisor. Supervision provides an intense (and intensive) learning situation. Feeling, or being, defensive will tend to limit any potential learning. For any student, there is a huge amount to learn. Anxiety about making mistakes, or about failing in some way, or not knowing something, is very understandable. Accepting the fact that there is much to learn may be a useful starting point. If you knew everything about counselling, then supervision would have little to offer, at least from a learning perspective.

However, supervision is not solely about training. It is a requirement for all counsellors, whether they are in training, or fully qualified. Supervision fulfils many functions beyond that of training you as a student. It also provides a framework for your practice, by linking it to a particular modality, such as cognitive behavioural therapy or an integrative approach, and to wider professional and ethical expectations. It provides necessary emotional support for what can be demanding, as well as satisfying, work. It provides a reflective space, in which you are able to take stock of your work with a client. Almost inevitably, you will leave each supervision session with much more than you took in.

Overcoming barriers to using supervision well

Nevertheless, using supervision may not be straightforward. Hawkins and Shohet have identified a number of barriers to counsellors making effective use of supervision (2012: 38–42). These include:

- previous experiences of supervision;
- personal inhibition and defensive routines;
- difficulties with authority;
- conflicts of roles;
- assessment;
- practical blocks;
- difficulties in receiving support;
- organisational blocks.

Developing your own 'internal supervisor'

Supervision textbooks will often refer to the process of developing your own 'internal supervisor', so that you become more able to reflect on your own practice and less immediately reliant on your supervisor for their support, reassurance and guidance. Casement (1993) makes an important distinction between developing an 'internalised' supervisor, i.e. simply taking into yourself the voice of your actual supervisor, and the process of developing your own internal supervisor, almost as a therapeutic 'satnav'. With the growth of your own internal supervisor, you gradually become better able to mesh your developing therapeutic instincts with a wider sense of what is professionally and ethically appropriate to do with each client (see Box 7.4).

Box 7.4   Developing an *internalised* supervisor or an *internal* supervisor?

Drawing upon an internalised supervisor means using someone else's thinking that may then tend to be superimposed upon what is happening. ... By contrast, internal supervision – being more autonomous – can help us to respond to the immediacy of the present moment in a session, in ways that are more appropriate to it. (Casement, 1993: 9–10)

Unpacking complex communication processes in therapy via supervision

Schön is another writer who has explored the process of development as a professional, and the particular role that supervision can play within this process for therapists. He provides an example, drawn from a therapist's taped supervision session with a more experienced supervisor, and explores some of the apparent difficulties in communication, which begin to emerge from this material (see Box 7.5).

Box 7.5   Schön: The client as a 'universe of one'

At the beginning of the session, when the Resident [i.e. the therapist] describes his patient as stuck in her relationship with her boyfriend and 'getting nowhere in therapy', the Supervisor asks,

In what way did she get stuck with you, I mean, in terms of the way she got stuck in the relationship?

With this slight change in the question, the Supervisor restructures the puzzle. Centring attention on the connection between 'stuck in the relationship' and 'stuck with you', he anchors the inquiry in the patient's transference, where the relationship between the patient and the therapist can serve as a window on the patient's life outside therapy. (Schön, 1983: 118–119)

This is perhaps a difficult, and rather complex, example to use as an illustration of the supervisory process. However, it is worth staying with, just as unravelling issues in supervision may also take some time and effort. First, some translation from a US cultural setting is needed. The Resident is a third-year psychiatrist in training, working within the US mental health system. The Supervisor is a psychoanalyst. The modality selected for therapy and for the related supervision of practice is therefore set within a psychoanalytic or, at the very least, *psychodynamic* frame. The choice of modality is important, as this provides the theoretical frame of reference for trying to understand what might be going on in the therapy. The Supervisor's response to the therapist's material illustrates their use of the concept of *transference*. This is offered as a potential link between the client's lived relationships *outside* therapy, namely with her boyfriend, and her relationship with the Resident, or therapist, *within* the therapeutic process. Transference here refers to the process of re-living what are often quite conflicted relationships by transferring their key qualities and emotions onto other, often apparently unconnected, relationships.

Schön unpicks some of the themes he perceives, in the somewhat prickly interaction between the therapist and the supervisor. He then provides further information in the form of a follow-up interview with the therapist, after the conclusion of the taped supervision session (see Box 7.6).

Box 7.6   Schön: The client as a 'universe of one' (continued)

What does the Resident [i.e. the therapist] make of this demonstration? After listening to the tape recording of the session, he complains that the Supervisor was not telling him what he wanted to hear. Then, upon reflection, he adds that he was not asking for what he wanted to know. He doubts that the Supervisor is an effective role model for him. He wants more help than he is getting, but feels angry when he asks for it. (Schön, 1983: 125)

Making sense of the therapeutic work with a client via supervision

The dominant tone of the therapist's evaluation of the supervision session seems to be one of dissatisfaction. It could be that the therapist does not understand the supervisor's use of the term 'transference' in this context, or perhaps he just doesn't agree with it. The therapist may also feel frustrated with himself for not being more assertive, in not asking more clearly for clarity and guidance, which might help him to work more effectively with the client. There could be any number of reasons for this apparent communication difficulty between supervisor and therapist. Alternatively, from an experiential point of view, it could even be a further example of 'parallel process'. This is another useful concept from a psychodynamic perspective. This refers to the possible existence of repeating, perhaps *unconscious*, patterns of miscommunication and dissatisfaction between client, boyfriend, therapist and supervisor:

- the client is described as 'being stuck in her relationship with her boyfriend';
- the client is described as 'getting nowhere in therapy';
- the therapist may feel he is also 'stuck' and 'getting nowhere' in his relationship with his supervisor;
- finally, it may even be the case that the supervisor feels 'stuck' and 'getting nowhere' in their supervisory relationship with the therapist.

At one level, the example provided by Schön might simply be taken as an illustration of obvious miscommunication at different levels, e.g. between client and boyfriend, client and therapist, and finally between therapist and supervisor. However, supervision hopefully offers a chance to unpick what might otherwise just be seen as unfathomable difficulties. By standing back from the situation and exploring the client–therapist relationship at an *experiential* rather than simply at a matter-of-fact or *cognitive* level, there is a chance to make sense of what might be going on at a more *relational* or *symbolic* level. Some real experiential learning might emerge, if the supervisor were to pick up and explore the therapist's frustration as 'live material' to be worked with and explored in the supervision session itself (see Figure 7.2).

Figure 7.2 repeats the key phrase 'getting nowhere' as maybe having wider significance than just reflecting the client's immediate experience. The analysis suggested here perhaps runs the risk of being too simplistic. Still, it might offer a way for *both* therapist and supervisor to reframe their shared experience. They could then begin to explore how both the therapist and client might begin to work with their 'stuckness', other than simply to feel frustrated and perhaps somewhat 'unheard'. Schön's example provides an illustration of how supervision can help to make very puzzling experiences look slightly different and to open them up to a more positive and fruitful therapeutic conversation. Over time, the therapist in this example could begin to develop their own 'internal supervisor' and take their lived and partly analysed experience of therapy into supervision for shared exploration with their supervisor. To progress your understanding of this kind of exploration of supervision, see the following exercise.

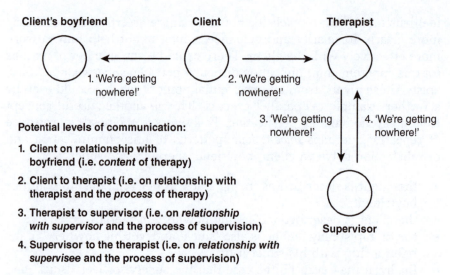

Client's boyfriend   Client   Therapist

1. 'We're getting nowhere!'   2. 'We're getting nowhere!'

3. 'We're getting nowhere!'   4. 'We're getting nowhere!'

Supervisor

Potential levels of communication:

1. **Client on relationship with boyfriend (i.e.** *content* **of therapy)**

2. **Client to therapist (i.e. on relationship with therapist and the** *process* **of therapy)**

3. **Therapist to supervisor (i.e. on** *relationship with supervisor* **and the process of supervision)**

4. **Supervisor to the therapist (i.e. on** *relationship with supervisee* **and the process of supervision)**

Figure 7.2   Unpacking potential levels of communication in supervision

Exercise   Reviewing your learning outcomes in supervision

Go back to the list of factors, identified by Hawkins and Shohet (2012), which may present barriers to using supervision effectively. Choose two factors which might explain the therapist's possible reluctance to accept the supervisor's interpretation of the underlying dynamic of the therapeutic process. Write brief notes and discuss your views with another student.

Now consider the list again. Which factors, if any, might apply to your own use of supervision? How might you address and begin to resolve these barriers?

Accessing counselling supervision which is independent of line management

Given the influence of organisational culture on counselling practice, which was explored in Chapter 2, it is important for counsellors to have access to a space where they can reflect on their work. According to the BACP *Ethical Framework for the Counselling Professions*, section 51, 'a substantial part or preferably all of supervision needs to be independent of line management' (2016: 11). There is a real risk, particularly when working on placement, or at the beginning of a counselling career, in assuming that the working practice in one setting is the norm, which applies across all, or most, work settings. Having access to counselling supervision, which sits *outside* the organisation, enables the counsellor to develop a more informed and critical understanding of counselling practice and policies. These might otherwise be taken for granted and not questioned. The example in Box 7.7 illustrates this.

Box 7.7 Accessing external supervision for school-based counselling

Sally is a counsellor working with pupils from 11 to 16 years of age within a school setting. She is supervised by Mandy, who is also a school counsellor within a different geographical area. They both agree that there is a need to work closely with the head of pastoral care in the school to ensure that parental consent is gained for the pupil to work with the counsellor. There is also provision for the counsellor to work with both parent and pupil together if the need arises. This procedure is not one that is evident in all school counselling services, however, Sally's school feels this is one way of involving parents in its work with the pupils. The culture of the school is one of openness and collaboration and therefore parental permission is regarded not with suspicion, but as the norm in all pupil transactions. Both Sally and Mandy are clear that if permission is not granted, the pupil will not be able to work with the counsellor. This might appear harsh, but in such an open culture is rarely a problem for Sally and her supervisor. (Copeland, 2005: 57)

The example in Box 7.7 shows some of the strengths and limitations of accessing supervision that is independent of line management. The school counsellor's line manager may be the head of pastoral care, so external supervision can help Sally to stand outside her immediate organisational context. She can then consider the therapeutic needs of her clients and her own stance as a practitioner. Within the organisational models discussed in Chapter 2, Sally's counselling work probably fits within a *task* culture that has been adapted to the predominantly *role*-based culture of the school (see discussion of these terms in Chapter 2). External supervision may help her to maintain appropriate boundaries for her therapeutic work. This might include managing staff's expectations for sharing information, as appropriate, or in following safeguarding requirements. However, a different external supervisor might also query the school's rule-based policy of *always* seeking parental consent for young people under age 16 to access counselling. This may conflict with the rights of the young person under the *Gillick* principle in English and Welsh law.

The format for counselling provision may not be a problem as such for Sally and her supervisor, but it may present a problem for her potential clients. The process of requiring young people under 16 to provide evidence of parental permission may have the unintended effect of deterring at least some young people from asking for this permission. Alternatively, they may be blocked from accessing school counselling, should their parents refuse, for whatever reason. From an ethical point of view, this policy would appear, in effect, to *veto* their adolescent children from accessing confidential counselling in a school setting. It would seem that this policy prioritises the rights of parents *over* the rights of the young people to be afforded their legal and ethical entitlements of privacy and confidentiality in accessing counselling.

There is also a risk that supervisory arrangements, in this case *external* to the school, may not recognise, or sufficiently challenge, the rule-based policy of the school. Arguably, this policy is acting to the disadvantage of those young people who are potential clients of the counselling service. Supervision that is *external* to the organisation, and therefore not based on a line management hierarchy of accountability, has a key role to play in identifying agency policies with problematic ethical and therapeutic effects. External supervision can be particularly important when on placement, where trainees may lack the experience to spot issues or policies that may conflict with sound ethical counselling practice.

Preparing for placement

Placements provide a crucial part of your overall learning experience as a student. In many ways, the placement experience, whether positive or negative, has a lasting impact on your future development as a therapist. It is also important as a key moment for your involvement with, and learning from, the training course. It is when you secure an appropriate placement and begin to engage with it fully that the course really 'takes off' as a learning experience. Increasingly, placements will offer, and sometimes require, participation in training activities. These might be directly related to the placement itself or be more generic training activities, related to risk management or working with specific client groups or client issues.

BACP *Core Curriculum* (2009): Practice placement

B5.3 The course seeking accreditation will have clear, written and published procedures for practice placements.

B5.4 The course must demonstrate how it approves its placement providers as appropriate for the particular course.

B5.5 There must be an explicit written agreement/contract between students, the placement provider and the course, which is available to all. This must include:

i. A description of the course including its rationale and philosophy, proce-dures and resources and the requirements of students for client work and assessment (e.g. supervisor reports, electronic media recording).

ii. A confirmation from the placement provider that its aims, orientation and philosophy are congruent with that of the course.

iii. Details of where accountability lies for:
   o the client work
   o reporting relationships
   o supervision arrangements
   o limits of confidentiality
   o complaints procedures
   o health and safety issues

iv. A contract between the course and the placement provider that details the requirements for reports on students, reciprocal feedback, meetings, etc.

v. Details of the placement providers' professional practice such as the ini-tial assessment of clients, methods of referral to students, note taking/record keeping requirements.

vi. Details of the type and range of client work undertaken by the placement provider, the kinds of client work contracts offered and any limits upon these in relation to student experience or other factors.

vii. Details of how clients are assessed for suitability to work with students. (2009: 8)

The kind of detail regarding placements, which is described as part of the BACP *Core Curriculum* (2009), is the joint responsibility of the train-ing course and of the placement agency. Usually, this will be spelled out in a three-way placement learning agreement or contract. This is signed and agreed by the student, tutor and placement manager. The fine detail of the expectations regarding your placement should also be spelled out in your course handbook. Appropriate forms for agreeing placements are usually available on the internal course website, for ease of access and reference.

The process of applying for, and being selected for, a placement has become increasingly formalised in recent years. The example in Box 7.8 is from a leading voluntary agency working with people with mental health issues. First, it sets out the person specification. This requires attendance at an appropriate counselling training course, access to exter-nal supervision, client skills relevant to short-term work, together with administration and teamwork skills, commitment and compliance with relevant agency policies. Many placement agencies will also require a recent Disclosure and Barring Service (DBS) check and evidence of professional indemnity insurance cover, although such insurance will generally be provided automatically by the agency for all staff and volunteers. Some placements will only accept students on the second year of their course. However, this blanket rule is worth questioning where it does not take account of prior relevant experience, perhaps as a social worker, teacher, youth worker, or mental health worker. Finally, all placements operate within a distinctive organisational culture, whether the placement is in a statutory setting or in a voluntary/third sector setting. It may be worth revisiting some of the material discussed in Chapter 2, on the different types of organisational context of counselling practice, to familiarise yourself with some of the particular issues this might raise for you as a student on placement.

Box 7.8   Person specification relating to counselling work

- Be attending a relevant and recognised counselling course.
- Be able to attend professional external supervision independent from the organisation and your place of study.
- Possess the skills to be able to work effectively with a client within seven sessions, or to recognise if this is unethical to do so and to not enter into a counselling relationship and refer to an appropriate service.
- Ability to work with clients through a variety of pathways.
- Basic administration skills.
- Ability to work on own and as part of a team.
- Be able to give regular commitment to providing some hours within the centre opening times.
- Adhere to all policies in place, especially Confidentiality, Health and Safety, and Boundaries, including following the cancellation policy without exception.
- Able to commit to the agreed time slots to meet with rotating client work load.

Source: Tameside, Oldham and Glossop Mind. Reprinted with permission.

The second part of the document sets out the more detailed aspects of the counselling role required of the student or volunteer. It notes the one-to-one nature of the counselling, as distinct from group or couples counselling, the agency limits for the number of sessions and the need for agreement with and compliance with the overall ethos of the organisation, regarding inclusiveness and recovery. There are standard requirements applicable to all placements regarding agency paperwork requirements, which often include completion of relevant outcome measures, such as CORE, policies and guidelines, CPD, recording and cancellation policy. Finally, candidates are required to access external supervision and to follow the BACP *Ethical*

Framework for the Counselling Professions (2016). Some placement agencies may provide in-house supervision, both group and individual, for which a charge may be made. Other agencies may have a policy of obtaining either payment or contributions by clients for all sessions. All of this detail should be very clearly spelled out in the application process so that you are fully aware of all aspects of the placement before starting actual work with clients (see Box 7.9).

Box 7.9 Role description of volunteer placement counsellors

Placement counsellor hours: To be confirmed at point of interview

Responsible to: Counselling Development Co-ordinator

Duties relating to the counselling work:

- To provide one-to-one counselling.
- To work within a variety of pathways, including short-term therapy of seven sessions.
- To promote social inclusion and recovery in all work carried out at the well-being centre.
- To accurately complete the relevant paperwork and statistical information.
- To attend regular independent supervision.
- To work within and adhere to policy and guidelines.
- To ensure all duties reflect a commitment to Equal Opportunities.
- Adhere to 2 x DNA [did not attend] and cancellation policy (without exception).
- To follow our standardised note taking.
- To be responsible for maintaining an appropriate level of informed CPD.
- Will be responsible for responding to any organisational changes.
- To effectively manage all data compliance and governance requirements of the organisation.
- To provide an ethical and professional counselling provision guided by the BACP Framework for Good Practice.

Source: Tameside, Oldham and Glossop Mind. Reprinted with permission.

Qualifying and registering as a counsellor

The end result of working with clients on placement, undergoing supervision and gaining skills, knowledge and self-awareness on a suitable training course is to equip you to finally become qualified as a counsellor or psychotherapist. There are currently two routes to achieving this goal by meeting BACP requirements. Students can complete a BACP-accredited training course, which is usually three or four years full-time at undergraduate level; or at postgraduate level, which is normally two years part-time; or, more unusually, one year full-time. BACP-accredited courses comprise a minimum of 450 class-contact hours, plus 100 hours of supervised practice on a recognised placement and individual, contracted supervision. The requirements for supervision are complex. There needs to be fortnightly supervision (including group supervision, course-based supervisory contact and individual supervision) of a minimum of one-and-a-half hours per month, at a ratio of one hour's supervision to each eight hours of client contact, i.e. a minimum of 12½ hours' supervision overall. In reality, your supervision hours may well need to be in excess of this, to take account of the need for emergency supervision, breaks in counselling on placement for personal reasons (e.g. illness or bereavement) or client DNAs (did not attend).

On completing training, the next step is to register as a counsellor with BACP. Registration is an important mark of achieving a properly recognised level of professional competence. The BACP Register is a voluntary register of practitioners, which is part of a register accreditation scheme that has been developed by the Professional Standards Authority for Health and Social Care. There are two main routes to achieving registration, depending on whether you have completed a BACP-accredited training course or a non-accredited training course (see Figure 7.3).

The Certificate of Proficiency provides the first level of official recognition of your professional competence as a counsellor. Beyond this, it is possible to progress to further levels of expertise, such as achieving accreditation as an individual practitioner, after gaining further post-qualifying experience (see Chapter 8). The Certificate of Proficiency provides a rigorous test of counsellor ability. It requires candidates to apply their knowledge and skills in order to discriminate between therapeutic responses which are deemed to be either appropriate to the client's situation or those following a counsellor's own personal agenda.

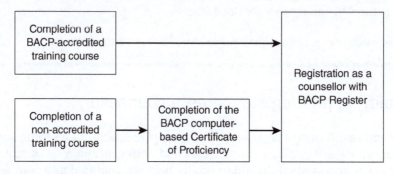

Figure 7.3 Two routes to achieving BACP registration as a counsellor

Case Study: At the beginning of your ninth session, Teresa disclosed that her husband had just been diagnosed with terminal lung cancer. What issue is likely to be the most significant to discuss? Choose only one, unless directed to 'please make another selection'

These are the options which the candidate can see and they must decide which of the four is the best choice to make.	The assessment is computer-based and is about making appropriate selections. The information in this column would be revealed when the corresponding option was selected.	The information in this column is for BACP use and is presented for your information. This information is never seen in an assessment.
1. The financial implications for Teresa.	1. Please make another selection.	Makes assumptions.
2. How long her husband is expected to live.	2. Please make another selection.	Fails to connect with possible client emotions.
3. The emotional impact of the diagnosis on Teresa.	3. Indicated.	Recognises the emotional significance of this for the client.
4. How her husband is coping.	4. Please make another selection.	Enquiry about a third party.

Figure 7.4 Example of the case study approach used for the BACP Certificate of Proficiency (COP) computer-based assessment for the registration of applicants to the BACP Practitioner Register (Aldridge, 2014: 27)

Reproduced with permission from BACP.

The latter responses might involve enquiring about third parties or satisfying one's own personal curiosity, rather than focusing directly on the client's perceived needs. The Certificate of Proficiency is taken as a computer-based test based on six fictitious, but realistic, case studies. Each case study has between six and eight questions. In some of the questions there are four potential responses, only one of which is geared to helping the client in the most effective therapeutic manner. The most appropriate response is assessed independently of the counsellor's preferred modality, such as person-centred, psychodynamic or integrative. An example of a question similar to the ones used in actual tests is shown in Figure 7.4.

Summary

This chapter has reviewed some of the main elements of becoming a counsellor, such as developing greater self-awareness and self-care. Supervision is a central aspect of both counsellor training and working once qualified, where the concept of developing an 'internal supervisor' can be a valuable resource and aid to practice. Some of the expectations and requirements of students in considering training placements were discussed. Finally, routes to achieving BACP registration as a counsellor were clarified.

Resources

Web resources

Weblink for Joan Wilmot on 'The Seven-Eyed Supervisor', from the Hawkins and Shohet model of supervision: www.youtube.com/watch?v=JJwhpz8NSV0

Research into counsellor self-awareness, self-care and professional development

Brownlee, E. (2016) 'How do counsellors view and practise self-care?', *Healthcare Counselling and Psychotherapy Journal*, 16(2), 15–17.

Small sample of interviews with practitioners (n: 7), regarding attitudes towards the practice of self-care, suggesting the importance of internalised introjects ('Put others first'), which may present barriers to achieving effective self-care.

Lowndes, L. and Hanley, T. (2010) 'The challenge of becoming an integrative counsellor: The trainee's perspective', *Counselling and Psychotherapy Research*, 10(3), 163–172.

Small sample of recently qualified integrative counsellors (n: 7), exploring particular challenges of developing confidence and competence in working within their chosen modality.

Lennie, C. (2007) 'The role of personal development groups in counsellor training: Understanding factors contributing to self-awareness in the personal development group', *British Journal of Guidance and Counselling*, 35(1), 115–129.

Mixed methods exploration of participants' experience of personal development (PD) groups (n: 88), identifying factors influencing their views of the personal value of PD groups in developing their self-awareness.

Wheeler, S. and Richards, K. (2007) *The Impact of Clinical Supervision on Counsellors and Therapists, Their Practice and Their Clients: A Systematic Review of the Literature*. Lutterworth: BACP (free pdf download available from: www.bacp.co.uk/research/Systematic_Reviews_and_Publications/Supervision.php).

Systematic review of high-quality research studies (n: 25) into clinical supervision, revealing limited evidence for improvements in supervisee self-efficacy, self-awareness, skill development or transferral of learning to practice.

Further reading

Moore, J. and Roberts, R. (eds) (2010) *Counselling and Psychotherapy in Organisational Settings*. Exeter: Learning Matters.

Descriptions of counselling practice in different settings, useful for preparing for placements. Agencies covered include a secondary school, a Further Education college, Higher Education, a voluntary agency, a residential treatment centre for addictions, an Employment Assistance Programmes and a prison.

Oldale, M. and Cooke, M. (2015) *Making the Most of Counselling and Psychotherapy Placements*. London: Sage.

Very useful practical guide to the process of searching and applying for placements and then deriving the maximum learning from them.

Reference section for supervisors

The BACP *Ethical Framework for the Counselling Professions* (2016) sets out the full detail of requirements for supervision, with key sections relating primarily to supervisors, rather than to students or supervisees. It has been repeated below for reference.

BACP *Ethical Framework for the Counselling Professions* (2016)

Supervision:

51. ...a substantial part or preferably all of supervision needs to be independent of line management.

54. All communications concerning clients made in the context of supervision will be consistent with confidentiality agreements with the clients concerned and compatible with any applicable agency policy.

55. Careful consideration will be given to the undertaking of key responsibilities for clients and how these responsibilities are allocated between the supervisor, supervisee and any line manager or others with responsibilities. ... These responsibilities will usually be reviewed at least once a year, or more frequently if necessary. (BACP, 2016: 11)

In addition, there is a BACP training curriculum for supervisors. The BACP Professional Standards *Counselling Supervision Training Curriculum* (2014) sets out the relevant aspects to be applied, including what are referred to as *metacompetences*. These are defined as the 'subtle judgments that a supervisor needs to make, including adapting the process and content of supervision' (BACP Professional Standards, 2014: 1). These include:

- Adapting the process and content of supervision – considering the supervisee's stage of development, identifying gaps in the knowledge, using professional judgment to monitor the supervisee's learning and emotional needs, balancing attention to process issues with the need to advance the supervisee's learning, using professional judgment to adapt supervision in response to feedback
- Giving feedback – balancing positive and negative feedback, prioritising areas for feedback
- Managing concerns about the supervisee's ability to use supervision
- Managing serious concerns about practice – using professional judgment to take appropriate action when the supervisee's clinical practice raises serious concerns, managing the possible adverse effects of this on the supervisory relationship, balancing the focus on the supervisee's educational needs with identifying practice that is harmful to clients. (BACP Professional Standards, 2014: 19)

Research

Bamblings, M., King, R., Raue, P., Schweitzer, R. and Lambert, W. (2006) 'Clinical supervision: Its influence on client-rated working alliance and client symptom reduction in the brief treatment of major depression', *Psychotherapy Research*, 16(3), 317–331.

Randomised controlled trial (n: 127) of both supervised and unsupervised counselling practice, showing more positive outcomes for clients of supervised therapists in terms of reduced levels of depression, higher rates for completion of therapy, and of client satisfaction levels.

Further reading

Copeland, S. (2005) *Counselling Supervision in Organisations: Professional and Ethical Dilemmas Explored*. London: Routledge.
Hawkins, P. and Shohet, R. (2012) *Supervision in the Helping Professions*. Fourth edition. Maidenhead: Open University Press.

8

Developing new roles in counselling and psychotherapy

Introduction

This chapter looks at the potential next steps for counsellors, once having finally achieved qualification and registration as a counsellor. These steps might include:

- working as a counsellor: employment, private practice or portfolio work;
- developing a new specialism and undertaking further training or individual accreditation as a counsellor;
- developing new roles as a group facilitator, counsellor trainer, supervisor, researcher or coach.

Learning context

The BACP *Core Curriculum* (2009) has relatively little to say about the development of new roles, as its main focus is primarily on the requirements for training as a counsellor. The BACP *Ethical Framework for the Counselling Professions* (2016) explicitly recognises the development of professional specialisms that are integrally linked to the role of counsellor, such as supervisor and trainer, and more recent specialisms, such as coach. This is consistent with the change in title from *Ethical Framework for Good Practice in Counselling and Psychotherapy* to the deliberately more inclusive phrase '*for the Counselling Professions*' (2002). Ethical requirements apply equally to practitioners working with clients in these new or associated roles and those providing counselling for clients in both individual and group formats.

BACP *Ethical Framework for Counselling and Psychotherapy* (2016)

Good practice:

2. This section of the Ethical Framework looks behind Our commitment to clients and Ethics to consider their implications for Good Practice in more detail.

3. It sets out what can be expected of all members and registrants of BACP as practitioners providing therapeutically-based services, particularly coaching, counselling, pastoral care and psychotherapy. This includes associated roles in supervision, education or training, management and research. (2016: 5)

Working as a counsellor:
Employment, private practice or portfolio work

Generally, the picture is one of guarded optimism for the continuing slow expansion of job opportunities in counselling and psychotherapy. In part, this reflects the sea-change in public attitudes towards recognising counselling as being both socially acceptable and personally helpful. Market research undertaken for BACP in 2004 identified that '83% of British adults have had or would consider having counselling or psychotherapy' (Future Foundation Projects, 2004: 17). In the same telephone survey (n: 1008), almost two-thirds of respondents said they knew someone who could benefit from therapy. Nine out of ten respondents accepted that other people may need counselling or psychotherapy (2004: 17). This huge demographic (and perhaps generational) shift highlights 'the mass acceptance of and appreciation for therapy in Britain today' (2004: 21). Older respondents and those from lower social classes (C2DE) were reported to be less likely to attend or to consider attending therapy. Despite this factor, there now seems to be clear evidence of an established and growing mass market for counselling and psychotherapy. This market has also been acknowledged, and perhaps in turn further stimulated, by government provision in the form of IAPT, and the rapid growth of counselling provision in areas such as the workplace and in secondary schools.

The estimates for continued employment growth are optimistic. According to the National Careers Service, 'the number of jobs in the sector is predicted to rise sharply between now and 2020' (Allen, 2015: 27) (see Figure 8.1). The category used in Figure 8.1 is for 'health support', which is clearly much broader than simply employment prospects

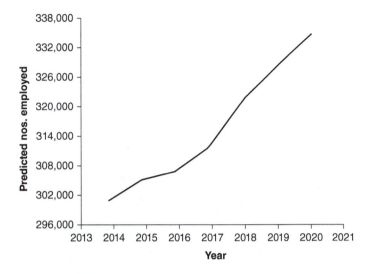

This graph shows the predicted numbers of people that will be working in
this sector between now and 2020.

Figure 8.1   Employment forecast for health support, 2014–2020

Source: https://nationalcareerservice.direct.gov.uk/advice/planning/jobprofiles/Pages/
counsellor.aspx

for counsellors and psychotherapists, but the overall trend is for continuing growth during the coming period.

However, gaining an accurate picture of employment opportunities
and patterns for counsellors is not easy. Employment of counsellors
appears to be highly fragmented. It is based on very distinct employment
sectors, such as counselling in the workplace, in university settings, in the
NHS, in schools and in private practice. In addition, many counsellors
may combine different patterns of part-time working, rather than hold
full-time employment that is restricted to one particular field of work.

In other more specific areas of practice, it seems clear that counsellor
employment will continue to be directly affected by government decisions
about investment in mental health planning, as the IAPT programme
demonstrates. The Mental Health Taskforce has called for parity between
physical health care and mental health care in the NHS in England, requiring an additional £1 billion investment in 2020–21 (Mental Health
Taskforce, 2016: 19). The detail of the required investment covers key areas
of high need, such as crisis care, dementia, self-harm, eating disorders and
autism, as set out in Figure 8.2. If implemented, the investment would
represent a significant area of potential employment of counsellors. This
would apply within what are often under-recognised and under-staffed

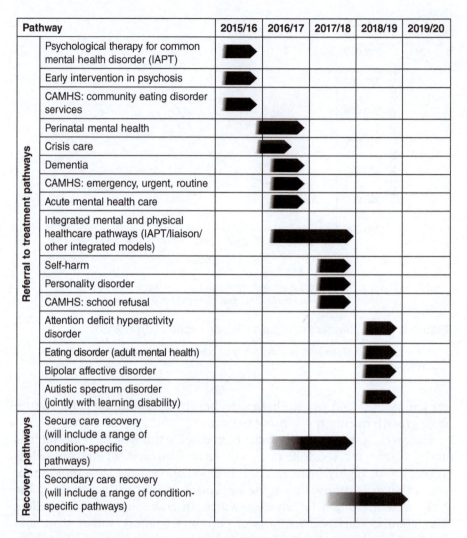

Pathway		2015/16	2016/17	2017/18	2018/19	2019/20
Referral to treatment pathways	Psychological therapy for common mental health disorder (IAPT)	➤				
	Early intervention in psychosis	➤				
	CAMHS: community eating disorder services	➤				
	Perinatal mental health		➤			
	Crisis care		➤			
	Dementia		➤			
	CAMHS: emergency, urgent, routine		➤			
	Acute mental health care		➤			
	Integrated mental and physical healthcare pathways (IAPT/liaison/ other integrated models)		➤			
	Self-harm			➤		
	Personality disorder			➤		
	CAMHS: school refusal			➤		
	Attention deficit hyperactivity disorder				➤	
	Eating disorder (adult mental health)				➤	
	Bipolar affective disorder				➤	
	Autistic spectrum disorder (jointly with learning disability)				➤	
Recovery pathways	Secure care recovery (will include a range of condition-specific pathways)		➤			
	Secondary care recovery (will include a range of condition-specific pathways)				➤	

Figure 8.2 Proposed mental health pathway and infrastructure development programme (Mental Health Taskforce, 2016: 36)

areas, particularly in areas of current demographic change, such as a rising demand for services for older people.

Working as a counsellor in private practice

One of the options for working as a counsellor, which appeals to many, is that of working independently, by going into private practice. There is intense competition for paid employment as a counsellor and an apparent

Table 8.1 Working in private practice (adapted from Wallace, 2015: 47)

Advantages	Disadvantages
Freedom to choose how many and which hours to work	Isolation of working alone
	Too few clients
Flexibility around other commitments	Requirement to work unsocial hours to meet client need
Freedom to offer as many sessions as are needed/wanted by clients	
A varied portfolio of work	Low income
Being able to work from home	High outgoings of being in business
Not being bound by the requirements of working within an organisation	

dearth of full-time, salaried positions. Private practice is an attractive prospect for many on completing their counselling training and registering with BACP. It appears to offer a number of distinct advantages, such as the opportunity of working from home, a degree of flexibility and control over client work and working hours, and professional autonomy in terms of clinical decision-making. However, there are also some disadvantages, which also need to be taken into account to get a fuller and more accurate picture of this option (Wallace, 2015) (see Table 8.1).

Wallace's findings are based on a questionnaire survey carried out in 2015 (n: 2,544) of members of the BACP Private Practice division. The findings suggest a niche area of practice that is undergoing rapid change. Most respondents, for example, used paper-based recording systems, although nearly a third were now interested in moving towards using an online system, such as Bacpac. Only one in ten respondents used standardised outcome measures, like CORE, to evaluate their work with clients, instead relying on verbal or written feedback.

Counsellors who have been successful in establishing their own private practice tend to stress the need to approach it as setting up a small business, which requires basic but sound financial, marketing and administrative skills. Rye (2011), for example, has calculated the average running costs of private practice at approximately £6,000 per year (at 2011 prices). Allowing for a maximum of 25 client hours per week, over 47 weeks a year, you would need to see 20 clients per week at £50 per hour in order to make a pre-tax income of £40,000 per year (Rye, 2011: 9). Estimating this number of regular paying clients assumes robust marketing and referral systems, which may take some years to put into place. Experienced counsellors in the field suggest that building such a private practice is a gradual process rather than something that can be set up overnight.

Finding paid employment as a counsellor: Exploring the example of workplace counselling

Increasingly, finding employment seems to be a question of adapting your skills and background for a specialist niche area of employment, or at least of combining a number of such specialisms within a broader range of work. One example of a relatively specialised area of work is that of counselling in the workplace. This is discussed simply as one specific example. You will need to undertake a similar survey for almost any area of potential employment as a counsellor, whether this is schools- or university-based, in IAPT or the NHS, or in a specialist voluntary or third sector organisation.

Workplace counselling is an area of employment for counsellors that has seen rapid growth during the past two decades. In part, this rise has been fuelled by litigation over workplace stress. The courts established that organisations providing confidential workplace counselling would be largely insured against such claims (Jenkins, 2008, 2010). In addition, research suggests that workplace counselling can be effective in reducing rising levels of stress and increasing employee satisfaction rates (McLeod, 2010). Counsellors working in the field, however, emphasise that it requires more than just a strong desire to work in this sector. Effective workplace counsellors must also have a keen sense of how organisations function, the distinctive nature of organisational cultures and how to communicate effectively at every level of the organisation, from the manual worker, through middle management, and up to senior executive level (see Box 8.1).

Box 8.1 Working as a workplace counsellor

I love the age range of my clients, covering the whole gamut of working lives. Such a richness of life experience. As a therapist in training, I enjoyed counselling very young people (and I still do in my current practice with students), but I definitely relish that richness, that variety that the workplace offers. ...

But there are, of course, challenges for a newcomer to workplace counselling. When I first walked into my office – yes, I notice that word 'office' too – I was a bit unconvinced about how 'therapeutic' it felt. There was a lamp, a rug, some paintings of peaceful scenes on the walls, the obligatory box of tissues ... and quite a bit of office furniture. And I'm in an office building. It makes me aware that in-house workplace counselling is very much a distinct branch of therapy.

But it's curious that I have such little contact with the organisation that has brought me together with my clients. I am an insider, but I am an outsider. I begin to form a picture of the way the organisation, and individuals within it, impact on staff. There may be a problem that is particular to one department, something that seems to be causing ripples of distress. I feel frustrated that I am dealing with the fallout, but not with the cause. But I have to be clear with myself. I'm not there as a workplace crusader. I'm not a union rep. I'm not asked to make judgments on the way people are treated – I just have to be there for my client, with all that that means. (Green, 2014: 27)

So how do you manage to get a job in workplace counselling? First, it is important to scope out the nature of the employment field and do some homework. Hughes (2015) suggests that the range of provision in work-place counselling is quite varied. It can include Employee Assistance Providers (EAPs), in-house counselling services, sessional and *ad hoc* work-place counselling, self-employed workplace counselling or, more rarely, retainer-contracted workplace counselling (Hughes, 2015: 5). Middleton goes on to offer a detailed outline of what potential EAP employers are looking for in applicants for workplace counselling (see Box 8.2).

Box 8.2   Requirements for finding work as a workplace counsellor

Recruiting counsellors to our network:

The three most important aspects that we require from our counsel-lors could be summed up as follows:

1. Experience and knowledge of working short term. This requires the ability to make both an assessment and a good ending, and in between the two, to achieve some focused work in the middle.
2. The ability to organise diaries and write timely notes.
3. An understanding of the business world and how organisations work.

Our selection process is quite rigorous. Regardless of background train-ing, we ask for:

- Accreditation by BACP or equivalent professional body;
- Five years' post-qualifying experience;
- A good understanding of short-term counselling;
- Two references (at least one must be a current supervisor);
- A minimum of £1,000,000 professional indemnity insurance;
- CRB [now Disclosure and Barring Scheme] check, followed by a telephone interview and photo of room;
- Suitable premises. (Middleton, 2013: 6)

Interestingly, the person specification provided in Box 8.2 once again stresses the importance of knowing about the dynamics of work by demonstrating 'an understanding of the business world and how organisations work'. This is repeatedly emphasised in the professional literature on workplace counselling. Having this awareness of organisational context is arguably crucial for work in *any* setting, whether this is in a school, a university, a voluntary organisation, or the NHS.

Adopting a model of 'portfolio employment'

This discussion may run the risk of overly emphasising some of the *problems* involved in finding paid employment as a counsellor. Certainly, it pays to be realistic about the nature of the job market, and about the limited number of full-time counselling posts in the field. 'One solution adopted by many counsellors is to develop a "portfolio career": that is, to use several part-time jobs or a combination of employed and freelance work to make up a full-time working week. Examples include combining working for an agency with private practice or teaching, or combining counselling work with work in a previous occupation, related or not' (Allen, 2015: 27).

This term, 'portfolio employment', keeps coming up in any informed discussion about job opportunities for counsellors. As suggested above, it refers to the process of taking on a number of different roles, e.g. as a counsellor, supervisor and trainer, and thus combining their respective income streams. This provides a high degree of variety, in that each working day tends to be different, with new contexts and fresh challenges. Portfolio employment could also reflect the situation of a counsellor who may be in a process of *transition*, i.e. in moving by degrees, from one main form of employment, perhaps as a teacher, nurse or manager, to various paid forms of counselling work, possibly including some private practice.

This term seems to have been first used by Charles Handy, a management expert, writing about working within voluntary organisations, where he referred to the rise of a new type of pattern of employment, namely 'a portfolio of work, some paid, some partly paid, some given for free' (Handy, 1988: 160) (see Box 8.3). In many ways, the term seems to sum up many of the opportunities, but also the frustrations, that are necessarily involved in working as a counsellor. It also captures some of the dilemmas facing counsellors caught in the 'accreditation trap' (discussed below), where counsellors are unable to gain paid employment until they have completed 450 hours of counselling practice, often undertaken as a volunteer after qualifying.

Box 8.3 Emerging new patterns of work in voluntary organisations: A management view

The heart of the core will probably always have to be paid full-time professionals, for only they can provide the necessary continuity and assurance of standards. But the core could be very small (as it already is in the best-regulated businesses), the contractual fringe much larger. Now the contractual fringe, made up of the self-employed and the small cooperative or self-managed group, *could* be the volunteers, increasingly well trained and well qualified, giving of themselves professionally for part of their time. The 'pay' which they would receive, in this version of the psychological contract, would be the training and experience that would allow them to feel, and be, professional. (Handy, 1988: 160–161, original emphasis)

Handy (1988) also identified some of the wider financial and funding pressures operating within many voluntary, or third sector, organisations. These pressures effectively limit the opportunities for providing paid employment to any other than a very narrow, central core, composed of managers and salaried senior staff. Key service-delivery tasks are then largely undertaken by a much wider periphery. This outer layer is made up of part-time paid employees, volunteers, or students on placement. Making the transition, from the outer periphery to the inner core of paid staff, therefore becomes an increasingly competitive process for those wanting paid work. In addition, funding for voluntary agencies has itself become much more short-term and project-driven, further accentuating the vulnerability of the organisation to periodic financial crisis.

Developing a new specialism and undertaking further training or individual accreditation as a counsellor

Other options for qualified counsellors include adding to your skill-set by developing a specialism, undertaking further training or undertaking the process of achieving accreditation as a counsellor.

Developing specialist competences

There is a growing recognition that certain areas of practice, such as working with children and young people, require additional levels of knowledge, skills and expertise beyond that acquired in working with adult clients.

This has led to the development of specific competences and a recognised curriculum for working with children and young people (BACP Professional Standards, 2016). In addition, there is an expectation for counsellors working with children and young people to have completed 50 hours of placement counselling with this client group and to have completed the relevant specialist curriculum. Some free distance-learning specialist training is already available via the MindEd counselling training resource (see Resources section at the end of this chapter). The process of devising specialist areas is likely to accelerate in the coming period, as successive groups of counsellors claim that a distinctive area of expertise is necessary to work with specific issues or with certain client groups.

Training for further counselling qualifications

One option is perhaps to look to pursue further academic qualifications. This may be partly because of the sheer pleasure of studying a subject like counselling. It could also be to improve employability and future job prospects in what is a highly competitive field. For many counsellors, it is a difficult choice to make, i.e. whether to focus on getting accreditation or to invest (both financially and emotionally) in undertaking further study. What form this study might take will depend on your previous history of study and on the level of academic qualification achieved. Students exiting with a Diploma in Counselling, or a variant of this, such as an Advanced Diploma, may want to study for a degree, as counselling increasingly moves towards becoming a graduate-only profession. Undergraduate degree courses can provide combined qualifications in counselling skills or counselling studies, taken together with health studies, psychology or complementary therapies. Some undergraduate courses lead to a degree in counselling and include a qualification in counselling on completion of a supervised placement and the associated assessment of practice.

Many students may have taken a less academic route, by completing a Diploma in a Further Education college, or via a private training provider. For those who do not have a degree, even perhaps in another unrelated subject, there is the option offered at some universities of taking additional modules to gain a 'top-up degree' in counselling studies. A similar route may be available for those students wanting to access postgraduate training by moving from their Diploma onto an MA or MSc qualification, again by taking additional advanced modules in ethics, professional practice and supervision. Having an MA or MSc should demonstrate a real facility in understanding and carrying out research to a current, or potential, employer.

Beyond Master's level, students can undertake a traditional PhD in counselling, usually based on their own very detailed research into a specific topic, for three years' full-time or five years' part-time study. An alternative to this route is to opt for a more practice-based Professional Doctorate in Counselling, where students are often experienced and often senior practitioners in their particular field. Students carry out a series of linked research studies and long essays to gain their ultimate qualification. Having or undertaking a PhD or Professional Doctorate is not a requirement for employment in the field, even at management level, outside employment as a counsellor trainer in a Higher Education setting.

For students with a first degree in psychology, there is an additional option available besides those outlined above. Psychology graduates can apply for MA or MSc courses, but also have the option of counting this training towards a qualification in counselling psychology. This can be achieved by following British Psychological Society requirements for the competence-based independent graduate route, under the guidance of a suitably qualified coordinating supervisor (see BPS guidance: www. bps.org.uk/system/files/Public%20files/Quals/qcop_candidate_hand book_aug_2012_with_hcpc_change.pdf). Alternatively, there is the route of applying for a Professional Doctorate in Counselling Psychology, via three years' full-time study. Private training providers, in turn, are increasingly aware of the shift towards a demand for graduate- or post-graduate-level training in counselling. A number of these have established academic validation from universities, such as Metanoia with Middlesex University, particularly with regard to teaching, supervising and assessing research at advanced levels.

Whether or not you opt for further academic study, counsellors generally are keen to learn about new areas of work and to update their knowledge, understanding and skills, and not simply because this is a formal requirement of professional membership. Counselling journals are full of adverts for generic and specialist training, from one-day workshops to more extended training programmes, for everything from bereavement to trauma work. It is always worth checking whether the training is accredited and by whom, e.g. by BACP or UKCP. It is important to know whether it simply requires attendance or carries a degree of assessment. Such assessment may take the form of supervised practice, completion of a case study or an assessment of a taped transcript of client work. As with any form of training, having attended any number of days' training does not necessarily equate with improved knowledge, skills or self-awareness. It is worth being selective about choosing further CPD. Look for the source of accreditation, the reputation of the trainer and the overall value of the training as an investment for your own developing practice.

Counselling for Depression

One example of further training which meets these criteria is the programme for training in Counselling for Depression (CfD). This has been developed in response to concerns about the much-disputed evidence base for counselling clients with depression that is judged not to be severe or chronic, according to medical criteria (Sanders and Hill, 2014). Counselling for Depression is a 'NICE recommended treatment programme for people with persistent sub-threshold depressive symptoms or mild to moderate depression' (Coles, 2012: 24). It comprises a five-day CPD training, followed by 80 hours of assessed and supervised practice, for Diploma-level-qualified counsellors with a minimum of two years' experience working with common mental health problems in a healthcare setting. Completion of CfD can be counted towards accreditation, which is outlined in more detail below.

Working towards individual accreditation as a counsellor

BACP accredits counselling organisations, workshops, courses at Diploma level and individual practitioners. Accreditation is sometimes described as the 'gold standard' for recognised practice as a counsellor. Hence, 'accreditation acknowledges mature competence and has become the hallmark of an independent, ethical practitioner' (Coles, 2012: 24). It can come as an unwelcome surprise to some counsellors that, having completed an often arduous and expensive counselling training, there is yet another hurdle to become fully recognised as an established practitioner. This is the step of working towards and finally achieving individual accreditation as a counsellor (see Box 8.4).

Box 8.4   Applying for individual accreditation as a counsellor

I have been a Person-Centred counsellor for 18 years, and have had my own practice for most of that time. I have only recently become BACP-accredited. I think there was some resistance on my behalf to the process due to feelings of (a) why do I need to prove to BACP that I am a competent counsellor and 'run through certain hoops'? (b) what will I gain from it?

As the deadline date for Registration drew near (I had not attended an accredited training course), I decided to make the full application for accreditation rather than do the computer exercise. I thought the challenge of doing pieces of reflective writing about my philosophy and practice would enable me to evaluate my work seriously. I also had a wonderful supervisor, who was 'on my case' regarding doing the accreditation and was not going to let me off the hook!

Once I had made the decision, I was determined to finish it without further procrastination (one of my failings). The challenge of completing

---

the philosophy assignment within 900 words was testing, to say the least. I still reread it now on occasions, to remind myself of its significance and the passion I have for the person-centred model. The two case studies I chose made me evaluate carefully what had contributed to any therapeutic change. This included listening to tapes again. It made me check on whether I was truly offering the Core Conditions and, if not, identify any which were not as prominent in my practice. That was a sobering exercise!

As regards what I have gained from accreditation, I would say (a) the sense of pride at achieving it and putting on paper what I do as a therapist; (b) I now work for those EAPs who require accreditation status; (c) through advertising my logo, including on my website, I have definitely had more enquiries, resulting in extra work.

Andrew Webb

In order to apply for BACP accreditation you must first be a Registered Member of BACP, have successfully completed a BACP-accredited or other appropriate professional training of at least 450 hours, and have been in practice for at least three years and completed a minimum of 450 supervised practice hours. In addition, you need to have an ongoing supervision arrangement in place for 1½ hours per month during your period of practice and to be covered by professional indemnity insurance.

The application requires evidence of the individual's training, practice and supervision, including a reflective practice section (www.bacp.co.uk/accreditation/Individual%20Practitioners/).

In the longer-term, it is possible to become a senior accredited member and to specialise as a practitioner and/or as a supervisor in group or individual supervision. These senior areas of practice include senior accredited practitioner counsellor/psychotherapist, or a specialist accredited counsellor/psychotherapist for children and young people, or in healthcare.

While working towards accreditation is a necessary step for most practitioners, it is worth mentioning what has been referred to as the 'accreditation trap'. This is the unintended effect of the requirement for 450 hours' counselling practice for accreditation. This requirement, combined with the problems experienced in finding paid, secure employment, may mean that some counsellors have to work unpaid in voluntary or third sector organisations in order to accrue the necessary hours to qualify for accreditation. The existence of this large pool of unpaid volunteer counsellors has produced sharp controversy within the profession, with pointed comparisons being made with other parallel professions. Teachers, social workers and nurses, as members of comparable 'semi-professions', are not required to accrue this level of additional qualifying hours to find employment, but usually undergo an initial probationary employment period before having this confirmed by their employer.

Developing new roles as a group facilitator, counsellor trainer, supervisor, researcher or coach

A further set of options relate to developing new roles in addition to your core skills as a counsellor. These include the roles of group facilitator, counsellor trainer or coach.

Developing a role as a group facilitator

Counsellors will be familiar with the nature of group work, at least as a participant, through their own experience of taking part in groups as part of their training. This can range from participating in skills practice triads through to community meetings and to personal development groups. Many counselling services will also offer clients access to therapeutic groups, as an addition or alternative to individual counselling. The interpersonal skills evident in group work, such as reflecting feelings, observing non-verbal communication and summarising content, clearly overlap with those used in one-to-one counselling. Many counsellors are attracted by the possibility of running groups for clients. This may be partly as a way of extending their own repertoire of skills and expertise, but also in order to offer a valuable and effective form of therapy to a wider number of clients. One small research study by King (n: 66) found that over half (53%) of the respondents working in the NHS and other settings had experience of facilitating groups (King, 2011: 29). Almost two-thirds of respondents (62%) were interested in offering group work as part of their therapeutic repertoire, while a slightly smaller proportion (45%) had received some form of training in group work, although much of this was of fairly limited duration (see Box 8.5).

Box 8.5   Working as a group facilitator

I worked as a Group Facilitator on the Counselling MA at Manchester University for over 16 years, taking up the role shortly after completion of my own MA in Counselling. One of the strengths of the Manchester course was the exploration of a range of counselling modalities, and I became intrigued by ideas about unconscious processes and the richness of psychodynamic theory. After completing the MA, I undertook a one-year Group Analysis training, and then a four-year Diploma in Psychodynamic Psychotherapy. These qualifications led to my registration as a psychoanalytic psychotherapist with UKCP (United Kingdom Council for Psychotherapy).

Groups are complex and challenging environments. They can be exhilarating, bewildering, containing, painful and healing in equal measure. My grounding in psychodynamic theory was crucial, helping me to function effectively as group conductor. It enabled me to orientate myself and to continue to be thoughtful in the face of often very powerful transference feelings and projections.

Counselling training invites students to question and re-evaluate their personal philosophies and beliefs. This inevitably impacts on their relationships. Students are challenged in a more personal way than in purely academic courses, and this can be stressful, albeit ultimately rewarding. The PD (Personal Development) group is a place where students can explore some of the thoughts and feelings that might be difficult to express in the wider learning community. Though not primarily therapy, PD provides a vital therapeutic breathing space.

Facilitating PD groups is undoubtedly complex, although it has been a privilege to undertake this role. There have been many positive aspects, but I would highlight three. First, I have hugely valued being part of a process in which students invest so much courage, honesty and trust. Secondly, witnessing individual students begin to own their potency and skill, and seeing the group recognise its own therapeutic potential and authority, is profoundly moving. Thirdly, the numerous personal and intellectual challenges that I've faced as a group facilitator have contributed in a very real way to my own professional development.

Maureen Charlton

For many counsellors, like Maureen Charlton, gaining experience as a group facilitator is an attractive next step in building your professional career. While you can gain experience by shadowing and co-working with more experienced colleagues, it is worth recognising that there are limits to this type of learning, and that formal training in leading groups is likely to be essential at some stage.

Working as a counsellor trainer

Having qualified in counselling, many counsellors are similarly attracted by the possibility of gaining experience and working as a counselling trainer. This may be at the initial levels of training others in counselling skills, or in a more specialist area, or in working at Diploma or post-qualifying level. The BACP *Core Curriculum* (2009) mainly focuses on organisational and academic requirements, such as the curriculum discussed throughout this book. In terms of staff working on BACP-accredited courses, the specific requirements are set out below.

BACP *Core Curriculum* (2009)

B2. Teaching and learning

B2.1 All course staff must be appropriately qualified and demonstrate competence between them to cover all elements of the course.

B2.2 All training staff for the course should be familiar with and agree to work with the current BACP *Ethical Framework for Good Practice in Counselling and Psychotherapy* (2009) (the *Ethical Framework*).

B2.3 Course staff must have regular meetings and access to other forms of support, consultation and professional development. (BACP, 2009: 6)

BACP *Ethical Framework for the Counselling Professions* (2016)

Training and education:

62. All trainers will have the skills, attitudes and knowledge required to be competent teachers and facilitators of learning for what is being provided.

67. All providers of training and education will model high levels of good practice in their work, particularly with regard to expected levels of competence and professionalism, relationship building, the management of personal boundaries, any dual relationships, conflicts of interest and avoiding exploitation. (BACP, 2016: 12)

The first set of requirements apply specifically for working on BACP-accredited Diploma-level training courses and would have relevance in broad generic terms for working on any form of counselling training. The *Ethical Framework for the Counselling Professions* (BACP, 2016) highlights the need to provide accurate information to prospective students to enable their informed choice and for the selection and assessment processes to be fair, respectful and transparent. George Brooks describes his experience of working as a counsellor trainer in Box 8.6.

Box 8.6 Working as a counsellor trainer

After training, and consequently qualifying, as a counsellor at a local training agency, I was asked to act as a co-trainer on the same course I trained on, partly I think because of my teaching background. It is so important for counsellors to utilise their expertise from previous work, if they have had it, to develop a portfolio approach to their new career. Since then I have become more aware that I wanted to at least begin my career with a portfolio approach, even though I am now beginning to consolidate my work between supervision and my counselling business in schools.

I did this for a few years and then, while doing my Master's at Manchester University in Educational Psychology, I was asked to apply for the part-time post of teaching associate on the MA Counselling programme.

I have always enjoyed working with trainee counsellors, as I am passionate about it and feel I have a lot to give in this respect and I have found that working as a counsellor trainer has been extremely good for me in terms of my own development in the field of counselling. I have a much better appreciation of theory and research, which has improved my practice, and this has enabled me to build a very successful business in schools. Finally, being a counsellor trainer has been important for me in helping me to stretch what I think I am capable of, consolidating my skills and giving me a confidence in myself that was not there before.

George Brooks

George Brooks' experience mirrors that of many counsellors who successfully make the transition from becoming a qualified counsellor to starting work as a counsellor trainer. In this case, having a prior qualification and experience as a teacher can be an advantage, although the demands of training counsellors are quite different from school-based teaching in many ways. Taking on the role of counsellor trainer requires a good understanding of group dynamics and a high level of confidence in one's own professional practice as a counsellor. Background experience in setting learning objectives and devising a varied, but purposeful, sequence of learning activities can be challenging for newcomers to training. In many ways, counsellor training is essentially a form of working with a *group*, but with the specific task of facilitating both group and individual learning. The essential components of counsellor training, such as clarity about task, roles and boundaries – i.e. time, space and membership – are common to any planned group work activity.

Many counsellors will already have expertise and confidence in their own modality and in their client work, but may lack experience in either working with groups or in training activities. One of the tried-and-tested ways of making this transition is similar to that of group work, namely by initially 'shadowing' a more experienced group worker or counsellor trainer. This can involve taking on another more experienced trainer's style and even, to some extent, their *persona*, before adapting this experience to shape a more unique and individual personal training style. Formal training as a teacher can be useful and is increasingly a requirement in Further and Higher Education settings for acquiring part-time, and later full-time, work as a trainer. In Higher Education settings, advanced qualifications, such as a PhD or Professional Doctorate, are now generally required, together with evidence of publication and research activity, or at least an aptitude for undertaking these activities.

Training to become a supervisor

All counsellors will have their own first-hand experience of undergoing supervision, as it is an essential part of the training process to become qualified as a counsellor. For many, training as a supervisor will seem to be the logical next step, having once gained some more counselling experience, perhaps by working in a range of settings or with a range of different client groups and issues. Training as a supervisor may seem likely to expand your awareness of the whole process of therapy, to add substantially to existing knowledge and skills, and to link in to practice, rather than move into what may be potentially unknown and less familiar areas, such as group work or training roles. Hazel Batchelor describes her own experience of making this transition from counsellor after undertaking supervision training (see Box 8.7).

Box 8.7 On being a supervisor

Some four years after I completed my counselling training, I decided to train to be a supervisor, undertaking the training at the same place, Manchester University, and qualifying as a supervisor in 2004. My counselling training was in integrative practice and I wanted a training that reflected this framework. The choice was also based on my knowledge of the tutors, whom I respected and liked. The model used on my course was Hawkins and Shohet's (2012) framework.

If someone contacts me about supervision, I arrange to meet with them, to see if we can work together, which involves both talking about ourselves and about the work we do and our theoretical orientations. When someone comes to a supervision session, we start by agreeing an agenda, so I expect the supervisee to have thought about what issues they need to bring to the session. We also consider how much time to allocate, as sometimes tricky issues, such as those that are shame-inducing, can fail to be addressed by too much consideration of less tricky issues. What I particularly enjoy when working with a supervisee is when we gradually unwrap an issue that is difficult and come to an understanding of why this is proving to be problematic. For example, it may be that it is too close to an unresolved issue for the counsellor so that the counsellor may need to address this issue in their own counselling. Knowing about and working with some of my supervisees over several years has also enabled sufficient trust and understanding to develop to allow me to safely challenge them and their practice, which will ultimately enhance their work with their client. I and my supervisees really value the insights

> that the depth of our relationship brings, paralleling the counselling rela-
> tionship but being quite different and distinct. I really enjoy being a super-
> visor, and I learn from my supervisees, just as I do from my clients.
>
> Hazel Batchelor

There is a huge range of training available for making the transition from counsellor to supervisor of counsellors, which Hazel Batchelor outlines above. The contact hours of supervisor training courses can vary from 12 to 500 hours (Coles, 2014). The relevant competences for supervisors have been devised and a curriculum put in place. This is set at the level of a postgraduate diploma and provides 60 hours of training. Candidates need to have one year's post-qualifying experience, and to have had a minimum of one-and-a-half hour's supervision themselves per month. The course requires a minimum of 40 hours' logged supervisory practice, 10 hours' consultative supervision, and completion of assignments, including a written assignment, audio-recording analysis and personal reflective journal (BACP Professional Standards, 2014).

Developing competence in undertaking counselling research

The growing role and acknowledgement of research has been a major feature of the professionalisation of counselling and psychotherapy. This research can be traced back to the earliest days of therapeutic work, whether with Freud's case studies, or Rogers' investigation of the necessary and sufficient conditions for client change. At a broader level, the *Ethical Framework for the Counselling Professions* (BACP, 2016) welcomes and seeks to support research activity by the counselling community. It emphasises the key role of informed consent and the principle of avoiding harm to participants (see below). The ethical requirements for research in counselling are also governed by a separate and additional set of BACP Guidelines (www.bacp.co.uk/research/ethical_guidelines.php).

BACP *Ethical Framework for the Counselling Professions* (2016)

70. When undertaking research we will be rigorously attentive to the quality and integrity of the research process, the knowledge claims arising from the research and how the results are disseminated.

71. All research that we undertake will conform to the BACP Ethical Guidelines for researching counselling and psychotherapy.

73. All research will be reviewed in advance to ensure the rights and interests of participants have been considered independently of the researcher.

74. The research methods used will comply with standards of good practice in any services being delivered and will not adversely affect clients. (2016: 13)

Many counsellors are, in a sense, already taking part in research at an informal and individual level, by asking their clients to routinely complete outcome measures and by reflecting on their own practice, in group and individual supervision. There are growing opportunities for counsellors to become involved in research within their own agencies (see Box 8.8). This can be through carrying out audits and evaluations of their service, e.g. for annual reports or as evidence used in bids for funding or for service expansion. Involvement in more formal academic research is a key part of postgraduate education at Master's level and beyond, where counsellors need to carry out small-scale interviews with practitioners and clients or devise larger-scale questionnaire surveys to inform practice. The latter can be extremely influential in shaping policy in developing counselling provision, as for example with the BACP survey for the Welsh Assembly. This resulted in the Welsh Assembly implementing statutory provision for secondary school-based counselling for all young people in Wales (BACP, 2007).

Box 8.8   Undertaking practice-based research as a counsellor

I [Jill Collins] work in a staff counselling service in a large university, providing time-limited counselling for 9,000 staff, and am part of a team of four counsellors with two trainee counsellors on placement, offering a mix of therapeutic approaches: cognitive analytic, integrative, person-centred and psychodynamic. In 2008, aware of the potential vulnerability of our service in a climate of financial cuts, we decided to undertake a piece of practice-based research to evaluate our service during a 12-month period, starting with a very basic question: 'Does what we do make a difference and, if it does, does this effect last?' We planned to answer this by assessing clients at their first and last session, and at three and six months afterwards. (Collins et al., 2011: 2)

The work undertaken by Jill Collins and her colleagues produced valuable evidence of the effectiveness of the counselling service within the wider university as an institutional setting. It had wider implications, beyond university counselling, to the broader setting of staff counselling in other contexts. This research was written up as a peer-reviewed paper for *Counselling and Psychotherapy Research* (Collins et al., 2012) and was also published in several of the BACP divisional journals in order to get the positive message out to interested readers and stake-holders. Taking part in this kind of research process requires a real commitment to see the work through to the end, the necessary research skills, access to external ethical review, and a degree of employer sup-port and recognition of the time and work involved by all participants.

However, if committing yourself to doing research seems somewhat academic and rather daunting at this stage, then a first tentative step might be to commit to reading at least one paper in the quarterly BACP journal *Counselling and Psychotherapy Research*, or even to discuss it with like-minded others in a journal club. In addition, you could join a practice research network (PRN), which gives access to current debates and findings in specific areas of practice, such as the PRN for school-based counselling for children and young people (www.bacp. co.uk/schools/).

Taking on a new role as a coach

Finally, there is the option of using many of your developed skills in counselling, but with a different focus – in the form of coaching. According to BACP, 'coaching may be characterised by interventions which are more likely to be developmental in nature, build on existing strengths, less likely to be accompanied by high levels of distress, and driven by the client's desire to develop their potential, and/or under-standing of themselves, their beliefs, behaviours and actions' (www. bacpcoaching.co.uk/position-statement). Many of the defining features of counselling, such as possessing clear ethics, making use of supervision, holding an awareness of relationship and context, and using explicit con-tracting, are also essential to effective coaching (Cox et al., 2010). Pam Winter writes about making her own transition below (see Box 8.9).

Box 8.9   My journey from counsellor to executive coach

I have worked as a person-centred/experiential counsellor/therapist for 30 years now and continue to practise and love my work. However, about seven years ago, I decided to also train as an executive coach, that is, working with employees in their organisations to enhance their personal and professional development in the context of work. This decision partly emerged from my experience of running a staff counselling service and

(Continued)

(Continued)

realising that many of the issues staff brought were related to the organisational context and culture, such as systemic issues, power relationships and group/team dynamics. These issues fascinated me, and I saw that it would be helpful to offer staff an opportunity to work with these interpersonal issues via coaching and take my work into organisations. I chose a Gestalt Coaching Diploma, which was perfect given my psychological and humanistic value base and orientation.

As my working background was also in teaching, I felt I could offer most in education settings and so my coaching clients are staff, managers and leaders in schools and academies. The work has a present and future focus, but is also about emotional support and time to reflect and think. Busy and often stressed staff value this time enormously and our work together is usually very stimulating and rewarding. I feel very passionate and committed to this work and it's a great balance and sometimes antidote to being a therapist. There is much pressure and responsibility on many employees today and I believe a need and opportunity for more therapists to work in organisations. Crucially, we can bring a deeper intrapersonal/psychological perspective into the workplace, which places both the human and the 'humane' back into organisations!

Pam Winter

As Pam Winter describes, coaching can provide not only a new area of work, but also a stimulating contrast to the very specific focus of one-to-one counselling. Like workplace counselling or, indeed, with any counselling, the organisational context of coaching plays a significant role, whether it is working with young people in a school, with people with disability who are returning to paid employment, or with staff in the context of major company restructuring. The BACP Coaching Division and its journal provide information and networking opportunities for counsellors wanting to make the transition to becoming a coach, or for those wanting to add coaching to their existing portfolio of skills.

Summary

This chapter has reviewed the changing context of counsellor employment and touched on a number of post-qualifying options, such as working as a counsellor in private practice, or finding paid employment as a counsellor, particularly by adopting a model of 'portfolio employment'. Other options include training for further counselling qualifications, developing a specialism, e.g. in working with children and young people, or by working towards individual accreditation as a counsellor. Some of the possible roles associated with the core practice of counselling include developing a role as a group worker, working as a counsellor trainer, undertaking training to become a supervisor, developing competence in undertaking counselling research, or taking on a new role as a coach.

Resources

Web resources

Counselling Mind-Ed (free online training material)

Jenkins, P. and Williams, A. (2014) *Key Differences in Counselling Adults and Children*. Mind-Ed (www.minded.org.uk).

Private practice

Rye, J. (2011) 'Adding it up', *The Independent Practitioner*, Autumn, pp. 6–9, http://bacppp.org.uk/_sitedata/1391515928%20Z3A0IvmuG/JournalsFrom OldSite/8221_adding%20it%20up.pdf

Weblink to video: Rye, J. (2013) 'Avoiding pitfalls and setbacks in private practice', Psychologists Protection Society CPD Event, available at: www.theprofessionalprac titioner.net/index.php/cpd-activities/15-cpd-activity-pitfalls-in-private-practice

Research

Ballinger, L. (2014) 'How person-centred counselling trainers understand and experience their roles in the present British context', *British Journal of Guidance and Counselling*, 42(2), 154–165.

Small interview survey (n: 5) of person-centred trainers with experience of a wide range of settings, contrasting the satisfying nature of the work with the personal pressures involved, such as high levels of stress and organisational constraints.

McLeod, J. (2010) 'The effectiveness of workplace counselling: A systematic review', *Counselling and Psychotherapy Research*, 10(4), 238–248.

Systematic review of research into workplace counselling, finding convincing evidence as an effective means of helping employees cope with their psychological, emotional and behavioural problems.

West, W. and Clark, V. (2004) 'Learnings from a qualitative study into counselling supervision: Listening to supervisor and supervisee', *Counselling and Psychotherapy Research*, 4(2), 20–26.

Small qualitative study (n: 3), using Interpersonal Process Recall to explore the potential meanings of one particular supervisor–supervisee dyad and explore the wider implications for supervision and qualitative research.

Further reading

Hanley, T., Lennie, C. and West, W. (2013) *Introducing Counselling and Psychotherapy Research*. London: Sage.

Standard user-friendly textbook on entering into research at Master's level.

Oldale, M. and Cooke, M. (2015) *Making the Most of Counselling and Psychotherapy Placements*. London: Sage.

Detailed, practical guide to the complexities of selecting, applying for and learning from your practice on placement.

References

Ainsworth, D. (2015) 'What went wrong at Kids Company?', *Civil Society*, 6 August, www.civilsociety.co.uk/finance/indepth/content/20171/the_fall_of_kids_company (accessed November 2015).

Aldridge, S. (2010) Counselling – An Insecure Profession? A Sociological and Historical Analysis. Thesis submitted for the degree of Doctor of Philosophy at the University of Leicester, November 2010.

Aldridge, S. (2014) *A Short Introduction to Counselling*. London: Sage.

Allan, C. (2016) 'The benefit cap isn't about reality, but how things look', *Guardian*, 9 November.

Allen, V. (2015) 'The work is out there', *Counselling at Work*, Spring, pp. 26–27.

American Psychiatric Association (APA) (2013) *Diagnostic and Statistical Manual of Mental Disorders*. Fifth edition (DSM-5). Washington, DC: APA.

American Psychological Association (2016) *Professional Health and Wellbeing for Psychologists*, www.apapracticecentral.org/ce/self-care/well-being.aspx (accessed November 2016).

Beauchamp, T. and Childress, J. (2008) *Principles of Biomedical Ethics*. Sixth edition. Oxford: Oxford University Press.

Bedor, C. (2015) 'Developing agency policy and practice and evaluating organisational policies on confidentiality and record keeping', in T. Bond and B. Mitchels (eds), *Confidentiality and Record Keeping in Counselling and Psychotherapy*. Second edition. London: BACP/Sage. pp. 105–117.

Brettle, A., Hill, A. and Jenkins, P. (2008) 'Counselling in primary care: A systematic review of the evidence', *Counselling and Psychotherapy Research*, 8(4), 207–214.

British Association for Counselling (1984) *Code of Ethics and Practice for Counsellors*. Rugby: BAC.

British Association for Counselling (1990) *Code of Ethics and Practice for Counsellors*. Rugby: BAC.

British Association for Counselling (1992) *Code of Ethics and Practice for Counsellors*. Rugby: BAC.

British Association for Counselling and Psychotherapy (BACP) (2002) *Ethical Framework for Good Practice in Counselling and Psychotherapy*. Rugby: BACP.

British Association for Counselling and Psychotherapy (2007) *Counselling in Schools: A Research Study into Services for Children and Young People, Commissioned by the Welsh Assembly Government*. Lutterworth: BACP.

British Association for Counselling and Psychotherapy (2009) 'Core Curriculum', in *Accreditation of Training Courses*. Fifth edition. Lutterworth: BACP. www.bacp.co.uk/docs/pdf/15014_corecurriculum07.pdf

British Association for Counselling and Psychotherapy (2012a) *What are Counselling and Psychotherapy?* Lutterworth: BACP, www.bacp.co.uk/crs/Training/whatiscounselling.php

British Association for Counselling and Psychotherapy (2012b) *Statement of Ethical Practice*, 18 September. Lutterworth: BACP.

British Association for Counselling and Psychotherapy (2016) *Ethical Framework for the Counselling Professions*. Lutterworth: BACP.

BACP Professional Standards (2014) *Counselling Supervision Training Curriculum*. Lutterworth: BACP.

BACP Professional Standards (2016) *An Evidenced Informed Curriculum Framework for Young People (11–18 Years): Young People (11–18 Years) Training Curriculum*. Lutterworth: BACP.

British Infertility Counselling Association (BICA) (2012) *Guidelines for Good Practice in Infertility Counselling*. Third edition. London: BICA.

Brownlee, E. (2016) 'How do counsellors view and practise self-care?', *Healthcare Counselling and Psychotherapy Journal*, 16(2), 15–17.

Carson, D. and Bain, A. (2008) *Professional Risk and Working with People*. London: Jessica Kingsley.

Casement, P. (1990) *On Learning from the Patient*. London: Routledge.

Casement, P. (1993) *Further Learning from the Patient: The Analytic Space and Process*. London: Tavistock/Routledge.

Centre for Suicide Research (CSR) (2013) *Assessment of Suicide Risk in People with Depression: A Clinical Guide*. CSR, Department of Psychiatry, University of Oxford, http://cebmh.warne.ox.ac.uk/csr/clinicalguide/docs/riskassessment.pdf

Cohen, S. (2008) 'IAPT: A brief history', *Healthcare Counselling and Psychotherapy Journal*, 8(2), 8–11.

Coles, H. (2012) 'Senior accreditation for healthcare practitioners', *Healthcare Counselling and Psychotherapy Journal*, 12(3), 24–25.

Coles, H. (2014) 'New framework for supervisor training', *Healthcare Counselling and Psychotherapy Journal*, 14(4), 26–27.

Collins, J., Dyer, C. and Shave, D. (2011) 'Counselling in the workplace: How time-limited counselling can effect change in wellbeing', *Counselling at Work*, Autumn, pp. 2–8.

Collins, J., Gibson, A., Parkin, S., Parkinson, R., Shave, D. and Dyer, C. (2012) 'Counselling in the workplace: How time-limited counselling can affect change in well-being', *Counselling and Psychotherapy Research*, 12(2), 84–92.

Cooper, M. (2008) *Essential Research Findings in Counselling and Psychotherapy*. London: Sage.

Copeland, S. (2005) *Counselling Supervision in Organisations: Professional and Ethical Dilemmas Explored*. London: Routledge.

Cowley, J. and Groves, V. (2016) 'The Cardiff model of short-term engagement', in D. Mair (ed.), *Short-Term Counselling in Higher Education: Context, Theory and Practice*. London: Routledge. pp. 108–126.

Cox, E., Bachkirova, T. and Clutterbuck, D. (eds) (2010) *The Complete Handbook of Coaching*. London: Sage.

Craig, D. (2017) 'Eyes on the prize: Achieving IAPT compliance within third sector mental health provision', *Healthcare Counselling and Psychotherapy Journal*, 15(1): 17–21.

Cromarty, K. and Richards, K. (2009) 'How do secondary school counsellors work with other professionals?', *Counselling and Psychotherapy Research*, 9(3), 182–186.

Culley, S. and Bond, T. (2011) *Integrative Counselling Skills in Action*. Third edition. London: Sage.

Department for Education (DfE) (2015) *Working Together to Safeguard Children: A Guide to Inter-Agency Working to Safeguard and Promote the Welfare of Children*. London: DfE. www.education.gov.uk/aboutdfe/statutory (accessed November 2016).

Department of Health (DoH) (2011) *Regulated Activity (Adults): The Definition of 'Regulated Activities' (Adults) as Defined by the Safeguarding Vulnerable Groups Act 2006 from 10 September 2012*. London: DoH.

Department of Health (2014) *Care and Support Statutory Guidance Issued under the Care Act 2014*. London: DoH.

Despenser, S. (2007) 'Risk assessment: The personal safety of the counsellor', *Therapy Today*, 18(2), 12–17.

Dreyfus, H.L. and Dreyfus, S.E. (1986) *Mind over Machine: The Power of Human Intuition and Expertise in the Era of the Computer*. New York: Free Press.

Dyer, C. (1995) 'Transsexual banned from prison work loses claim', *Guardian*, 1 November.

Etzioni, A. (1969) *The Semi-Professions and Their Organization: Teachers, Nurses and Social Workers*. London: Collier Macmillan.

Foster, J.G. (1971) *Enquiry into the Practice and Effects of Scientology*. London: HMSO.

Fox, C. and Butler, I. (2007) '"If you don't want to tell anyone else you can tell her": Young people's views on school counselling', *British Journal of Guidance and Counselling*, 35(1), 97–114.

Furedi, F. (2003) 'Get rid of professional stabilisers', *Times Higher Education*, 17 October, pp. 22–23.

Furedi, F. (2004) *Therapy Culture: Cultivating Vulnerability in an Uncertain Age*. London: Routledge.

Future Foundation Projects (2004) *The Age of Therapy: Exploring Attitudes Towards and Acceptance of Counselling and Psychotherapy in Modern Britain*. London: Future Foundation.

Gibbard, I. and Hanley, T. (2008) 'A five-year evaluation of person-centred counselling in routine clinical practice in primary care', *Counselling and Psychotherapy Research*, 8(4), 215–222.

Gore-Smith, J. (2015) 'Setting up a cooperative', *Therapy Today*, 26(6), 30–31.

Green, H. (2014) 'The new counsellor', *Counselling at Work*, Spring, p. 26.

Griffith, R. and Tengnah, C. (2010) *Law and Professional Issues in Nursing.* Second edition. Exeter: Learning Matters.

Gross, E. (1967) 'When occupations meet: Professions in trouble', *Hospital Administration*, 12(Summer), 40–59.

Hall, O. and Swindells, J. (2013) 'Inside out: Two views of a prison placement', *Therapy Today*, 24(9), 25–27.

Handy, C. (1988) *Understanding Voluntary Organisations.* Harmondsworth: Penguin.

Happiness Research Institute (2015) *The Facebook Experiment: Does Social Media Affect the Quality of Our Lives?* Copenhagen, Denmark: Happiness Research Institute.

Harris, P. (2012) 'Psychiatrist who backed "gay cure" admits research fatally flawed', *Observer*, 20 May.

Harrison, R. (1972) 'Understanding your organization's character', *Harvard Business Review*, May–June, pp. 119–128.

Hawkins, P. and Shohet, R. (2012) *Supervision in the Helping Professions.* Fourth edition. Maidenhead: Open University Press.

Health and Care Professions Council (HCPC) (2001) *New Professions Process*, www.hpc-uk.org/aboutregistration/aspirantgroups/newprofessions process/ (accessed November 2016).

Her Majesty's Government (HMG) (2015a) *Revised Prevent Duty Guidance for England and Wales.* London: HMG.

Her Majesty's Government (HMG) (2015b) *Information Sharing: Advice for Practitioners Providing Safeguarding Services to Children, Young People, Parents and Carers.* London: HMG.

Heyward, C. (1994) *When Boundaries Betray Us: Beyond Illusions of What is Ethical in Therapy and Life.* New York: Harper Collins.

Hill, A., Brettle, A., Jenkins, P. and Hulme, C. (2008) *Counselling in Primary Care: A Systematic Review of the Evidence.* Lutterworth: BACP.

Howard, A. (2000) *Philosophy for Counselling and Psychotherapy.* London: Macmillan.

Hughes, R. (2015) 'The bigger picture: Finding work', *Counselling at Work*, Winter, p. 5.

Information Commissioner's Office (ICO) (2009) *The Guide to Data Protection.* Wilmslow: ICO.

Information Commissioner's Office (2012) 'ICO's top tips for improving data protection', posted 14 September 2012, https://ico.org.uk/for-organ isations/charity/ (accessed November 2016).

Information Commissioner's Office (2014) *Monetary Penalty Notice*, 28 February, https://ico.org.uk/about-the-ico/news-and-events/news-and-blogs/2014/03/british-pregnancy-advice-service-fined-200-000/ (accessed November 2016).

Information Commissioner's Office (2016) *Overview of the General Data Protection Regulation.* Wilmslow: ICO.

Jenkins, P. (1996) 'Counselling and the law', in S. Palmer, S. Dainow and P. Milner (eds), *Counselling: The BAC Counselling Reader*. London: BAC/ Sage. pp. 451–457.

Jenkins, P. (2006) 'Contracts, ethics and the law', in C. Sills (ed.), *Contracts in Counselling and Psychotherapy*. Second edition. London: Sage. pp. 109–116.

Jenkins, P. (2007a) *Counselling, Psychotherapy and the Law*. Second edition. London: Sage.

Jenkins, P. (2007b) 'Supervision in the dock? Supervision and the law', in K. Tudor and M. Worrall (eds), *Freedom to Practise: Volume 2: Developing Person-Centred Approaches to Supervision*. Ross-on-Wye: PCCS Books. pp. 176–194.

Jenkins, P. (2008) 'Organisational duty of care: Workplace counselling as a shield against litigation?', in A. Kinder, R. Hughes and C. Cooper (eds), *Employee Well-being Support: A Workplace Resource*. Chichester: Wiley. pp. 99–110.

Jenkins, P. (2010) 'Stress and the law', in A. Weinberg, V. Sutherland and C. Cooper (eds), *Organisational Stress Management: A Strategic Approach*. London: Palgrave. pp. 37–52.

Jenkins, P. (2015a) 'Client confidentiality and data protection', in R. Tribe and J. Morrissey (eds), *Handbook of Professional Practice for Psychologists, Counsellors and Psychotherapists*. Second edition. London: Routledge. pp. 47–57.

Jenkins, P. (2015b) 'The legal context of therapy', in R. Tribe and J. Morrissey (eds), *Handbook of Professional Practice for Psychologists, Counsellors and Psychotherapists*. Second edition. London: Routledge. pp. 58–69.

Jenkins, P. (2015c) 'Law and policy', in S. Pattison, M. Robson and A. Beynon (eds), *The Handbook of Counselling Children and Young People*. London: Sage/BACP. pp. 259–276.

Jenkins, P. and Palmer, J. (2012) '"At risk of harm?" An exploratory study of school counsellors in the UK, their perceptions of confidentiality, information sharing and risk management', *British Journal of Guidance and Counselling*, 40(5), 545–559.

Jenkins, P. and Swindells, J. (2015) 'Legal and ethical issues in therapeutic work in the criminal justice system', in P. Jones (ed.), *Interventions in Criminal Justice: A Handbook for Counsellors and Therapists Working in the Criminal Justice System*. Volume Two. Hove: Pavilion Press. pp. 13–34.

Johns, R. (2010) *Using the Law in Social Work*. Fourth edition. Exeter: Learning Matters.

Jones, E. (1987) *The Life and Work of Sigmund Freud*. Harmondsworth: Penguin.

Kakabadse, A. (1982) *Culture of the Social Services*. Aldershot: Gower.

Keeping, C. (2014) 'The processes required for effective interprofessional working', in J. Thomas, K. Pollard and D. Sellman (eds), *Interprofessional Working in Health and Social Care*. Second edition. London: Palgrave Macmillan. pp. 22–34.

Khele, S., Symons, C. and Wheeler, S. (2008) 'An analysis of complaints to the British Association for Counselling and Psychotherapy, 1996–2006', *Counselling and Psychotherapy Research*, 8(2), 124–132.

King, S. (2011) 'Counsellors and group work: The lost domain?', *Healthcare Counselling and Psychotherapy Journal*, 11(2), 28–30.

Kirkbride, R. (2016) *Counselling Children and Young People in Private Practice: A Practical Guide*. London: Karnac.

Lago, C. and Kitchin, D. (1998) *The Management of Counselling and Psychotherapy Agencies*. London: Sage.

Layard, R. (2006) 'Happiness', *Open Mind*, November–December, pp. 6–8.

Lees, J. (1999) 'What is clinical counselling in context?', in J. Lees (ed.), *Clinical Counselling in Context*. London: Routledge. pp. 6–19.

London Multi-Agency (LMA) (2015) *Safeguarding Policies and Procedures*. London: LMA.

McLeod, J. (2010) 'The effectiveness of workplace counselling: A systematic review', *Counselling and Psychotherapy Research*, 10(4), 238–248.

McLeod, J. (2013) *An Introduction to Counselling*. Fifth edition. Maidenhead: Open University Press.

McLeod, J. and Machin, L. (1998) 'The context of counselling: A neglected dimension of training, research and practice', *British Journal of Guidance and Counselling*, 26(3), 325–336.

Meara, N., Schmidt, L. and Day, J. (1996) 'Principles and virtues: A foundation for ethical decisions, policies and character', *The Counseling Psychologist*, 24(1), 4–77.

Mental Health Taskforce (2016) *The Five Year Forward View for Mental Health*. https://www.england.nhs.uk/wp-content/uploads/2016/02/Mental-Health-Taskforce-FYFV-final.pdf

Middleton, S. (2013) 'The heart of the business', *Counselling at Work*, Spring, pp. 4–7.

Moore, J. and Roberts, R. (eds) (2010) *Counselling and Psychotherapy in Organisational Settings*. Exeter: Learning Matters.

National Institute for Health and Clinical Excellence (NICE) (2009) *Depression in Adults: Recognition and Management. Clinical Guideline CG 90*, www.nice.org.uk/guidance/cg90 (accessed November 2016).

Office of the Public Guardian (2015) *Safeguarding Policy*. Birmingham: OPG.

Pan American Health Organization (Regional Office of World Health Organization) (2012) '"Cures" for an illness that does not exist', 17 May, www.paho.org/hq/index.php?option = com_content&view = article&id = 6803%3A 2012-therapies-change-sexual-orientation-lack-medical-justification-threaten-health&catid = 740%3Apress-releases&Itemid = 1926&lang = en (accessed November 2016).

Pattison, S., Rowland, N., Richards, K., Cromarty, K., Jenkins, P. and Polat, F. (2009) 'School counselling in Wales: Recommendations for good practice', *Counselling and Psychotherapy Research*, 9(3), 169–173.

Pybis, J., Cooper, M., Hill, A., Cromarty, K., Levesley, R., Murdoch, J. and Turner, N. (2015) 'Pilot randomised controlled trial of school-based humanistic counselling for psychological distress in young people: Outcomes and methodological reflections', *Counselling and Psychotherapy Research*, 15(4), 241–250.

Reeves, A. (2013) *An Introduction to Counselling and Psychotherapy: From Theory to Practice*. London: Sage.

Rizq, R. (2012) 'The perversion of care: Psychological therapies in a time of IAPT', *Psychodynamic Practice*, 18(1), 7–24.

Rogers, C. (2004) *Psychotherapy and Counselling: A Professional Business*. London: Whurr.

Rosofsky, I. (2009) *Nasty, Brutish and Long: Adventures in Old Age and the World of Eldercare*. New York: Penguin.

Roth, A., Hill, A. and Pilling, S. (2009) *The Competences Required to Deliver Effective Humanistic Psychological Therapies*. London: University College London, www.ucl.ac.uk/CORE (accessed November 2016).

Rye, J. (2011) 'Adding it up', *The Independent Practitioner*, Autumn, pp. 6–9.

Sanders, P. and Hill, A. (2014) *Counselling for Depression: A Person-Centred and Experiential Approach to Practice*. London: BACP/Sage.

Sands, A. (2000) *Falling for Therapy: Psychotherapy from a Client's Point of View*. Macmillan: London.

Schön, D. (1983) 'Psychotherapy: The patient as a universe of one', in D. Schön, *The Reflective Practitioner: How Professionals Think in Action*. London: Temple Smith. Chapter 4, pp. 105–127.

Seighart, P. (1978) *Statutory Regulation of Psychotherapists: A Report of the Professions Working Party*. London: Tavistock.

Sivis-Cetinkaya, R. (2015) 'Ethical dilemmas of Turkish counsellors: A critical incidents study', *British Journal of Guidance and Counselling*, 43(4), 476–491.

Smith, G., Bartlett, A. and King, M. (2004) 'Treatments of homosexuality in Britain since the 1950s – an oral history: The experience of patients', *British Medical Journal*, 328(21 February), 427–429.

Socarides, C. (n.d.) 'The erosion of heterosexuality', www.orthodoxytoday.org/articles/SocaridesErosion.php (accessed November 2016).

Sommerbeck, L. (2003) *The Client-Centred Therapist in Psychiatric Contexts: A Therapist's Guide to the Psychiatric Landscape and its Inhabitants*. Ross-on-Wye: PCCS Books.

Spitzer, R. (2003) 'Can some gay men and lesbians change their sexual orientation? 200 participants reporting a change from homosexual to heterosexual orientation', *Archives of Sexual Behaviour*, 32(5), 403–417.

Streatfield, N. (2012) 'Measuring outcomes', *Therapy Today*, 20(1), 28–31.

Strudwick, P. (2010) 'The ex-gay files', *Life, Independent*, 1 February, pp. 2–5.

Thomas, J., Pollard, K. and Sellman, D. (eds) (2014) *Interprofessional Working in Health and Social Care*. Second edition. London: Palgrave Macmillan.

Thorne, B. (1987) 'Beyond the core conditions', in W. Dryden (ed.), *Key Cases in Psychotherapy*. London: Croom Helm. pp. 48–77.

Thorne, B. (1993) 'Body and spirit', in W. Dryden (ed.), *Questions and Answers on Counselling in Action*. London: Sage. pp. 112–117.

Vesey, G. and Foulkes, P. (1999) *Dictionary of Philosophy*. Glasgow: Harper Collins.

Wallace, P. (2015) 'Working in private practice', *Therapy Today*, 26(8), 47.

Walton, M. (1997) 'Organisation culture and its impact on counselling', in M. Carroll and M. Walton (eds), *Handbook of Counselling in Organisations*. London: Sage. pp. 92–110.

Walton, M. (2010) 'Beyond the face before you: Considering the internal dynamics of your organisation', *Counselling at Work*, Spring, pp. 16–19.

Wenger, E. (1998) *Communities of Practice: Learning, Meaning and Identity*. Cambridge: Cambridge University Press.

Wenger, E., McDermott, R. and Snyder, W. (2002) *Cultivating Communities of Practice: A Guide to Managing Knowledge*. Boston, MA: Harvard Business School Press.

Wilkinson, R. and Pickett, K. (2010) *The Spirit Level: Why Equality is Better for Everyone*. Harmondsworth: Penguin.

World Health Organization (WHO) (2010) *International Statistical Classification of Diseases and Related Health Problems*. Tenth edition. Geneva: WHO.

Yates, E. (2014) 'Ready to enter the online world?', *Children and Young People*, September, pp. 35–37.

Index